THEOLOGICAL ESSAYS

OTHER SHEDD TITLES FROM SOLID GROUND

COMMENTARY ON THE EPISTLE TO THE ROMANS
THE DOCTRINE OF ENDLESS PUNISHMENT
HISTORY OF CHRISTIAN DOCTRINE (two volumes)
HOMILETICS AND PASTORAL THEOLOGY
ORTHODOXY AND HETERODOXY
SERMONS TO THE NATURAL MAN
SERMONS TO THE SPIRITUAL MAN

THEOLOGICAL ESSAYS

William G.T. Shedd

Solid Ground Christian Books
Birmingham, Alabama USA

Solid Ground Christian Books
PO Box 660132
Vestavia Hills AL 35266
205-443-0311
sgcb@charter.net
www.solid-ground-books.com

THEOLOGICAL ESSAYS

William G.T. Shedd (1820-1894)

Originally published by Scribner, Armstrong & Co. 1877

Cover design by Borgo Design
Contact them at borgogirl@bellsouth.net

ISBN- 978-159925-199-8

PREFACE.

THE substance of this volume has been before the public some twenty years or more. The opinions expressed in it relate to some of the most important and difficult themes in theology and theological philosophy. The editions through which it has passed prove that there is a considerable circle of readers who are interested in such problems, and in that particular mode of presentation in which they here appear. The author has seized the opportunity afforded by a new publication to revise and enlarge these papers. No change, however, has been made in the dogmatic positions. The reader will find the historical Calvinism defended in the essays upon Original Sin and Atonement; yet with an endeavor to ground these cardinal themes in the absolute principles of reason, as seen in the nature of both God and Man. Sin must take its origin, from first to last, in the finite will, and atonement is the necessary requirement of eternal justice. In these two essays, the writer, if he has done nothing else, has at least shown the sincerity of his belief that theology and philosophy have no inherent contradiction, and that the more exact and strict type of theology is the one of all which is most defensible at the bar of reason and logic; agreeing with Selden, that "without school divinity a divine knows nothing logically, nor will be able to satisfy a rational man out of the pulpit."

PREFACE.

The essay upon Evolution was first published in 1856, under the title of "The Philosophy of History." This has been recast, amplified, and carefully revised. The recent misuse to which the doctrine of evolution has been put by the sceptical physics of the day, has imparted a fresh interest to the subject. The author, in his discussion, discriminates the idea of evolution from that of creation, and from that of improvement or normal progress—with both of which it has been identified and confounded—and having evinced that an evolution is never creative, or originant from nothing, shows the applicability of the term either to an improvement or to a deterioration, either to a development of good or to a development of evil. In this way, a doctrine which of late has been violently forced into the service of pantheism is seen to be in harmony with the first truths of theism.

The remaining essays in the volume are somewhat more popular in their tone and contents. That upon the influence of Theological Studies, the author is glad to know, has given to some minds an impulse towards the ministry, and the service of the Church. The article upon the influence of Symbols, though in its form having a prevailing reference to a particular denomination, owing to the circumstances of its preparation, has a universal bearing, particularly at a time when the question respecting the value and need of creed statements is being raised. The subject of Clerical Education is examined, first, in reference to the need of its being scientific and professional, in distinction from lay education; and secondly, in reference to the duty incumbent upon the Church to facilitate it by institutions and endowments.

It will thus be seen that the contents of this volume are theological, either theoretically or practically. The writer for

PREFACE.

more than a quarter of a century has been engaged in theological instruction, which has overflowed, more or less, into authorship. An author in the more abstruse departments of literature gradually makes his own circle of readers, as a logical preacher gradually forms his own congregation. Both have the advantage of homogeneousness in readers and hearers, and escape the evils of a miscellaneous concourse. To that circle upon whom from experience he finds he may rely, and whose favorable verdict is his chief concern, the writer would express his hearty thanks for their past interest in his thoughts, and the hope that he may ever continue to retain it.

UNION THEOLOGICAL SEMINARY,
NEW YORK, Nov. 1, 1877.

Table of Contents

The Method, and Influence of Theological Studies	7
The Nature, and Influence of the Historic Spirit	53
The Idea of Evolution Defined, and Applied to History	121
The Doctrine of Original Sin	211
The Atonement a Satisfaction for the Ethical Nature of both God and Man	265
Symbols and Congregationalism	319
Clerical Education	355

THE METHOD, AND INFLUENCE, OF THEOLOGICAL STUDIES.

A DISCOURSE DELIVERED BEFORE THE LITERARY SOCIETIES OF THE
UNIVERSITY OF VERMONT, AUGUST 5, 1845.

GENTLEMEN OF THE SOCIETIES:

THE subject to which I invite your attention is: *The method, and influence, of Theological Studies.*

Theology more than any other science, suffers from false views of its scope and contents. In the opinion of many, it is supposed to have little or no connection with other sciences, and to exert but a very small and unimportant influence upon other departments of human knowledge. Its contents are supposed to be summed up in the truths of *natural* theology. It is thought to be that isolated and lifeless science which looks merely at the *natural* attributes of God and man, and which consequently brings to view no higher relations, and no deeper knowledge, than those of mere nature. Of course, for such minds theology must be a very unimportant and simple science, treating merely of those superficial qualities which do not reach into the depths of God and man, and of those merely secondary and temporal relationships that rest upon them. Said a member of the Directory appointed by France during its Revolution to remodel Christianity, " I want a simple religion: one with a couple of doctrines." Theology, as understood by many, is the science of the French Director's religion.

But such is not the scope, or the character, of that " sacred and inspired divinity " which Lord Bacon asserts to be " the sabbath and port of men's labors and peregrinations." Nature; the natural attributes of God and man, and the natural laws and relations of creation forms but a minor and insignificant part of its subject matter. This lower region of being is but the suburb. The metropolis and royal seat of theology is the *supernatural* world; a region full of *moral* being, sustaining most profound and solemn relations to reason and law.

Before proceeding, then, to speak of the true method of theological study, and of its great and noble influences, it will be needful to discuss more at large the real spirit and character of the science itself; and for this somewhat abstract discussion, I bespeak your forbearing and patient attention. It is needed in order to a clear apprehension of the enlarging and elevating influence of the science. Far am I from recommending to the educated man, the pursuit of those seemingly religious studies which never carry him out of the sphere of natural theology, and which cannot awaken enthusiasm of feeling or produce profundity of thought. I am pleading for those really theological studies, which by means of their *supernatural* element and character give nerve to the intellect and life to the heart.

Theology is the science of the supernatural. That we may obtain a clear knowledge of its essential character, let us for a moment consider the distinction between the natural and the supernatural.

That which makes these different from each other in kind, so that the line which divides them divides the universe into two distinct worlds, is this fact: — the natural has no *religious* element in it, while the supernatural is entirely composed of this element. There is and there can be in mere nature nothing religious. There is and there can be in that which is supernatural nothing that is not religious.* When we have said this, we have given the essential difference between the natural and supernatural.

The common notion that by the natural is meant the material and visible, and by the supernatural, the immaterial and invisible, is false. Nature may be as invisible and immaterial as is spirit. Who ever saw or ever will see the natural forces of gravitation, electricity, and magnetism? Who ever saw or ever will see that natural principle of life, of which all outward and material nature is but the manifestation? Back of this world of nature which we apprehend by the five senses, there is an invisible world which is nature still; which is not supernatural; neither the object of supernatural science nor of supernatural interests, because there is no moral element in it. When we have stripped the world of its materiality, and have dissolved all that is visible into unseen forces and vital laws, we have not reached any higher region than that of nature. We have not yet entered the supernatural and religious world. He who worships the vital principle or adores the force of gravity; nay, he who has no higher emotions than those of the natural religionist, which are called forth by the beauty

---

* Religion is from *religo*: — natural laws have no *religious*, or *binding* force, and in the sphere of nature there can be no such things as *duty, guilt* or *praiseworthiness.*

and glory of visible nature, or by the cloudy and mystic awfulness of invisible nature, is as really an idolater, as is the most debased heathen who bows down before a visible and material idol. And that system of thought which never rises into the world of moral or supernatural reality, is as truly material (whatever may be its professions to the contrary), as is the most open and avowed materialism.

It seems like stating truisms to make such statements as these; and yet some of the most seductive and far-reaching errors in philosophy and theology have arisen from the non-recognition, or the denial, of any thing higher than invisible nature. Ideal Pantheism, a system received by minds of a really profound order, and which boasts of its spirituality, results from the error in question. Hence, although it admits of, and produces, a mystic adoration and a vague dreamy awe, it is utterly incompatible with really spiritual feeling and truly moral emotion.

But the reality, and nature, of the distinction between the natural and supernatural, is still more clearly seen by a contemplation of the Divine attributes; partly because at this point the distinction itself is more marked and plain, and partly because from this point the vital errors in theological and philosophical science take their start.

Although, at first sight, it may appear bold and irreverent, yet a thorough investigation will show that it results in the only true fear and adoration of God, to say that his natural attributes considered by themselves are of no importance at all for a moral being. Taken by themselves, they have no religious quality, and therefore, as such, cannot be the ground of theological science or religious feeling. Considered apart from his supernatural attributes, what meaning have the omnipresence, the omnipotence, and even the adaptive intelligence, of the Deity, for me as a religious being? Of what interest, is the possessor of these merely natural attributes, to me as a rational and moral being, until I know the *supernatural character and person* which reside in them, and make them the vehicle of their operations? I may see the exhibitions of Infinite Power in the heavens above me, and on the earth around me; I may detect the work of an Infinite Intelligence in this world of matchless design and order; but what are these isolated qualities to me as one who possesses *moral* reason and sustains *supernatural* relations? Let that Infinite Power thunder and flash through the skies, and let that Infinite Intelligence clothe the world in beauty and glory; these merely natural attributes are nothing to me, in a religious point of view, until I know *who* wields them, and what *supernatural* and *holy* attributes make them their bearer and agent. Then will I fear spiritually, and then will I adore morally.

This fundamental distinction between the natural and the supernatural is of vital importance to theological science. If not clearly seen and rigidly recognized in theology, this science comes to be nothing more than an investigation of the *natural* attributes of the Deity, and treats merely of those relations of man to the Creator, which the vilest reptile that crawls has in common with him. For if we set aside the supernatural attributes of God, man sustains only the same relations to him that the brute does. He, in common with the brutes that perish, is the creature of the Divine Power, and in common with them is sustained by the Divine Intelligence; that attribute which causes merely natural wants to be supplied by their correlative objects. The mere supervention of consciousness will make no difference between man and brute in relation to the Deity, unless consciousness bring with it the knowledge of his higher *supernatural* attributes. If we set aside his relations to the Wisdom, Holiness, Justice and Mercy of God, we find man on a level with brute existence in all respects. He comes into being, reaches his maturity, declines, and dies, as they do, by the operation of the natural attributes of the Creator manifesting themselves in natural laws, and this is all that can be said of him in reference to his Maker.

The more we contemplate the Divine Being, the more clearly do we see that his supernatural are his constituting attributes; the very Divinity of the Deity. If they are denied, the Creator is immediately confounded with the creature; for his natural attributes, without his moral ones, become the soul of the world, its blind, though unerring principle of life. Or if they are misapprehended, and the difference between the two classes is supposed to be only one of degree, and consequently that there is no essential distinction between nature and spirit, fatal errors will inevitably be the result. There will be no sharply and firmly drawn line between the natural and spiritual worlds, natural and spiritual laws, and natural and spiritual relationships. A mere naturalism must run through theology, philosophy, science, literature and art, depriving each and all of them of their noblest characteristics.

The reality and importance of this distinction between the natural and the supernatural, are to be seen in a less abstract and more interesting manner in the actual life of men. Man is by creation a religious being; and even in his religion we discover his proneness to deny or misapprehend the distinction in question. The religion of the natural man is strictly *natural* religion. It refers solely to the *natural* attributes of God. There is no man who is not pleasurably affected by the manifestation of the Power and intelligent Design of the Deity, as seen in the natural world; and all men who have not been taught experimentally, that there are higher attributes than these, and a higher religion than this, are content with such religion. " As is the earthy, such are they that are earthy." They are strictly natural men, and seek that in God which corresponds to their character. The spirit, or the supernatural part of man, has not yet been renewed and vivified by a supernatural influence, and therefore there is no search after the spiritual attributes of God. The moment that the *supernatural* dawns upon such men, and the *moral* attributes of God appear in their awful and solemn relations to law, guilt, and atonement, they are troubled; and unless mercifully prevented, descend into the low regions of nature, to escape from a light and a purity which they cannot endure.

It will be evident even from this brief discussion that the distinction between the natural and the supernatural is a valid and fundamental one; that the natural world is essentially different from the supernatural, and that theology, as the science of the supernatural, possesses a scope, contents, and influence, as vast and solemn as the field of its inquiry.

And think for a moment what this field is! It is not the earth we tread upon, nor the heavens that are bent over it, all beautiful and glorious as they are. It is not that unseen world of living forces and active laws which lies under the visible universe, giving it existence and causing its manifold motions and changes. This is indeed a deeply mysterious realm, and is a step nearer the Eternal than all that we see with the eye or touch with the hand is; but it is not the proper home of theologica inquiry.

Above the kingdoms of visible and invisible nature, there is a world which is the residence of a personal God, with supernatural attributes, and the seat of spiritual ideas, laws, and relations. It is, to use the language of Plato, "that super-celestial place which no one of the poets has hitherto worthily sung, or ever will," where righteousness itself, true wisdom and knowledge, are to be seen in their very essence.* This is the proper field of theological inquiry, and as the mind ranges through it, it comes in sight of all that invests man's spirit with infinite responsibilities, and renders human existence one of awful interest.

But what is the proper method of theological studies?

If what has been said relative to the two great kingdoms into which the universe is divided, be true, it is plain that theological studies must commence in that supernatural world whose realities form its subject matter, and that the true method is to descend from spirit to nature, in our investigations. The contrary process has been in vogue for the last century and a half, and the saying "from nature we ascend to nature's God," has come to be received as an axiom in theological science.

If this assertion means anything, it means that by a careful observation of all that we can apprehend by the five senses, in space, we shall obtain a correct and full knowledge of God. The *spirit* of the assertion is this: Nature is first in the order of investigation, because its teachings are more surely correct, and its proofs are

---

* Phædrus. Opera viii. p. 30. See the whole of the beautiful description of this ὑπερουράνιος τόπος: a passage vividly reminding of 1 Cor. ii.

more to be relied on, than those of the supernatural. Let us test it by rigidly applying it to the investigation of the being and character of God. What is there in nature which teaches, or proves, the existence of the Holiness of God; or his Justice; or his Mercy? What is there in the world in which we live as beings of nature and sense, which necessarily compels us to assume the personality of God? It is true that we are taught by all that exists in " the mighty world of eye and ear," that there are power and adaptive intelligence *somewhere*, but whether they are seated in a self-conscious and personal being, or are only the eternal procession of a blind and unconscious life, we cannot know anything that nature teaches. You see a movement in the natural world: say the growth of a plant or the blowing of a flower. What does that natural movement teach (considered simply by itself, and with no reference to a higher knowledge from another source,) and what have you a right to infer from it? Simply this: that there is a *merely natural* power adequate to its production; but whether that power has any connection with the *moral character of a spiritual person*, you cannot know from anything you see in the natural phenomenon. Now extend this through infinite space, and will the closest examination of all the physical movements occurring in this vast domain, *taken by itself*, lead up to a personal and holy God? What is there in the law of gravity which has the least tendency to lead to the recognition of the law of holiness? Is there any similarity between the two in kind? What can the motions of the sun and stars, the unvarying return of the seasons, the birth, growth, and death, of animated existence, *taken by themselves*, teach regarding the supernatural attributes of God? Take away from man the knowledge of God which is contained in the human spirit and in the written word and leave him to find his way up to a personal and spiritual Deity by the light of nature alone, and he will grope in eternal darkness, if for no other reason, because he cannot even get the idea of such a Being.

For the truth is, that between the two kingdoms of nature and spirit a great gulf is fixed, and the passage from one to the other is not by degrees, but by a leap; and this leap is not up, but down. There is one theory which assumes that the universe is but the development of one only substance; and if this is a correct theory, then it is true that we can " ascend from nature up to nature's God." For all is continuous development, with no chasm intervening, and the height may consequently be reached from the bottom by a patient ascent. There is another and the true theory, which rejects this doctrine of development, and substitutes in its place that of creation, whereby nature is not an emanation, but springs forth into existence for the first time, at the fiat of the Creator, who is now distinct from the work of his hands. Nature is now, in a certain sense, separate from God, and instead of being able to prove his moral existence, or to manifest his supernatural and constituting attributes, requires a previous knowledge of the Creator, from another source, in order to its own true apprehension.*

Now the true method of obtaining a correct knowledge of an object, is to follow the method of its origin, and therefore true theological science follows the footsteps of

---

* Whether the absolute is the *ground* or the *cause* is the question which has ever divided philosophers. That it is the *ground* but not the *cause* is the assertion of Naturalism; that it is the *cause* and not the *ground* is the assertion of Theism. Jacobi. Von den Gött. Dingen. Werke. iii. 404, together with the references.

God. It *starts* with the assumption of his existence, and the knowledge of his character derived from a higher source than that of mere nature, that it may find in the works of his hands the illustration of his already known attributes, and the manifestation of his already believed being. True theology descends from God to nature, and rectifies and interprets all that it finds in this complicated and perplexing domain, by what it knows of its Maker from other and higher sources.

Take away from the human spirit that knowledge of the moral attributes of God which it has from its constitution, and from revelation, and compel it to deduce the character of the Supreme Being from what it sees in the natural world, and will it not inevitably become skeptical? As the thoughtful heathen looked abroad over a world of pain and death, was he not forced resolutely to reject the natural inference to be drawn from this sight, and to cling with desperate faith to the dictum of a voice speaking from another quarter, saying: "See what thou mayest in nature apparently to the contrary, He *is* Just; He *is* Holy; He *is* Good."

This false method of theological study proceeds from a belief common to man, resulting partly from his corruption and partly from his present existence in a world of sense. It is the common belief of man that reality in the strictest sense of the term is to be predicated of material things, and in his ordinary thought and feeling, that which is spiritual is unreal. The solid earth which the "swain treads upon with his clouted shoon" has substantial existence, and its material objects are real, but if we watch the common human feeling regarding such objects as the soul and God, we detect (not necessarily a known and determined infidelity, but) an inability to make them as real and substantial as the sun in the heavens, or the earth under foot. Lord Bacon in describing the idols of the tribe; the false notions which are inherent in human nature; says, that "man's sense is falsely asserted to be the standard of things."* It is, however, under the influence of the notion that it is, that man goes to the investigation of truth, and especially of theological truth. Every thing is determined by a material standard, and established from the position of materialism. It is assumed that nature is more real than spirit; that its instructions and evidences are more to be relied on than those of spirit; and that from it, as from the only sure foothold for investigation, we are to make hurried and timid excursions into that dim undiscovered realm of the supernatural which is airy and unreal, and filled with airy and unreal objects.

This is a low and mean idol, and if the inquirer after spiritual truth bows down to it he shall never enter the holy of holies. Spirit is more real than matter, for God is a spirit. Supernatural laws and relations are more real than those of nature, for they shall exist when nature, even to its elements, shall be melted with fervent heat.

Why then should we, as did the pagan mythology, make earth and the earth-born Atlas support the old everlasting heavens? They are self-supported and embosom and illumine all things else. Why should we attempt to rest spiritual science upon natural science; the eternal upon the temporal; the absolute upon the empirical; the certain upon the uncertain? Is all that is invisible unreal, and must a thing become the object of the five senses, before we can be certain of its reality? Not to go out of the natural world; by what in this do

* Novum Organum, Aph. 41.

main are we most vividly impressed with the conception of reality, and how is the notion of *power* awakened? Not by anything we see with the eye or touch with the hand, but by the knowledge of that *unseen* force and law which causes the motions of the heavens, and makes the "crystal spheres ring out their silver chimes." Not by an examination of the phenomena of the mineral, vegetable, and animal kingdoms, but by the idea of that one vast *invisible* life manifesting itself in them. Even here, upon a thoughtful reflection, that which is unseen shows itself to be the true reality. And to go up higher into the sphere of human existence: where is the substantial reality of man's being? In that path which, in the language of Job, "no fowl knoweth, and which the vulture's eye hath not seen." In that unseen world where human thought ranges, where human feelings swell into a vastness not to be contained by the great globe itself, and where human affections soar away into eternity. No! reality in the high sense of the term belongs to the invisible, and in the very highest sense, to the invisible things of the supernatural world. There is more of reality in the feeblest finite spirit than in all the material universe, for it will survive "the wreck of matter and the crash of worlds." The supernatural is a firmer foundation upon which to establish science than is the natural; its data are more certain, and its testimony more sure than those of nature. None but an open ear, it is true, can hear the voices and the dicta that come from this highest world, but he who has once heard never again doubts regarding them. He *cannot* doubt, if he would. He has heard the tones, and they will continue to sound through his soul, with louder and louder reverberations, through its whole immortality.

Perhaps it will be objected that, granting spiritual

things to be the true realities, yet the mind cannot see them except through a medium, and cannot be certain of their existence except by means of deductions from a palpable and tangible reality like that of the material world. But is it so? Does the spirit need a medium through which to behold the idea and law of Right, for example; and must it build up a series of conclusions based upon deductions drawn from the world of sense, before it can be certain that there is any such reality?— Does not the human spirit see the idea of Right as directly and plainly as the material eye sees the sun at high noon; and when it sees it, is it not as certain of its existence as we are of that of the sun? If man does not see this spiritual entity, this supernatural idea, directly and without a medium, he will never see it, and if it does not of itself convey the evidence of its reality, it can be drawn from no other quarter.

The same may be said of all spiritual entities whatever; of all the objects of the supernatural world. The rational spirit may and must behold them by direct intuition in their own pure white light. It has the organ for doing this. Not more certainly is the material eye designed for the vision of the sun, than the rational spirit is designed for the vision of God. The former is expressly constructed to behold matter, and the latter is just as expressly constructed to behold spirit. Nor let it be supposed that the term "behold" is used literally in reference to the act of the material eye, and merely metaphorically in reference to the act of the spirit. The term is no more the exclusive property of one organ than of the other. Or if it is to belong to one exclusively let us rather appropriate it to that organ which sees eternal distinctions. If the term "sight" is ever metaphorical, surely it is not so when applied to the vision of immutable truths and everlasting realities.

Man, both by nature and by the circumstances in which he is placed, finds it difficult thus to contemplate abstract ideal truth, and when it eludes his imperfect vision he charges the difficulty upon the truth and not upon himself. But for all this the ideal is real, and man is capable of this abstract vision. Upon his ability to free himself from the disturbing influences of sense, to be independent of the physical senses in the investigation of spiritual things, and to see them in their own light by their correlative organ, depends his true knowledge of the supernatural. It is on this ground that Plato asserts it to be the true mark of a philosophic mind to desire to die, because the mind is thereby withdrawn from the distraction of sense, and in the spiritual world beholds the Beautiful, the True, and the Good, in their essence. — Hence with great force he represents those spirits which have not been entirely freed from the crass and sensuous nature of the body, as being afraid of the purely spiritual world and its supernatural objects, and as returning into the world of matter to wander as ghosts among tombs and graves, loving their old material dwelling more than the spirit-land.*

The knowledge which comes from a direct vision of spiritual objects is sure, and needs no evidence of its truth from a lower domain. He who has once in spirit obtained a distinct sight of such realities as the Good, the Beautiful, the True, and their contraries, will never again be in doubt of their existence, or as to their natures. These are entities which once seen compel an everlasting belief. These are objects

---

* Phædon, Opera I. pp. 115. 116, 139.

>   that wake
> To perish never;
> Which neither listlessness nor mad endeavor,
>   Nor man nor boy,
> Nor all that is at enmity with joy,
> Can utterly abolish or destroy.

The true method then of theological studies is to commence in and with the supernatural and to work outward and downward to the natural. The theologian must study his own spirit by the aid of the written word. He will ever find the two in perfect harmony and mutually confirming each other. The supernatural doctrines of theology must be seen in their own light; must bring their own evidence with them, and theology must be a self-supported science.

Whatever may be said in opposition to this method by those who magnify natural theology to the injury of spiritual religion, it has always been the method of inquiry employed by the profoundest and most accurate theologians. Augustine lived at a period when natural science was but little cultivated and advanced, but even if he had possessed all the physical knowledge of the present day, that inward experience with its throes, agonies, and joys, so vividly portrayed in his "Confessions," would still have kept his eye turned inward. The power of Luther and Calvin lies in their realizing views of supernatural objects seen by their own light; and nothing but an absolutely abstract and direct beholding of supernatural realities could have produced the calm assurance and profound theology of that loftiest of human spirits, John Howe.

But what has been the result of the contrary method? Have not those who commenced with the study of natural theology, and who made this the foundation of their inquiries into the nature and mutual relations of

God and man, always remained on the spot where they first stationed themselves? Did they, by logically following their assumed method, ever rise above the sphere of merely natural religion into that of supernatural, and obtain just views either of the Infinite Spirit as personal and therefore tri-une; or of the Finite Spirit as free, responsible and guilty? Did they ever acquire rational views of holy and just law; of law as strictly *supernatural;* and so of its relations to guilt and expiation?

An undue study of natural science inevitably leads to wrong theological opinions. Unless it be pursued in the light which spirit casts upon nature, the student will misapprehend both nature and spirit. Who can doubt that if Priestley had devoted less time to the phenomena of the natural world, and far more to those of the supernatural; less attention to physical laws as seen in the operations of acids and alkalies, and far more attention to the operation of a spiritual law as revealed in a guilty conscience; he would have left a theology far more nearly conformed to the word of God and the structure of the human spirit.

I have been thus particular in speaking of the supernatural element in theological studies, for the purpose of showing where their power lies, and whence their influence comes. I turn now to consider the influence of these studies as they have been characterized, upon education and the educated class in the state.

Genuine education is immediately concerned with the essence of the mind itself, and its power and work appear in the very substance of the understanding. It starts into exercise deeper powers than the memory, and it does more for the mind than merely to fill it. It enters rather into its constituent and controlling principles; rouses and develops them, and thus establishes a basis for the mind's perpetual motion and progress. Whether there be much or little acquired information is of small importance, comparatively, if the mind has that which is the secret of mental superiority, the power of originating knowledge upon a given subject for itself, and can fall back upon its own native energies for information. That process whereby a mind acquires the ability to fasten itself with absorbing intensity upon any legitimate object of human inquiry, and to originate profound thought and clear conceptions regarding it, is education.

The truth of this assertion will be apparent if we bear in mind that knowledge, in the high sense of the term, is not the remembrance of facts, but the intuition of principles. Facts are that through which principles manifest themselves, and by which they are illustrated, but to take them for the essence of knowledge is to mistake the body for the soul. The true knowledge of nature, art, philosophy, and religion, is an insight into their constituent principles, of which facts and phenomena are but the raiment; the "white and glistering" raiment in which the essence is transfigured and through which it shines.

Now, principles are entities that do not exist either in space or time. They cannot be apprehended by any organ of sense, and therefore they are not in space. — They cannot in a literal sense be said to be old or new. Principles are eternal and therefore they are not in time. Where then are they? In the intellectual world: — a world that is not measured by space or limited by periods of time, but which has, nevertheless, as real an existence as this globe. In the world of mind, all those principles which *constitute* knowledge are to be sought for. They lie in the structure of mind, and therefore the development of the mind is but the discovery of principles, and education is the *origination* of substantial knowledge out of the very being who is to be educated.*

Thus, by this brief examination of the true nature of knowledge, do we come round in a full circle to the spot whence we started, and see that he alone is in the process of true education who is continually looking within, and by the gradual *evolution* of his own mind is continually unfolding those principles of knowledge that lie imbedded in it. Such an one may not have amassed great erudition, but he possesses a working intellect which, unencumbered by amassed materials, overflows all the more freely with original principles. We *feel* that such a mind is educated, for its products, are alive and communicate life. From a living impulse it originates a knowledge, regarding any particular subject to which it directs itself, that commends itself to us as truth, by its congeniality and affinity with our own mind, and by its kindling influence upon it.

Accustomed, from the domination of a mental philosophy which rejects the doctrine of innate ideas, to consider learning as something carried into the mind instead of something drawn out of it, it sounds strangely to speak of *originating* knowledge. But who are the really learned statesmen, philosophers, and divines? Not those who merely commit to memory the results of past inquiry, but those in whom after deep reflection the principles of government, philosophy, and religion, rise into sight, with the freshness, inspiration, and splendor, of a new discovery. In asserting however that learning is the product of the mind itself, I mean that it is relatively so.

---

* This is Plato's meaning when he asserts that learning is recollection :— the reminding of the human spirit of those great principles which are born with it, and which constitute its rationality.— Phædon Opera I. p. 125, *et seq.* Cudworth's Im. Mor. Book iii, Chap. 3.

It is not asserted that every truly learned mind discovers *absolutely* new principles, and consequently that the future is to bring to light a great amount of knowledge unknown to the past. Far from it. The sum of human knowledge, with the exception of that part relating to the domain of natural science, is undoubtedly complete, and we are not to expect the discovery of any new fundamental principles in the sphere of the supernatural.— But it is asserted with confidence that these old principles must be discovered afresh *for himself*, by every one who would be truly educated. " He who has been born," says an eloquent writer, " has been a first man, and has had the world lying around him as fresh and fair as it lay before the eyes of Adam himself." In like manner, he who has been created a rational spirit, has a world of rational principles encircling him, which is as new and undiscovered for him as it was for the first man. In the hemisphere of his own self-reflection and self-consciousness, the sun must rise for the first time, and the stars must send down their very freshest influences, their very first and purest gleam.

For education, in the eminent sense of the term, is dynamic and not atomic. It does not lie in the mind in the form of congregated atoms, but of living, salient, energies. It is not therefore poured in from without, but springs up from within. The power of pure thought is education. Indeed the more we consider the nature of mental education, the more clearly do we see that it consists in the power of pure, practical reflection; the ability so to absorb the mind that it shall sink down into itself, until it reaches those ultimate principles, bedded in its essence, by which facts and all acquired and remembered information are illuminated and vivified. It cannot be that he who remembers the most, is the most thoroughly educated man, or that the age which is in possession of the greatest amount of books and recorded information, is the most learned. No! learning is the product of a powerful mind, which, by self-reflection and absorption in pure, practical thought, goes down into those depths of the intellectual world, where, as in the world of matter, the gems and gold, the seeds, and germs, and roots, are to be found. It is related that Socrates could remain a whole day utterly lost in profound reflection.* This was the education in that age of no books, to which, through his scholar Plato, himself educated in the same way, is owing a system of philosophy, substantial with the very essence of learning; a system which for insight into ultimate principles is at the head of all human knowledge.

Such being the nature of education, it is evident that theological studies are better fitted than any others, to educe a rational mind. For they bring it into immediate communication with those supernatural realities and truths which are appropriate to it, and which possess a strong power of development. There is in the human mind a vast amount of latent energy forming the basis for an endless progress, and this will lie latent and dormant unless the forces of the supernatural would evolve it. The world of nature unfolds merely the superficies of man, leaving the hidden depths of his being unstirred, and only when the windows of heaven are opened are the fountains of this great deep broken up. For proof of this assertion, consider the influence which the theological doctrine of the soul's immortality exerts upon the spirit. When man realizes that he is immortal he is supernaturally roused. Depths are revealed in his being which he did not dream of, down into which he looks with solemn awe, and energies which had hitherto slum

---

* Convivium. Platonis Opera vii. p. 278.

bered from his creation are now set into a play at which he stands aghast. Never do the tides of that shoreless ocean, the human soul, heave and swell as they do when it feels what the scripture calls "the power of an endless life." The same remark holds true of all properly theological doctrines. An unequalled developing influence rains down from this great constellation.

And the intellect as well as the heart of man feels the influence. Hence that period in a man's life which is marked by a realizing and practical apprehension of the doctrines of spiritual religion is also marked by a great increase of intellectual power. A manlier and more substantial cultivation begins, because the being has become conscious of his high origin and the awfulness of his destiny, and a stronger play of intellectual power is evoked, because the stream of supernatural influence flows through the whole man, and both head and heart feel its vivification. The value of theological studies, in an intellectual point of view, does not consist so much in the amount of information as in the amount of energy imparted by them. The doctrines of theology, like the solar centres, are comparatively few in number, and while the demand they make upon the memory is small, the demand they make upon the power of reflection is infinite and unending. For this reason, theological studies are in the highest degree fitted to originate and carry on a true education. There is an invigorating virtue in them which strengthens while it unfolds the mental powers, and therefore the more absorbing the intensity with which the mind dwells upon them, the more it is endued with power.

This truth is very plainly written in literary history. If we would see that period when the mind of a nation was most full of original power, we must contemplate its theological age. We ever find that the national intellect is most energetically educed in that period when the attention of educated men is directed with great earnestness to theological studies, while that period which is characterized by a false study, or a general neglect, of them, is one of very shallow education. Compare the education of the English mind during the sixteenth and seventeenth centuries, with its education in the eighteenth. The great difference between the two, is owing to the serious and profound reflection upon strictly theological subjects that prevailed in the first period, and to the absence of such reflection in the second. The former was a theological age in the strict sense of the term; a period when the educated class felt very powerfully the vigor proceeding from purely supernatural themes. The latter was a period when, through the influence of a system of philosophy which teaches that every thing must be learned through the five senses, a mere naturalism took the place of supernaturalism, and when, as a matter of course, the mind of the literary class was not the subject of those developing and energizing influences which proceed only from supernatural truths.

Again, that we may still more clearly see the vigorous character imparted to education by purely theological studies, let us consider two individuals who stand at the head of two different classes of literary men, and afford two different specimens of intellectual culture: — Lord Chancellor Bacon and Lord Chancellor Brougham.

The education of Bacon is the result, in no small degree, of the influence of the truths of supernatural science. There was no naturalism in the age of Bacon; there was none in his culture; and there is none in his writings. He lived at a period when the English mind was stirred very deeply by religious doctrines, and when the truths of the supernatural world were very absorbing topics of thought and discussion, not only for divines, but for statesmen. We of this enlightened nineteenth century, are in the habit of calling those centuries of reformation, dark, in comparison with our own; but with all the darkness on some subjects, it may be fearlessly asserted that since the first two centuries of the history of Christianity, there has never been a period when so large a portion of the race have been so *deeply* and *anxiously* interested in the truths pertaining to another world, as in those two centuries of reformation; the sixteenth and seventeenth. With all the lack of modern improvements and civilization, there was everywhere a firm belief in the supernatural, and a sacred reverence for religion. Even the very keenness and acrimony of the theological disputations of that period prove that men believed, as they do not in an indifferent age, that religious doctrines are matters of vital interest.

Bacon lived in this age; in its first years, and felt the first and freshest influences of the great awakening. His intellect felt them, and hence its masculine development and vigor. The products of his intellect felt them, and hence the solid substance, strong sinew, and warm blood, of which they are made.

The education of Brougham has been obtained in a very different age from that of Bacon: an age when the faith and interest which the learned class once felt in the realities of another world, have transferred themselves to the realities of this. It has also been the result, in no small degree, of the belief and the study of the half-truths of natural theology. While then the recorded learning of Bacon bears the stamp of originality, is drenched and saturated with the choicest intellectual spirit and energy, makes an epoch in literary history, and sends forth through all time an enlivening power, the recorded learning of Brougham is destitute of fresh life, being the result of a diligent acquisition, and not of profound contemplation, gives off little invigorating influence, and cannot form a marked period in the history of literature.

Thus far we have considered the developing and energizing influence of theological studies; but if we should stop here, we should be very far from discovering their full worth. There is a merely *speculative* development and energy of the mind which is heaven-wide from genuine education, and really prevents growth in true knowledge.

There have ever been, and, so long as man shall continue to be a fallen spirit, there ever will be, two kinds of thought. The one speculative and hollow; the other practical and substantial. The one wasting itself upon the factitious products of its own energy; the other expending itself upon those great realities which are veritable, and have an existence independent of the finite mind. The natural tendency of the intellect, *when not actuated by a rational and holy will*, is to produce purely speculative thought, and in this direction do we see all intellect going which does not feel the influence of moral and spiritual truth. The speculative reason is a wonderful mechanism, and if kept within its proper domain, and applied to its correlative objects, is an important instrument in the attainment of truth and culture, but if suffered to pass over its appointed limits, and to occupy itself with the investigation of subjects to which it is not adapted, it brings in error rapidly and *ad infinitum*, preventing the true progress and repose of the spirit. There is no end to the manufactures of the speculative faculty, or to the productive energy of its life, when once the process of speculation is begun. Nay, it is the express doctrine of Fichte (the most intensely and purely speculative intellect the world has yet seen) that the finite mind having the principle of its own movement within itself, by working in accordance with its own indwelling laws, is able to *create*, and actually *does create the grea universe itself!* The history of philosophy disclose much of such speculative thought, and hence the dissatisfaction of philosophy with what it has hitherto done, and its striving after a substantial and genuine knowledge. Man as a moral being cannot be content with these hollow speculations, for spirit as well as nature abhors a vacuum. Thought must be filled up with substantial verity, and knowledge must become practical, in order to the repose and true education of the mind.

Yet notwithstanding the unsatisfying nature of speculative thinking, an intellectual life and enthusiasm are generated by it which invest it with a charming facination for the mind that is led on by a merely speculative interest. What though the thinker is bewildered and lost in the mazes of speculation; he is bewildered and lost in wonderful regions, the astounding nature of whose objects represses, for a time, the feelings of doubt and dissatisfaction. He is like the pilgrim lost in "the gorgeous East," who is *delightedly* lost amid the luxuriant entanglements and wild enchantments of the oriental jungle. In this exciting world of speculation, the energies of the intellect are in full action, the thirst and curiosity for knowledge are keen, and under the impulse of these the thinker says with Jacobi; "though I know the insufficiency of my philosophizing, still I can only philosophize right on."*

---

* Jacobi, quoted by Tholuck. Vermischte Schriften. ii. 427; and see a similar remark by Kant, Kritik der reinen Vernunft. p. 196. The philoso

It is possible to evoke intellectual energy so powerfully and habitually that the action shall become organic, and the intellect shall be instinctively busy with the production and reproduction of speculations; and though the thinker gets no repose of soul by it, yet he is so much under the power of the intellectual appetite that he will not cease to gratify it. There is no more mournful chapter in the history of literary men than that which records their unending speculative struggles; their efforts to find peace of mind and true education in the application of merely speculative energy to the solution of the great problems of moral existence. The process of speculation continually becomes more and more impeded, as at every advance still more mysterious problems come into sight, not soluble by this method; the over-tasked intellect at length gives out, and its gifted possessor falls into the abyss of unbelief like an archangel.

It is not enough therefore that the latent power of the mind is developed merely; it must be developed by some substantial objects, and it must be expended upon some veritable realities. In other words, the thought of man must be called forth by the ideas and principles of the supernatural world, and the mind of man must find repose and education in moral truth.

pher, (says Chalybäus in the conclusion of his lecture upon Jacobi, Vorlesungen p. 77.) as well as the poet, can say of himself:—
        Ich halte diesen Drang vergebens auf,
        Der Tag und Nacht in meinem Busen wechselt,
        Wenn ich nicht sinnen oder dichten soll,
        So ist das Leben mir kein Leben mehr!
        Verbiete du dem Seidenwurm, zu spinnen —
        Wenn er sich schon dem Tode näher spinnt,
        Das köstlichste Geweb' entwickelt er
        Aus seinem Innersten, und läszt nicht ab
        Bis er in seinen Sarg sich eingeschlossen.

The reader of Plato is struck with the earnestness with which this truly philosophic and educated mind insists upon knowing *that which really is*, as the end of philosophy. It matters not how consecutive and consistent with itself a system of thought may be, if it has no correspondent in the world of being, and does not find a confirmation in the world of absolute reality. The form may be distinct, and the proportions symmetrical, but the thing is spectral and unsubstantial, and though it be dignified with the name of philosophy, it is nevertheless a pure figment. Though not the product of the fancy but of a far higher faculty, a merely speculative philosophical system is but a fiction; a creation of the brain, to which there is, objectively, nothing correspondent. As an instance of such philosophizing, take the system of Spinoza. No one can deny that as a merely speculative unity, it is perfect, and perfectly satisfies the wants of that part of the human understanding which looks for nothing but a theoretical whole. All its parts are in most perfect harmony with each other, and with the whole. This system is conceived and executed in a most systematic spirit, and if man had no moral reason which seeks for something more than a merely speculative unity, it would be for him the true theory of the universe. But why is it not, and why cannot the human mind be content with it? Because a rational spirit cannot *rest* in it. There is in this system, great and architectural as it is, no repose or home for a moral being, and therefore it is not truth; for absolute truth is infallibly known by the absolute and everlasting satisfaction it affords to the moral spirit.

Another great aim of education, therefore, is the calm repose of the mind; its settlement in indisputable truth. This can proceed only from the study of the purely spiritual truths of theology, because such is their nature that there can be no real dispute regarding them, whereas merely speculative dogmas are susceptible of, and awaken, an endless ratiocination. There has always been, for example, even among thoughtful men a keen dispute regarding some points in the mode of the Divine existence, but none at all regarding the Divine character. The doctrine of the subsistence of creation in the creator has ever awakened honest disputations among sincere disputants, but the doctrine that God is holy has never been doubted by a conscientious thinker. This holds true of all speculative and practical doctrines. Within the sphere of theory and speculation there is room for endless wanderings, and no foundation upon which the spirit can stand still and firm. Within the sphere of practice and morality there need be no doubt nor error, and the sincere mind, by a direct vision of the truths of this practical domain of knowledge, may enter at once and forever into rest.

The influence of purely theological studies, in producing an education that ministers repose and harmony to the mind, is great and valuable. The intellectual energy is not awakened by abstractions, nor is it expended upon them, but upon those supernatural realities which are the appropriate objects of a rational contemplation, and which completely satisfy the wants of an immortal being. For that which imparts substantiality to thought, is religion, and all reflection which does not in the end refer to the moral and supernatural relations of man, is worthless. Though a fallen spirit, man still bears about with him the great idea of his origin and destiny. This allows him no real peace or satisfaction but in religious truth, and there are moments, consequently, in the life of the educated man, when he feels with deep despondency the need of the purer culture, and the more satisfactory reflection, of better studies. If any, short of strictly theological studies, can give repose of mind, they would have given it to the poet Goethe. Yet that mind, singularly symmetrical and singularly calm by nature, after ranging for half a century through all regions save that strictly supernatural world of which we have spoken, and after obtaining what of culture and intellectual satisfaction is to be found short of spiritual truths; that mind, so richly and variously gifted, at the close of its existence on earth confessed that it had never experienced a moment of genuine repose.

The German poet is not the only one whose education did not contribute to repose and peace of mind. The literary life has not hitherto been calm and satisfied. From all times, and from all classes of educated minds, there comes the mournful confession that " he that increaseth knowledge increaseth sorrow," and that all learning which does not go beyond the consciousness of the natural man and have for its object the Good, the True, and the Divine, cannot satisfy the demands of man's ideal state. From Philosophy, from Poetry, and from Art, is heard the acknowledgment that there is no repose for the rational spirit but in moral truth. The testimony that the whole creation groaneth and travaileth in pain, together, is as loud and convincing from the domain of letters, as it is from the cursed and thistle-bearing ground. From the immortal longing and dissatisfaction of Plato, down to the wild and passionate restlessness of Byron and Shelley, the evidence is decisive that a spiritual and religious element must enter into the education of man in order to inward harmony and rest.

Time forbids a longer discussion of this part of the

subject. It may be said as a result of the whole, that a thorough study of theology as the science of the supernatural, results in a profundity and harmony of education which can be obtained in no other way, and if the culture which comes from poetry and fine literature generally be also mingled with it, a truly beautiful as well as profound education will be the result of the alchemy.

I turn now to consider the influence of theological studies upon Literature. And let me again remind you that I am speaking of *purely* theological studies, as they have been defined. There is an influence proceeding from so-called theological studies, which deprives literature of its depth, power, beauty, and glory; the *quasi* religious influence of naturalism, of which the poetry of Pope, the philosophy of Locke, the divinity of Priestley, and the morality of Paley, are the legitimate and necessary results.

The fact strikes us in the outset, that the noblest and loftiest literature has always appeared in those periods of a nation's existence, when its literary men were most under the influence of theological science. Whether we look at Pagan or Christian literature, we find this assertion verified. The mythology and theology of Greece exerted their greatest influence upon Homer, the three dramatists, and Plato; and these are the great names in Grecian literature. If Cicero is ever vigorous and original he is in his ethical and theological writings. The beautiful flower of Italian literature is the " unfathomable song" of the religious Dante. The beauty and strength of English literature are the fruit of those two pre-eminently theological centuries:—the sixteenth and seventeenth. The originality and life which for the last century has given German literature the superiority over other literatures of this period, must be referred mainly to the tendency of the German mind toward theological truth. And judging *a priori*, we should conclude that such would be the fact. We might safely expect that the human mind would produce its most perfect results, when most under the influences that come from its birth-place. We might know beforehand, that truth and beauty would flow most freely into the creations of man's mind, when he himself is in most intimate communication with that world where these qualities have their eternal fountain.

1. The first and best fruit of the influence of theology upon literature is *profundity*. This characteristic of the best literature of a nation is immediately noticed by the scholar, so that its decrease or absence is, for him, the chief sign of deterioration. In that glorious age of a nation when the solemn spirit of religion informs everything; when, compared with after ages, the nation seems to be very near the supernatural world in feeling and sentiment; when prophet, poet, and priest, are synonymes; then arises its most profound literature.

By a profound literature, is meant one that addresses itself to the most profound faculties of the human soul. The so-called polite literature, is the lightest and most unessential product of the human mind. It is the work of the inferior part of the understanding, deriving little life or vigor from its deepest powers, and having no immediate connection with its highest cultivation. It occupies the attention of man in his youthful days, affording an ample field in which the fancy may rove and revel, and starting some of the superficial life of the intellect, but in the mature and meditative part of his existence, when the great questions relating to his origin and destiny are raised, he leaves these gay and pleasant studies for that more profound literature which comes home to deeper faculties and wants.

A survey of literature generally, at once shows that but a very small portion of it is worthy to be called profound. How very little of the vast amount which has been composed by the literary class, addresses itself to the primitive faculties of the human soul! The greater part merely stimulates curiosity, exercises the fancy, and perhaps loads the memory. Another portion externally polishes and adorns the mind. It is only a very small portion, which by speaking to the Reason and the rational and creative Imagination, and rousing into full play of life those profound powers, ministers strength, true beauty, and true culture to the soul.

Consider for a moment the character of the English literature of the present day. I do not now refer to the dregs and off-scourings which are doing so much to debauch the English mind, but to the bloom and flower. And I ask if it does anything more for the scholar than to externally adorn and embellish his education? Has it the power to educate? Does it have a strong tendency to *develop* a historical, a philosophical, a poetical, or artistic capability if it lie in the student? Must not a more profound literature be called upon to do this, and must not the scholar who would truly develop what is in him, go back to the study of Homer and Plato; of Dante; of Shakspeare, Bacon, and Milton? If he contents himself with the study of the best current literature, will he do anything more than produce a refinement destitute of life; a culture without vigor; and will he himself in his best estate be anything more than an intellectual voluptuary, utterly impotent and without vivifying influence upon letters?

There is then a profound portion of literature speaking to the deeper part of man, from which he is to derive a profound literary cultivation. A brief examination will show that its chief characteristics arise from its being impregnated by theology; not necessarily by the formal doctrines of theology, but by its finer essence and spirit. Theology, it has been said, is the science of the supernatural and therefore of the strictly mysterious. The idea of God, which constitutes and animates the science, is a true mystery. But that which is truly mysterious is truly profound, and deepens everything coming under its influence. Indeed mystery, in the philosophical sense of the term, is the author of all great qualities. Sublimity, Profundity, Grandeur, Magnificence, Beauty, cannot exist without it. Like night, it induces a high and solemn mood, and is the parent and nurse of profound and noble thought. That literature which is pervaded by it, becomes deep-toned, and speaks with emphasis to the deeper powers of man. Even when there is but an imperfect permeation by this influence; when mystery is not fully apprehended, and the mind is not completely under its power; even when the Poet feels

"What he can ne'er express, yet cannot all conceal,"

there is a noble inspiration in his lines, which, with all its vagueness, deepens the feelings and elevates the conceptions. It is related of Fichte, that in very early childhood he would stand motionless for hours, gazing into the distant ether.* As such he is a symbol of the soul which is but imperfectly possessed by that mystery which surrounds every rational being. Those vague yearnings and obscure stirrings of the boy's spirit, as with strained eye he strove to penetrate the dark depths of infinite space, typify the workings of that soul which in only an imperfect degree partakes of this "vision and

* Fichte's Leben. I. 7.

faculty divine." And as those motions in this youthful spirit awaken interest in the observer, betokening as they do no common mood and tendency, so even the vague and shadowy musings of the mind which is but feebly under the influence of mystery: — a Novalis, or a Shelley,— are not without their interest and elevation.

But when a genius appears in the history of a nation's literature, who sees the great import and feels the full power of those true mysteries which are the subject matter of theological science, then creations appear which exert an inspiring influence upon all after ages, and by their profundity and power betoken that they are composed of no volatile essence, and produced by no superficial mental energy. They are not to be comprehended or admired at a glance, it is true, and therefore are not the favorites of the falsely educated class, but ever remain the peculiar property and delight of that inner circle of literary men in whom culture reaches its height of excellence.

It may appear strange to attribute the noblest characteristics of literature to the mysteries of theology, but a philosophical study of literature convincingly shows that from this dark unsightly root grows "the bright consummate flower." It is the spirit of this solemn and dark domain, which, by connecting literature with the moral and mysterious world, and by giving it a direct or indirect reference to the deepest and most serious relations of the human spirit, renders it profound, and raises it infinitely above the mass of common light literature.

2. This same influence of theology imparts that *earnest and lofty purpose* which resides in the best literature. The chief reason why the largest portion of the productions of the literary class contributes nothing to true cul-

tivation, and is destitute of the highest excellence, is the fact that it is not animated by a purpose. The poet composes a poem with no specific and lofty *intention* in his eye, but merely to give vent to a series of personal states and feelings. He writes for his own relief and gratification, not realizing, as Milton did, that " poetic abilities, wheresoever they be found, are the inspired gift of God, rarely bestowed; and are of power *beside the office of a pulpit*, to imbreed and cherish in a great people the seeds of virtue and public civility," and should be used for this noble purpose. The literary man generally, does not even dream that he is obligated to work with a good and elevated object in his eye, but is exempt from the universal law of creation, which obligates every finite spirit to live and labor for truth and God.

But sin always takes vengeance, and all literature which is purposeless, and does not breathe an earnest spirit, is destitute of the highest excellence. It will want the solemnity, the enthusiasm, the glow, the grandeur, and the depth, which proceeds only from a lofty and serious intention in the mind of the author. And this purpose can dwell only in the mind which is haunted by the higher ideas and truths of supernaturalism. It is in vain for the literary man to seek his inspiration in the earthly, or the intellectual, world. He must derive it from the heaven of heavens.

Both in heathen and in Christian literature, we find the noblest productions to be but the embodiment of a purpose; and the purpose is always intimately connected with the moral world. The Iliad proposes to exhibit the battle of heaven and earth, of gods and men, united in defence of the rights of injured hospitality. This proposition pervades the poem, and greatly contributes to invest it with the highest attributes of literature. The Grecian drama is serious and awful with the spirit of law and vengeance. Its high *motive*, is to teach all those solemn and fearful truths regarding justice and injustice which constitute the law written on the heart, and are the substance of the universally accusing and condemning conscience of man. Pagan though the Greek drama be, yet when we consider the loftiness and fixedness of its intention to bring before the mind all that it can know of the supernatural short of revelation, we hesitate not to say that it is immeasurably ahead of much of so-called Christian literature, in its doctrine and influence, as well as in its literary characteristics. As the scholar contemplates the elevated moral character running through this portion of Grecian literature, and contrasts it with much of that which is called Christian in distinction from heathen, he is led to take up that indignant exclamation of Wordsworth uttered in another connection,

> I'd rather be
> A Pagan, suckled in a creed outworn.

Of all literary men who have written since the promulgation of the Christian religion, Milton seems to have most strongly felt the influences of theology, and he more than all others was animated and strengthened by a high moral aim. In his literary works he distinctly and intentionally has in view the advancement of truth and the glory of God. These were "his matins duly, and his even-song." And to this noble purpose, as much as to his magnificent intellectual powers, are owing the profundity, loftiness, grandeur, truth, and beauty, which, in the literary heavens make his works like his soul, " a star that dwells apart."

We live in an age when theology has become entirely

dissevered from literature, and when supernatural science forms no part of the studies of the cultivated class. There was a period when literary men devoted the best of their time to the high themes of religion, and when literature took a deep hue and tincture from theology. There was a period when such a man as Bacon wrote theological tracts and indited most solemn and earnest prayers; when such a man as Raleigh composed devotional hymns; when such a man as Spenser sung of the virtues and the vices; when such a man as Shakspeare expended the best of his poetic and dramatic power in exhibiting the working of the moral passions; and when such a man as Milton made the fall of the human soul the "great argument" of poetry. There was a time when literature was in a very great degree impregnated by theology. But that time has gone by, and the productions of later ages show, by their ephemeral and inefficient character, that they have not that truly spiritual element which makes literature ever fresh and invigorating. Whatever may be the embellishment, the charm, and the fascination, of modern literature, for the student in certain stages of his growth, it does not permanently rouse and enliven like the old. It may satisfy the wants of the educated man for a time, but there does come a period in the history of every mind that is truly progressive in its character, when it will not satisfy, and the student must "provide a manlier diet." The mind when in the process of true unfolding cannot be ultimately cheated. Wants, which in the first stages of its development were dormant, while more shallow cravings were being met by a weak aliment, eventually make themselves felt, and send the subject of them after more substantial food. The favorite authors of the earlier periods of education are thrown aside as the taste becomes more severe, the sympathies more refined, and profounder feelings are awakened; the circle diminishes, until the scholar finally rests content with those few writers in every literature, who speak to the deeper spirit, because full of the vigor and power of the higher world.

The student while in the enjoyment of it may not distinctly know whence comes the charm and abiding spell of the older literature; but let him transfer himself into periods of national existence when faith in the supernatural had become unbelief, and when literary men had lost the solemn and earnest spirit of their predecessors, and he will know that religion is the life of literature, as it is of all things else. He will discover that the absence of an enlarging and elevating influence in letters, is to be attributed to the absence of that theological element with which the human mind, notwithstanding the corruption of the human spirit, has a quick and deep affinity.

I have thus, gentlemen of the societies, spoken of the true method of Theological Studies, and of their great and noble influences upon education and literature. If I have spoken with more of a theological tone than is usually heard upon a literary festival like the present occasion, I might excuse myself by simply saying, in the language of Bacon, that every man is a debtor to his profession. But I confess to a most sincere and earnest desire of awakening in the minds of those who are soon to become a part of the educated class of the land, an interest and love for that noblest and most neglected of the sciences: — theology. This science has come to be the study of one profession alone, and of one that unhappily includes but a very small portion of the educated class. And yet in the depth and breadth of its relations, as well as in the importance of its matter, it is the science of the sciences. God is the God of every man, and the science which treats of Him and his ways deeply concerns every man, and especially every one who in any degree is raised above the common level, by the opportunity and effort to cultivate himself. It is a great error to suppose that theological studies should be the exclusive pursuit of the clergy, and that the remainder of the literary class in the state should feel none of the enlargement and elevation of soul arising from them. — When the idea of a perfect commonwealth shall be fully realized — if it ever shall be on earth — theology will be the light and life of all the culture and knowledge contained in it. Its invigorating and purifying energy will be diffused through the whole class of literary men, and through them will be felt to the uttermost extremities of the body politic. All other sciences will be illuminated and vivified by it, and will then reach that point of perfection which has ever been in the eye of their most genial and profound votaries.

For a knowledge of the aims of the most gifted and enthusiastic students of science, discloses the need of the influence of theology, in order to the perfection of science, as well as of letters. That which makes Burke one of the few great names in political science, is the solemn and awful view he had of law as strictly supernatural in its essence; of law, in his own language, as " prior to all our devices, and prior to all our contrivances, paramount to all our ideas, and all our sensations, antecedent to our very existence, by which we are knit and connected in the eternal frame of the universe, out of which we cannot stir." * It was his high aim therefore to render political science religious in its character, and to found government upon a sacred and reverential sentiment towards law, in the breasts of the governed. Politics in his eye,

---

* Speech in the impeachment of Hastings. Works, iii, p. 327.

and government in his view, are essentially different from the same things, as viewed by that large class of political men who do not appear to dream, even, that there is a supernatural world, or that there are supernatural sanctions and supports to government. But the speculative views regarding politics advanced by Burke will never be practically realized among the nations, until the influence of the high themes of spiritual theology is felt among them, and political science will not be a perfect scheme, until constructed in the light and by the aid of theological doctrine. The sanction, the sacredness, the authority, and the binding power, of law, as the foundation of government and political science, for which Burke plead so eloquently, come from the supernatural world, and are not apprehensible except in the light of that science which treats of that world. The fine visions and lofty aspirations of Burke, relative to government and political science, depend therefore upon the practical and theoretical influence of theology for their full realization.

Let me briefly refer to another instance, in which we see that the high aims of a most profound and genial student will be attained only under the influence of the science of the supernatural. It has been the high endeavor of Schelling to spiritualize natural science; to strip nature of its hard forms, and by piercing beneath the material, to behold it as immaterial ideas, laws, and forces.* This is not only a beautiful, but it is the true, idea of nature and natural science. Schelling however has failed to realize it *in a perfect manner.* However great may be his merit in infusing life into this domain

---

* System des transcend. Idealismus, p. 5 For a full exhibition of this method of natural science, see Carus's Physiologie, Erster Theil.

of knowledge, and in overthrowing the mechanical view of nature, he has not constructed his system so as to maintain a pure theism, and therefore when viewed in connection with the true system of the universe, with which every individual science must harmonize, its falsity, in the great whole of knowledge, is apparent. And the imperfection of this system is owing, first, to the absence of a sharp and firm line of distinction between the natural and the supernatural, and secondly, to the want of that protection from pantheism, which a truly profound philosopher can find only in the purely supernatural doctrines of theology.

It is not true then that the theologian by profession is alone concerned with theology. He who would obtain correct views in political or natural science, as well as he who would be a mind of power and depth in the sphere of literature; in short, *the student generally;* has a vital interest in the truths of supernatural science.— And it is this conviction, gentlemen, which I would fix and deepen in your minds. Your attention might have been directed to some more popular theme; to some one of the aspects of polite literature, present or hoped for; but I preferred to direct your thoughts to a range of neglected but noble studies, confident that if any permanent interest should be thereby awakened in your minds towards them, a substantial benefit would be conferred upon you. I would then, not with the feigned earnestness which too generally characterizes appeals upon such an occasion as the present, but with all the solemn earnestness of the Sabbath, urge you to the serious pursuit of theological studies. It matters not, which may be the particular field in which you are to labor as educated men; the influence of these studies is elevating and enlarging in any field, and upon all the public professions.

If the Law is to be the special object of your future study, your idea of human law will be purified and corrected by your study of the divine law, and the general spirit and bearing of your practice will be elevated by those high studies which, more than any others, generate high principles of action.

Should you enter the arena of Political life, the influence of these studies will be most salutary. In this sphere, a man at the present day needs a double portion of pure and lofty principle, and should anxiously place himself under the most select influences. If the *serious* political spirit of Washington, and Jay, and Madison, is ever again to actuate our politics, it will be only through the return of that reverence for law, as flowing from a higher reality than the naturally corrupt will of man, and that faith in government as having its ground and sanctions in the supernatural and religious world, which characterized them. If politics is ever to cease to be a game, and is ever again to be considered as one of the solemn interests pertaining to human existence, it will be only when our young men enter this field under the influence of studies, and a discipline, that purge away low and sordid views, and induce a serious integrity and a self-sacrificing patriotism. If then you would sustain a relation to the government of your country, honorable to yourselves, and beneficial to it, imbue your minds and baptize your views and opinions with the theological spirit. Then you will be a statesman in the old and best sense of the word; not a mere office holder or seeker of office; but one in whom the great idea of the state resides and lives, and who by its indwelling power is full of the patriotic sentiment, and inspired by the noble spirit of allegiance to government and country.*

Finally, if you are to be one of the ministers and interpreters of Nature, or one who devotes himself to the cultivation of Fine Letters, the influence of these studies will be great and valuable. In the light of the supernatural, you will best interpret nature, and under the power of theology, you will be best enabled to contribute a profound and lofty addition to literature.

No one who watches the signs of the times, and especially the rapid and dangerous change now going on in the public sentiment of our country relative to the foundations of religion, government, and society, can help feeling that under Providence, very much is depending upon the principles and spirit which the educated young men take out with them into active life. Bacon, long ago, said that the principles of the young men of a nation decided its destiny, and the course of human events since his day has verified his assertion. It is certainly true in its fullest sense of this nation and its young men. Unless an upbuilding and establishing influence proceeds from the educated class, the disorganizing elements which are already in a furious fermentation in society will eventually dissolve all that is solid and fixed in it; and unless this class feel some stronger and purer influence than that of this world; unless it feels the power of the objects and principles of the other world; it will hasten rather than counteract the coming dissolution. Merely human culture, and merely natural

* Das Wort Staatsmann ist hier in dem Sinn des antiken πολιτικὸς genommen, und es soll dabei weniger daran gedacht werden, dasz einer etwas bestimmtes im Staat zu verrichten hat, was völlig zufällig ist, als dasz einer vorzugsweise in der Idee des Staats lebt. Schleiermacher. Reden. p. 28.

science, cannot educe that moral weight and force in the cultivated class, without which the state cannot long hold together. These must come from the general influence of theological science upon the minds of the educated; from the infusion into culture of that reverence for God, and that purifying insight into supernatural truth, without which culture becomes skeptical and shallow, powerless for good and all-powerful for evil.

In closing, permit me to remind you that you need the influence of these studies personally, without reference to your relations to the world at large. You need them in order to attain the true end of your own existence. However sedulously you may cultivate yourselves in other respects, you will not be cultivated for eternity, without the study and vital knowledge of theology. It has been foreign to the main drift of my discourse, and to the occasion, to speak of that deepest, that saving, knowledge of supernatural religion which proceeds from being taught by the Eternal Spirit. I have spoken only of the general and common influence of the doctrines of purely supernatural, in distinction from those of merely natural, theology. They have a great power in themselves, apart from their special vivification by the Divine Spirit. This is worthy of being sought after, and to this I have urged you. But if you would feel the full power of theology; if you would secure the freest, fairest, and holiest development of your spirits; if you would accomplish the very utmost of which you are capable, for your country and for man, in the sphere in which you shall be called to labor; if you would secure a strength which you will soon find you need in the struggle into which you are about to enter: — the struggle with the real world, and the still fiercer struggle with your real selves; then study theology experimentally. The discipline to which you have been subjected in the course of your training in this University, so far as human influence can do so, leads and urges you in this direction; for it is the plan and work of one of those elect and superior spirits (few and rare in our earthly race) who have an instinctive and irresistible tendency to the Supernatural.* This has been the tendency of your training, and if you will only surrender yourselves to this tendency, heightened and made effectual by special divine influences, as it will be for every scholar who seeks them with a solemn spirit, you will fully realize the idea of a perfect education.

* The allusion is to the late President Marsh.

THE NATURE, AND INFLUENCE, OF THE HISTORIC SPIRIT.

AN INAUGURAL DISCOURSE DELIVERED IN ANDOVER THEOLOGICAL SEMINARY, FEB. 15, 1854.

THE purpose of an Inaugural Discourse is, to give a correct and weighty impression of the importance of some particular department of knowledge. Provided the term be employed in the technical sense of Aristotle and Quinctilian, the Inaugural is a demonstrative oration, the aim of which is to justify the existence of a specific professorship, and to magnify the specific discipline which it imparts. It must, consequently, be the general object of the present discourse to praise the department, and recommend the study, of History.

As we enter upon the field which opens out before us, we are bewildered by its immense expanse. The whole hemisphere overwhelms the eye. The riches of the subject embarrass the discussion. For this science is the most comprehensive of all departments of human knowledge. In its unrestricted and broad signification, it includes all other branches of human inquiry. Everything in existence has a history, though it may not have a philosophy, or a poetry; and, therefore, history covers and pervades and enfolds all things as the atmosphere does the globe. Its subject-matter is all that man has thought, felt, and done, and the line of Schiller is true even if taken in its literal sense: the final judgment is the history of the world.*

If it were desirable to bring the whole encyclopaedia of human knowledge under a single term, certainly history would be chosen as the most comprehensive and elastic of all. And if we consider the mental qualifications required for its production, the department whose nature and claims we are considering, still upholds its superiority, in regard to universality and comprehensiveness. The historic talent is inclusive of all other talents. The depth of the philosopher, the truthfulness and solemnity of the theologian, the dramatic and imaginative power of the poet, are all necessary to the perfect historian, and would be found in him, at their height of excellence, did such a being exist. For it has been truly said, that we shall sooner see a perfect philosophy, or a perfect poem, than a perfect history.

We shall, therefore, best succeed in imparting unity to the discourse of an hour, and in making a single and, therefore, stronger impression, by restraining that career which the mind is tempted to make over the whole of this ocean-like arena, and confining our attention to a single theme.

It will be our purpose, then, to speak,

First, Of that peculiar spirit imparted to the mind of an educated man, by historical studies, which may be denominated the historic spirit; and

Secondly, Of its influence upon the theologian.

The historic spirit may be defined to be: the spirit of

* Resignation.

the race as distinguished from that of the individual, and of all time as distinguished from that of one age.

We here assume that the race is as much a reality as the individual; for this is not the time nor place, even if the ability were possessed, to reopen and reargue that great question which once divided the philosophic world into two grand divisions. We assume the reality of both ideas. We postulate the real and distinct, though undivided, being of the common humanity and the particular individuality. We are unable, with the Nominalist, to regard the former as the mere generalization of the latter. The race is more than an aggregate of separate individualities. History is more than a collection of single biographies, as the national debt is more than the sum of individual liabilities. Side by side, in one and the same subject; in every particular human person; exist the common humanity with its universal instincts and tendencies, and the individuality with its particular interests and feelings. The two often come into conflict with an earnestness, and at times in the epic of history with a terrible grandeur, that indicates that neither of them is an abstraction; that both are solid with the substance of an actual being, and throb with the pulses of an intense vitality.

The difference between history and biography involves the distinct entity and reality of both the race and the individual. Biography is the account of the peculiarities of the single person disconnected from the species, and is properly concerned only with that which is characteristic of him as an isolated individual. But that which is national and philanthropic in his nature; that which is social and political in his conduct and career; all that links him with his species and constitutes a part of the development of man on the globe; all this is historical and not biographic. Speaking generally in order to speak briefly, all that activity which springs up out of the pure individualism of the person, makes up the charm and entertainment of biography, and all that activity which originates in the humanity of the person furnishes the matter and the grandeur of history.

History, then, is the story of the race. It is the exhibition of the common generic nature of man as this is manifested in that great series of individuals which is crowding on, one after another, like the waves of the sea, through the ages and generations of time. The historic muse omits and rejects everything in this march and movement of human beings that is peculiar to them as selfish units; everything that has interest for the man, but none for mankind; and inscribes upon her tablet only that which springs out of the common humanity, and hence has interest for all men and all time.

History, therefore, is *continuous* in its nature. It is so because its subject-matter is a continuity. This common human nature is in the process of continuous evolution, and the wounded snake drags its slow length along down the ages and generations. No single individual; no single age or generation; no single nationality, however rich and capacious; shows the whole of man, and so puts a stop to human development. The time will, indeed, come, and the generation and the single man, will one day be, in whom the entire exhibition will close. The number of individuals in the human race is predetermined and fixed by Him who sees the end from the beginning. But until the end of the series comes, the development must go on continuously, and the history of it, must be continuous also. It must be linked with all that has gone before; it must be linked with all that is yet to come. As it requires the whole series of individuals, in order to a complete manifestation of the species, so it requires the whole series of ages and periods, in order to an entire account of it.

But while history is thus continuous in its nature, paradoxical as it may appear, it is at the same time *complete* in its spirit. Observe that we are speaking of the abstract and ideal character of the science; of that quality by which it differs from other branches of knowledge. We are not speaking of any one particular narrative that has actually been composed, or of all put together. History as actually written is not the account of a completed process, because, as we have just said, the development is still going on. Still, the *tendency* of the department is to a conclusion. History looks to a winding up. We may say of it, as Bacon says of unfulfilled prophecies: "though not fulfilled punctually and at once, it hath a springing and germinant accomplishment through many ages." It contains and defines general tendencies; it intimates, at every point of the line, a final consummation. The historical processes that have actually taken place, all point at, and join on upon, the future processes that are to be homogeneous with them. That very continuity in the nature of this science, of which we have spoken, results in this completeness, or tendency to a conclusion, in its spirit. Like a growing plant, we know what it will come to, though the growth is not ended. For it is characteristic of an evolution, provided it is a genuine one, that seize it when you will, and observe it at any point you please, you virtually seize the whole; you observe it all. Each particular section of a development exhibits the qualities of the whole process, and the organic part contemplated by itself throbs with the general life. Hence it is that each particular history; of a nation, or an age, or a form of government, or a school of philosophy, or a Christian doctrine; when conceived in the spirit of history, wears a finished aspect, and sounds a full and fundamental tone. And hence the proverb: man is the same in all ages, and history is the repetition of the same lessons.

So universal and virtually complete in its spirit is this science, that a distinguished modern philosopher has asserted that it may become a branch of *à priori* knowledge, and that it actually does become such in proportion as it becomes philosophic. Being the account, not of a dislocation, but of a development, and this of *one* race; being the exhibition of the unfolding of one single idea of the Divine mind; the history of the world, he contends, might be written beforehand by any mind that is master of the idea lying at the bottom of it. The whole course and career of the world, is predetermined by its plan, and supposing this to be known, the historian is more than "the prophet looking backward," as Schlegel calls him; he is the literal prophet. He does not merely inferentially foretell, by looking back into the past, but he sees the whole past and future *simultaneously* present in the Divine idea of the world, of which by the hypothesis he is perfectly possessed.

This philosopher believed in the possibility of such an absolutely perfect and *à priori* history, because he taught that the mind of man and the mind of God are one universal mind, and that the entire knowledge of the one may consequently be possessed by the other. While, however, the philosopher erred fatally in supposing that any being but God the Creator, can be thus perfectly possessed of the organic idea of the world, or that man can come into an approximate possession of it except as it is revealed to him by the Supreme mind, in providence and revelation, we must yet admit that the world is constructed according to such an idea or plan, and that for this reason, coherence, completeness, and universality, are the distinguishing characteristics of its development.

While, therefore, we deny that history as actually written, or as it shall be, comes up to this absolute and metaphysical perfection, it would be folly to deny that it has made any approximation towards it, or that it will make still more. So far as the account has been composed under the guiding light of this divine idea, which is manifesting itself in the affairs of men; so far, in other words, as it has been written in the light of providence and revelation; it has been composed with truth, and depth, and power. Historians have been successful in gathering the lessons and solving the problems of their science in proportion as they have recognized a providential plan in the career of the world, and have had some clear apprehension of it. The most successful particular narratives seem to be parts of a greater whole.— They have an easy reference to general history; evidently belong to it; evidently were written in its comprehensive spirit and by its broad lights. So much does this science abhor a scattering, isolating, and fragmentary, method of treating the subject-matter belonging to it, that those histories which have been composed without any historic feeling; with no reference to the Divine plan and no connection with the universe; are the most dry and lifeless productions in literature. Disconnection, and the absence of a unifying principle, are more marked, and more painfully felt, in historical composition, than in any other species of literature. Even when the account is that of a brief period, or mere point, as it were, in universal space, the mind demands that it be rounded and finished in itself; that it exhibit, in little, that same complete and coherent process, which is going on more grandly, on the wider arena of the world at large.

History, then, is the exhibition of the *species*. Its lessons may be relied upon as the conclusions to which the human race have come. In these historic lessons, the narrowness of individual and local opinions has been exchanged for the breadth and compass of public and common sentiments. The errors to which the single mind; the isolated unit, as distinguished from the organic unity; is exposed, are corrected by the sceptical and critical processes of the general mind.

What, for illustration, is its teaching in regard to the presence and relative proportions in a political constitution of the two opposite elements, permanence and progression? Will not the judgment, in regard to this vexed question, that is formed on *historic* grounds, be, to say the least, safer and truer, than that formed upon the scanty experience of an individual man? Will not the decision of one who has made up his mind after a thoughtful study of the ancient tyrannies and republics of Greece and Rome, of the republican states of Italy in the middle ages, of the politics of Europe since the formation of its modern state-system, be nearer the real truth than that of a pledged and zealous partisan, on either side of the question; than that of the ancient Cleon or Coriolanus; than that of the modern Rousseau or Filmer? And why will it be nearer the truth? Not merely because these men were earnest and zealous. Ardor and zeal are well in their place. But because these minds were individual and local; because they were not historic and general in views and opinions.

Take another illustration from the department of philosophy. A great variety of theories have been projected respecting the nature and operations of the human mind so that it becomes difficult for the bewildered inquirer to know which he shall adopt. But will he run the hazard of fundamental error, if he assumes that that theory is the truth, so far as truth has been reached in this domain, which he finds substantially present in the philosophic mind in all ages? if he concludes that the historic philosophy is the true philosophy? And will it be safe for the individual to set up in this department, or in the still higher one of religion, doctrines which have either never entered the human mind before, or, if they have, have been only transient residents?

The fact is, no one individual mind is capable of accomplishing, alone and by itself, what the *race* is destined to accomplish only in the slow revolution of its cycle of existence. It is not by the thought of any one individual, though he were as profound as Plato and as intuitive as Shakspeare, that truth is to obtain an exhaustive manifestation. The whole race is to try its power, and, in the end, or rather at every point in the endless career, is to acknowledge that the absolute is not yet fully known; that the knowledge of man is still at an infinite distance from that of God. Much has been said, and still is, of the spirit of the age; and extravagant expectations have been formed in regard to its insight into truth and its power of applying it for the progress of the species. But a single age is merely an individual of larger growth. There is always something particular, something local, something temporary, in every age, and we must not look here for the generic and universal any more than in the notions of the individual man. No age is historic, in and by itself. Like the individual, it only contributes its portion of investigation and opinion, to the sum total of material which is to undergo the test, not of an age, but of the ages.

Considerations like these go to show, that there is in that which is properly historic, nothing partial, nothing defective, nothing one-sided. It is the individual which has these characteristics; and only in proportion as the individual man becomes historic in his views, opinions and impressions; only as his culture takes on this large and catholic spirit, does he become truly educated. It is the sentiment of mankind at large, it is the opinion of the race, which is to be accepted as truth. When, therefore, the mind of the student, in the course of its education, is subjected to the full and legitimate influence of historical studies, it is subjected to a rectifying influence. The individual eye is purged, so that it sees through a crystalline medium. That darkening, distorting matter, composing oftentimes the idiosyncracy rather than the individuality of the intellect, is drained off.

Having thus briefly discussed the nature of the historic spirit by a reference to the abstract nature of the science itself, let us now seek to obtain a more concrete and lively knowledge of it, by looking at some of its actual influences upon the student. Let us specify some of the characteristics of the historical mind.

I. In the first place, the historical mind is both reverent and vigilant.

The study of all the past raises the intellect to a loftier eminence than that occupied by the student of the present; the man of the time. The vision of the latter is limited by his own narrow horizon, while that of the former goes round the globe. As a consequence, the historic mind is impressed with the vastness of truth. It knows that it is too vast to be all known by a single mind, or a single age; too immense to be taken in at a single glance, much less to be stated in a single proposition. Historic studies have, moreover, made it aware of the fact that truth is modified by passing through a variety of minds; that each form taken by itself is imperfect, and that, in some instances at least, all forms put together do not constitute a perfect manifestation of the "daughter of time." The posture and bearing of such a mind, therefore, towards all truth, be it human or divine, is at once reverent and vigilant. It is seriously impressed by the immensity of the field of knowledge, and at the same time is adventurous and enterprising in ranging over it. For it was when the human imagination was most impressed by the vastness of the globe, that the spirit of enterprise and adventure was most rife and successful. Before the minds of Columbus and De Gama, before the imagination of the Northmen and the early English navigators, space stretched away westward and southward like the spaces of astronomy, and was invested with the awfulness and grandeur of the spaces of the Miltonic Pandaemonium. Yet this sense of space, this mysterious consciousness of a vaster world, was the very stimulation of the navigator; the direct cause of all modern geographical discovery. The merely individual mind, on the contrary, seeing but one form of truth, or, at most, but one form at a time, is apt to take this meagre exhibition for the full reality, and to suppose that it has reached the summit of knowledge. It is self-satisfied and therefore irreverent. It is disposed to rest in present acquisitions and therefore is neither vigilant nor enterprising.

II. And this naturally suggests the second characteristic of the historical mind: its productiveness and originality.

Such a mind is open to truth. The first condition to the advancement of learning is fulfilled by it; for it is the fine remark of Bacon, that the kingdom of science.

like the kingdom of heaven, is open only to the child; only to the reverent, recipient, and docile, understanding. Perhaps nothing contributes more to hinder the progress of truth than self-satisfied ignorance of what the human mind has already achieved. The age that isolates itself from the rest of the race and settles down upon itself, will accomplish but little towards the development of man or of truth. The individual who neglects to make himself acquainted with the history of men and of opinions, though he may be an intense man within a very narrow circumference, will make no real advance and no new discoveries. Even the ardor and zealous energy, often exhibited by such a mind, and, we may say, characteristic of it, contribute rather to its growing ignorance, than its growing enlightenment. For it is the ardor of a mind exclusively occupied with its own peculiar notions. Its zeal is begotten by individual peculiarities, and expended upon them. Having no humble sense of its own limited ability, in comparison with the vastness of truth, or even in comparison with the power of the universal human mind, it closes itself against the great world of the past, and, as a penalty for this, hears but few of the deeper tones of the "many voiced present." In the midst of colors it is blind; in the midst of sounds it is deaf.

That mind, on the contrary, which is imbued with the enterprising spirit of history, contributes to the progress of truth and knowledge among men, by entering into the great process of inquiry and discovery which the race as such has begun and is carrying on. It moves onward with fellow-minds, in the line of a preceding advance, and consequently receives impulse from all the movement and momentum of the past. It joins on upon the truth which has actually been unfolded, and is thereby enabled to make a positive and valuable addition to the existing knowledge of the human race.

For the educated man, above all men, should see and constantly remember, that progress in the intellectual world, does not imply the discovery of truth *absolutely* new; of truth of which the human mind never had even an intimation before, and which came into it by a mortal leap, abrupt and startling, without antecedents and without premonitions. This would be rather of the nature of a Divine revelation than of a human discovery. A revelation from God is different in kind from a discovery of the human reason. It comes down from another sphere, from another mind, than that of man; and, although it is conformed to the wants of the human race, can by no means be regarded as a natural development out of it; as a merely historical process, like the origination of a new form of government, or a new school of philosophy. A discovery of the human mind, on the contrary, is to be regarded as the pure, spontaneous, product of the human mind; as one fold in its unfolding.

It follows, consequently, that progress in human knowledge, progress in the development of human reason, does not imply the origination of truth absolutely and in all respects unknown before. The human mind has presentiments; dim intimations; which thicken all along the track of human history like the hazy belt of the galaxy among the clear, sparkling, mapped, stars. These presentiments are a species and a grade of knowledge. — They are not distinct and stated knowledge, it is true, but they are by no means blank ignorance. The nebulae are *visible*, though not yet resolved. Especially is this true in regard to the mind of the race; the general and historic mind. How often is the general mind restless and uneasy with the dim anticipation of the future discovery? This unrest, with its involved longing, and its potential knowledge, comes to its height, it is true, in the mind of some one individual who is most in possession of the spirit of his time, and who is selected by Providence as the immediate instrument of the actual and stated discovery. But such an one is only the secondary cause of an effect, whose first cause lies lower down and more abroad. There were Reformers before the Reformation. Luther articulated himself upon a process that had already begun in the Christian church, and ministered to a want, and a very intelligent want too, that was already in existence. Columbus shared in the enterprising spirit of his time, and differed in degree, and not in kind, from the bold navigators among whom he was born and bred. That vision of the new world from the shores of old Spain; that presentiment of the existence of another continent beyond the deep; a presentiment so strong as almost to justify the poetic extravagance of Schiller's sonnet,* in which he says, that the boding mind of the mariner would have *created* a continent, if there had been none in the trackless West to meet his anticipation; that prophetic sentiment, Columbus possessed, not as an isolated individual, but as a man who had grown up with his age and into his age; whose teeming mind had been informed by the traditions of history, and whose active imagination had been fired by the strange narratives of anterior and contemporaneous navigation.

Another proof of the position that the individual mind owes much of its inventiveness and originality to its ability to join on upon the invention and origination already in existence, is found in the fact, that some of

---

* Columbus.

the most marked discoveries in science have occurred simultaneously to different minds. The dispute between the adherents of Newton and Leibnitz respecting priority of discovery in the science of Fluxions, is hardly yet settled; but the candid mind on either side will acknowledge that, be the mere matter of priority of detailed discovery and publication as it may, neither of these great minds was a servile plagiary. The Englishman, in regard to the German, thought alone and by himself; and the German, in regard to the Englishman, thought alone and by himself. But both thought in the light of past discoveries, and of all then existing mathematical knowledge. Both were under the laws and impulse of the general scientific mind, as that mind had manifested itself historically in preceding discoveries, and was now using them *both* as its organ of investigation and medium of distinct announced discovery. The dispute between the English and French chemists, respecting the comparative merits of Black and Lavoisier, is still kept up; but here, too, candor must acknowledge that both were original investigators, and that an earlier death of either would not have prevented the discovery.

Now in both of these instances the minds of individuals had been set upon the trail of the new discovery by history; by a knowledge of the then present state and wants of science. They had kept up with the development of science; they knew what had actually been achieved; they saw what was still needed. They felt the wants of science, and these felt wants were dim anticipations of the supply, and finally led to it. It was because Newton and Leibnitz both labored in a historical line of direction, that they labored in the same line, and came to the same result, each of and by himself. For this historical basis for inquiry and discovery is common to all. And as there is but one truth to be discovered, and but one high and royal road to it, it is not surprising that often several minds should reach the goal simultaneously.

A striking instance of the productive power imparted to the individual mind by its taking the central position of history, is seen in the department of philosophy. In this department it is simply impossible, for the individual thinker to make any advance unless he first make himself acquainted with what the human mind has already accomplished in this sphere of investigation. Without some adequate knowledge of the course which philosophic thought has already taken, the individual inquirer in this oceanic region is all afloat. He does not even know where to begin, because he knows not where others have left off; and the system of such a philosopher, if it contain truth, is most commonly but the dry repetition of some previous system. Originality and true progress here, as elsewhere, are impossible without history. Only when the individual has made his mind historic by working his way into that great main current of philosophic thought, which may be traced from Pythagoras to Plato and Aristotle, from Aristotle to the Schoolmen, and from the Schoolmen to Bacon and Kant, and moving onward with it up to the point where the next stage of true progress and normal development is to join on; only when he has thus found the proper point of departure in the present state of the science, is he prepared to depart, and to move forward on the straight but limitless line of philosophic inquiry. It is for this reason that the speculative systems of Germany exhibit such productiveness and originality. Whatever opinion may be held respecting the correctness of the Germanic mind in this department, no one can deny its fertility. The Teutonic philosopher first prepares for the appearance of his system, by a history of philosophy in the past, and then aims to make his own system the crown and completion of the entire historic process; the last link of the long chain. It is true that, in every instance thus far in the movement of this philosophy, the intended last link has only served as the support of another and still other links, yet only in this way of historic preparation could such a productive method of philosophizing have been attained. Only from the position of history, even though it be falsely conceived, can the speculative reason construct new and original systems.

A good illustration of the defectiveness which must attach to a system of philosophy, when it is not conceived and constructed in the light of the history of philosophy, is seen in the so-called Scotch school. A candid mind must admit that the spirit and general aim of this system was sound and correct. It was a reaction against the sensual school, especially as that system had been run out to its logical extreme in France. It recognized and made much of first truths, and that faculty of the mind which the ablest teacher of this school loosely denominated Common Sense, and still more loosely defined, was unquestionably meant to be a power higher than that which "judges according to sense." But it was not an original system, in the sense of grasping with a stronger and more *scientific* grasp than had ever been done before, upon the standing problems of philosophy. It is true that it addressed itself to the solution of the old problems, in the main, in the right spirit and from a deep interest in the truth, but it did not go low enough down, and did not get near enough to the heart of the difficulty, to constitute it an original and powerful system of speculation. Its greatest defect is the lack of a *scientific* spirit, which is indicated in the fact that, although it has exerted a wide influence upon the popular mind, it has exerted but little influence upon the philosophic mind, either of Great Britain or the Continent.

And this defect is to be traced chiefly to the lack of an extensive and profound knowledge of the history of philosophic speculation. The individual mind, in this instance, attempted a refutation of the acute arguments of scepticism, without much knowledge of the previous developments of the sceptical understanding and the counter-statements of true philosophy. A comprehensive and reproductive study of the ancient Grecian philosophies, together with the more elaborate and profound of the modern systems, would have been a preparatory discipline for the Scottish reason that would have armed it with a far more scientific and original power. Its aim, in the first place, would have been higher, because its sense of the difficulty to be overcome would have been far more just and adequate. With more knowledge of what the human intellect had already accomplished, both on the side of truth and of error, its reflection would have been more profound; its point of view more central; its distinctions and definitions more philosophical and scientific; and its refutations more conclusive and unanswerable.*

---

* This deficiency in scientific character, in the Scotch philosophy, is felt by its present and ablest defender, Sir William Hamilton. More deeply imbued with the spirit of the department than either Reid or Stewart was, because of a wider and more thorough scholarship than either of them possessed, he has been laboring to give it what it lacks. But it is more than doubtful whether any mind that denies the possibility of metaphysics as distinguished from psychology, will be able to do much towards imparting a *necessary* and *scientific* character either to philosophy generally, or to a system which is popular rather than philosophic, in its foundations and superstructure.

Thus we might examine all the departments of human knowledge, singly by themselves, and we should find that, in regard to each of them, the individual mind is made at once recipient and original by the preparatory discipline of historical studies and the possession of the historic spirit. Even in the domain of Literature and Fine Art, the mind that keeps up with the progress of the nation or the race ; the mind that is able to go along with the great process of national or human development in this department; is the original and originant mind. Although in Poetry and Fine Art, freshness and originality seem to depend more upon the impulse of individual genius and less upon the general movement of the national or the universal mind, yet here, too, it is a fact, that the founders of particular schools ; we mean schools of eminent and historic merit; have been men of extensive study, and liberal, universal sympathies. The great masters of the several schools of Italian Art, were diligent students of the Antique, and had minds open to truth and nature in all the schools that preceded them. They, moreover, cherished a historic feeling and spirit, by a most intimate and general intercourse with each other. The earnest rivalry that prevailed, sprung up from a close study of each other's productions. The view which Cellini presents us of the relations of the Italian artists to each other, and of the general spirit that prevailed among them, shows that there was very little that was bigoted and individual in those minds so remarkable for originality and productiveness within their own sphere.

A very fine and instructive illustration of the truth we are endeavoring to establish, is found in the department of literature in the poet Wordsworth. This man was a *student*. He cultivated the poetic faculty within him as sedulously as Newton cultivated the scientific genius within him. He retired up into the mountains, when he had once determined to make poetry the aim of his literary life, and by the thoughtful perusal of the English poets, as much as by his brooding contemplation of external nature, enlarged and strengthened his poetic power. By familiarizing himself with the spirit and principle, the *inward history*, of English poetry, he became largely imbued with the national spirit. And he was thorough in this course of study. He not only devoted himself to the works of the first English poets, the Chaucers, Spensers, Shakspeares and Miltons; but he patiently studied the productions of the second class, so much neglected by Englishmen, the Draytons, the Daniels, and the Donnes. The works of these latter are not distinguished for passion in sentiment or beauty in form, but they are remarkable for that thoroughly English property, thoughtful sterling sense. Wordsworth was undoubtedly attracted to these poets, not merely because he believed, with that most philosophic of English critics who was his friend and contemporary, that good sense is the body of poetry, but because he saw that an acquaintance with them was necessary to a thorough knowledge of English poetry considered as a historic process of development, as one phase of the English mind. For, although a poem like the Polyolbion of Drayton can by no means be put into the first class with the Faery Queen of Spenser, it yet contains more of the English temper, and exhibits more of the flesh and muscle of the native mind. These writers Wordsworth had patiently studied, as is indicated by that vein of strong sense which runs like a muscular cord through the more light and airy texture of his musings. It was because of this historical training as a poet, that Wordsworth's poetry breathes a far loftier and ampler spirit than it would have done had it been like that of Byron, for example, the product of an intense, but ignorant and narrow, individualism. And it was also because of this training, that Wordsworth, while preserving as original an individuality, certainly, as any writer of his time, acquired a much more national and universal poetic spirit than any of his contemporaries, and was the most productive poet of his age.

The result, then, of the discussion of the subject under this head is, that the individual mind acquires power of discernment and power of statement only by entering into a process already going on; into the great main movement of the common human mind. In no way can the educated man become genially recipient, and at the same time richly productive, but by a profound study of the development which truth has already attained in the history of man and the world.

III. The third characteristic of the historical mind is its union of moderation and enthusiasm.

One of the most distinct and impressive teachings of history is, that not every opinion which springs up and has currency in a particular age, is true for all time. History records the rise and great popularity, for a while, of many a theory which succeeding ages have consigned to oblivion, and which has exerted no permanent influence upon human progress. There always are, among the opinions and theories prevalent in any particular period, some, and perhaps many, that have not truth enough in them to preserve them. And yet these may be the very ones that seize upon the individual and local mind with most violence and most immediate effect. Because they are partial and narrow, they for this reason grasp the popular mind more fiercely and violently. Were they broader and more universal in their character, their immediate influence might be less visible, because it would extend over a far wider surface, and go down to a much lower depth. A blow upon a single point makes a deep dint, but displaces very few particles of matter, while a steady heavy pressure over the whole surface, changes the position of every atom, with but little superficial change.

The proper posture, therefore, of the individual mind, and, especially, of the educated mind, towards the current opinions of the age in which he lives, is, that of moderation. The educated man should keep his mind equable, and, in some degree, aloof from passing views and theories. He ought not to allow theories that have just come into existence to seize upon his understanding with all that assault and onset with which they take captive the uneducated, and, especially, the unhistoric mind. Of what use are the teachings of history if they do not serve to render the mind prudently distrustful in regard to newborn opinions, at the same time that they throw it wide open and fill it with a strong confidence towards all that has historically *proved* itself to be true? Is it for the cultivated man, the man of broad and general views, to throw himself without reserve and with all his weight, into what, for aught he yet knows, may be only a cross-current and eddy, instead of the main stream of truth?

Now it is only by the possession of a historic spirit that the individual can keep himself sufficiently above the course of things about him, to enable him to judge correctly concerning them. Knowing what the human mind has already accomplished in a particular direction, in art or science, in philosophy or religion, he very soon sees whether the particular movement of the time in any one of these directions, will or will not coincide with the preceding movement and be concurrent with it. He occupies a height, a vantage ground, by virtue of his extensive historical knowledge, and he stands upon it, not with the tremor and fervor of a partisan, but with the calmness and insight of a judge. Suppose the activity of an age, or of an individual, manifests itself in the production of a new theory in religion, of some new statement of Christian doctrine, the mind that is well versed in the history of the Christian church, and of Christian doctrine, will very quickly see whether the new joins on upon the old; whether it is an advance in the line of progress or a deviation from it. And his attitude will be accordingly. He will not be led astray with the multitude or even with the age. Through all the fervor and zeal of the period, he will preserve a moderate and temperate tone of mind; committing himself to current opinions no faster than he sees they will amalgamate with the truth which the human mind has already and confessedly discovered in past ages; with historic truth.

This moderation in adopting and maintaining current opinions is an infallible characteristic of a true scholar, of a ripe culture. And it is the fruit of that criticism and scepticism which is generated by historical study. For it is one of the effects of such studies to render the mind critical and sceptical; not, indeed, in respect to truth that has stood the test of time, but to truth that has just made its appearance. It would be untrue to say that the study of history genders absolute doubt and unbelief in the mind; that it tends generally and by its very nature to unsettle faith in the good and the true. This would be the case if there were no truth in the science; if it were substantially the record of dissension and disagreement; if, above the din and uproar of discordant voices, one clear and clarion-like voice did not make itself heard as the voice of universal history. We are all familiar with the story told of Raleigh, who is said to have destroyed the unpublished half of his work, because of several persons who professed to describe an occurrence in the Tower Court, which he had also witnessed from his prison window, each gave a different version of it, and his own differed from theirs. But history is not thus uncertain and unreliable. It teaches but one lesson. It reveals but one truth. Down through the ages and generations it traces one straight line, and in this one line of direction lies truth, and out of it lies error. Its record of the successes and triumphs of truth certainly teaches a correct lesson, and its record of the successes and triumphs of error is but the dark background from which truth stands out in still more bold and impressive reality. Whatever may be the case with particular accounts by particular individuals, the main current of this science runs in one direction, and its great lesson is in favor of truth and righteousness.

Not, then, towards well-tried and well-established truth, but towards apparent and newly-discovered truth, does history engender criticism and scepticism. The past is secure. That which has verified itself by the lapse of time, and the course of experiment, and the sifting of investigation, is commended as absolute and universal truth to the individual mind, and history bids it to believe and doubt not. But that which is current merely; that which in the novelty and youth of its existence is carrying all men away; must stand trial, must be brought to test, as all its predecessors have been. Towards the opinions and theories of the present, so far as they vary from those of the past, the historical mind is inquisitive, and critical, and sceptical, not for the purpose, be it remembered, of proving them to be false, but with the generous hope of evincing them to be true. For the scepticism of history is very different from scepticism in religion. The latter is always in some way biassed and interested. It springs out of a desire, conscious or unconscious, to overthrow that which the general mind has found to be true, and is resting in as truth. Scepticism in religion has always been in the minority; at war with the received opinions of the race, and consequently with all that is historic. There never was an individual sceptic, from Pyrrho to Strauss, who was not unhistorical; who did not take his stand outside of the great travelled road of human opinion; who did not try to disturb the human race in the possession of opinions that had come down from the beginning, besides having all the instincts of reason to corroborate them. But the scepticism of history has no desire to overthrow any opinion that has verified itself in the course of ages, and been organically assimilated, in the course of human development. All such opinion and all such truth constitutes the very substance of the science itself; its very vitality and charm for the human mind; and, therefore, can never be the object of doubt or attack for genuine historic scepticism. On the contrary, these sifting and critical methods have no other end or aim but to make a real addition to the existing stock of well-ascertained truth, and to prevent any erroneous opinion or theory from going into this sum-total, and thus receiving the sterling stamp and endorsement. This criticism and scepticism is simply for self-protection. These sceptical and sifting processes are gone through with, to preserve an all-sided science pure from the individual, the local, and the temporary, and to keep it universal and absolute in its contents and spirit.

Now it might seem at first glance, that this moderation of mind towards current opinions would preclude all earnestness and enthusiasm in the educated man; that the historic spirit must necessarily be cold and phlegmatic. It might seem that it would be impossible for such a mind to take an active and vigorous interest in the age in which it lived, and that it would be out of its element amid the stir and motion going on all around it. This is substantially the objection which the half-educated disciple of the present brings against history and historical views and opinions.

But this is a view that is false from defect; from not containing the *whole* truth. It arises from not taking the full idea of the science into the mind. This idea, like all strictly so-called ideas, contains two opposites, which, to the superficial glance, look like irreconcilable contraries, but to a deeper and more adequate intuition, are not only perfectly reconcilable, but are opposites in whose conciliation consists the vitality and fertility of the idea, and of the science founded upon it. History, as we have seen, is both continuous and complete; and continuity and completeness are opposite conceptions. — It is, in the first place, the record of a development that must unintermittently go on, and cannot cease, until the final consummation. And it is, in the second place, complete in its spirit, because at every point in the continuous process there are indications of the consummation; tendencies to an ultimate end. No part of history is irrelative. Even when it is but the account of a particular period, a small section of the great historic process, it exhibits this complete and universal spirit by clinging to what precedes and pointing to what succeeds; by its large discourse of reason looking before and after. But the objector does not reconcile these opposites in his own mind; he does not take this comprehensive and full view of the subject. Whether he acknowledges it or not his view really is, that the many several ages of which history takes cognizance, have no inward connection with each other, nor any common tendency, and consequently that the whole entire past, in relation to the present, is a nonentity. It is gone, with all that it was and did, into "the dark backward and abysm" of time, and the present age, like every other, starts independent and alone upon its particular mission. His view of history is atomic. — On his theory, there is no such thing as either connected evolution or explanatory termination, in the course of the world. There is no human race, no common humanity, to be manifested in the millions of individuals, and the multitudes of ages and epochs. On this theory, there is and can be nothing in the past, in which the present has any *vital* interest; nothing in the past which has any *authority* for the present; nothing in the past which constitutes the root of the present, and nothing in the present which constitutes the germ of the future. History, on this theory, has no principle; no organization. It is a mere catalogue of events; a mere list of occurrences.

It is because the imperfectly educated disciple of the present, really takes this view, that he asserts that historic views and opinions are deadening in their influence upon the mind, and that the historic spirit is a lifeless spirit. If he believed in a living concatenation of events and a vital propagation of influences, he would not say that that which is truly historical, is virtually dead and buried. If he believed that no one age, any more than any one individual, contains the whole of human development within itself, but is only one fold of the great unfolding, he would suspect, at least, that there might be elements in the past so assimilated and wrought into the nistory of universal man that they are matters of living interest for every present age. If he believed that truth is reached only by the successive and consentaneous endeavors of many individual minds, each making use of all the labors of its predecessors, and each taking up the standing problem where its predecessors had dropped it; if the too zealous disciple of the present believed that truth is thus reached only by the efforts of the race; of the universal mind in distinction from the individual; he would find life all along the line of human history; he would see that in taking into his mind a historic view or opinion he was lodging there the highest intensity of mental life; the very purest and densest reason of the race.

Instead, therefore, of being cold, phlegmatical and lifeless, the historical mind is really the only truly living and enthusiastic mind. It is the only mind that is in communication. It is the only mind that is not isolated. — And in the mental world, intercommunication is not more necessary to a vital process, and isolation or breaking off is not more destructive of a vital process, than in the world of nature. That zeal, begotten by the narrow views of an individual, or a locality, or an age, which the unhistorical mind exhibits, is an altogether different thing from the enthusiasm of a spirit enlarged, educated, and liberalized, by an acquaintance with all ages and opinions. Enthusiasm springs out of the contemplation of a whole; zeal from the examination of a part. And there is no surer test and sign of intellectual vitality than enthusiasm; that deep and sustained interest which is grounded in the broad views and profound intuitions of history.

But while the well-read student of history preserves a wise and cautious moderation, in the outset, towards current opinions, yet, because of this genial and enthusiastic interest in the truth which the human mind has actually and without dispute arrived at, he in the end comes to take all the interest in the views and theories of the present, which they really deserve. The historical mind does no ultimate injustice. So far and so fast as it finds that the new movement of the present age is a natural continuation of the unfinished development of the past, does he acknowledge it as a step in advance, and receives the new element into his mind and into his culture with all the enthusiasm and all the feeling with which he adopts the great historic systems of antiquity. In this way the historical mind is actually more truly alive and interested even in relation to the present, than the man of the present. It appreciates the real excellence of the time more intelligently and profoundly, and it certainly has a far more inspiring view of the connection of this excellence with the excellence that has preceded it, and which is the root of it. How much more inspiring and enlivening is that vision which sees the progress of the present linked to that of all the past, and contributing to make up that long line of development extending through the whole career of the human species, than that vision which sees but one thing at a time, and does not even know that it has any living references, or any organic connections whatever!

As an exemplification of the preceding remarks, contemplate for a moment the historian Niebuhr. His was a genuinely historical mind. He conceived and constructed in the true spirit of history. He always viewed events in the light of the organization by which they were shaped and of which they were elementary parts. He saw by a native sagacity, in which respect he never had a superior, the idea lying at the bottom of a historical process; such, for example, as the separate foundation of the city of Rome; the rise and formation of the

Roman population; the growth and consolidation of the plebeians; and built up his account of it, out of it and upon it. His written history thus corresponds with a fresh and vital correspondence with the actual history; with the living process itself. In this way he reproduced human life in his pages, and the student is carried along through the series with all the interest and charm of an actor in it. So sagacious was his intuition that, although two thousand years further off from them in time, he has unquestionably so reconstructed the very facts of the early history of Rome, as to bring them nearer the actual matter of fact, than they appear in the legendary pages of Livy. It was the habit of his mind, both by nature and by an acquisition as minute as it was vast, to look at human life as an indivisible process, and to connect together all the ages, empires, civilizations, and literatures, of the secular world by the bond of a common development; thus organizing the immense amount of material contained in human history into a complete and symmetrical whole.

But slow and sequacious as the movements of such an organizing and thoroughly historic mind were, and must be from the nature of the case, we do not hesitate to affirm that the historian Niebuhr was one of the most vividly alive and profoundly enthusiastic minds in all literary history. He was not spared to complete his great work as it lay in him to have done, and as he would have done, immense as it was, had he lived to the appointed age of man. He left it a fragment. He left it a Torso which no man can complete. But from that fragment has gushed, as from many living centres, all the life and power not only of Roman history, but of history generally, since his day. It gave an impulse to this whole department which it still continues to feel, besides reproducing itself in particular schools and particular individuals. It is the work which more than any other one production, shaped the opinions of the most vigorous and enthusiastic of English historians, the late Dr. Arnold. And that serious spirit which we find in the science itself since the days of Niebuhr, when compared with the moral indifference characterizing it before his day and to a great extent during his day, is to be traced to his reverent recognition of a personal Deity in history, and his deep belief in the freedom and accountability of man.

But the man himself, as well as his works, was full of life, and he showed it nowhere more plainly than in his direct address to the minds of his pupils. " When he spoke," says one of them, " it always appeared as if the rapidity with which the thoughts occurred to him, obstructed his power of communicating them in regular order or succession. Nearly all his sentences, therefore, were anacoluths; for, before having finished one, he began another, perpetually mixing up one thought with another, without producing any one in its complete form. This peculiarity was more particularly striking when he was laboring under any mental excitement, which occurred the oftener, as, with his great sensitiveness, he felt that warmth of interest in treating of the history of past ages, which we are accustomed to witness only in discussions on the political affairs of our own time and country." The writer, after speaking of the difficulty of following him, owing to his rapid, and it should be added, entirely extemporaneous delivery (for he spoke without a scrap of paper before him), remarks, that " notwithstanding this deficiency of Niebuhr as a lecturer, there was an indescribable charm in the manner in which he treated his subject; the warmth of his feelings, the sympathy which he felt with the persons and things he was speaking of, his strong conviction of the truth of what he was saying, his earnestness, and, above all, the vividness with which he conceived and described the characters of the most prominent men, who were to him living realities, with souls, feelings and passions like ourselves, carried his hearers away, and produced effects which are usually the results only of the most powerful oratory.*"

How different from all this is the impression which we receive from the mind of one who, notwithstanding his great defects, must yet thus far be regarded as the first of English historians; from the mind of Gibbon. After a candid and full allowance of the ability of that mind and the great value of the History of the Decline and Fall of Rome, it must yet be said that it was not a vivid and vital mind, nor is its product. The autobiography of Gibbon, indeed, exhibits considerable native liveliness, but the perusal of his history does not even suggest the existence of such qualities as earnestness and enthusiasm. One is disposed to conclude from the picture which he gives of himself, that the historian had been endowed by his Maker with a more than average share of mental freshness and vitality, and most certainly if there had been in exercise enough of this quality; enough of the *vis vivida vitæ;* to have vivified his immense well-selected and well-arranged material, he would have approximated nearer than he has to the ideal of historical composition. But there was not, and, therefore, it is, that, throughout the whole of this great work, there reigns, so far as the human and moral interest of history is concerned, so far as all its higher religious problems are concerned, an utter sluggishness, apathy, and lifelessness; an apathy and

---

* Dr. Leonhard Schmitz. Preface to Vol. IV. of Niebuhr's Rome.

lifelessness as deep, unvarying, and monotonous, as if the forces of the period he described, the principles of decline and decay, had passed over into his own understanding and made it the theatre of their operations. We doubt whether there is another work in any literature whatever, possessing so many substantial excellences, and yet characterized by such a total destitution of glowing inspiration and earnest enthusiasm, as the History of the Decline and Fall of the Roman Empire.

The explanation of this fact will corroborate the truth of the position, that the *genuinely* historic mind is the only truly living and enthusiastic mind. Though nominally a historian, Gibbon was really utterly unhistorical in his spirit. His religious scepticism, besides paralyzing whatever natural vigor and earnestness of conception may have originally belonged to him, made it impossible for him to regard the processes of human life as so many parts of one grand plan of the world formed by one supreme presiding mind. History for him, consequently, had no organization and no moral significance. It was, therefore, strictly speaking, no *history* at all for him; no course of development with a divine plan at the bottom of it and a divine purpose at the termination of it. It was neither continuous in its nature, nor complete in its spirit and tendency. Everything that occurred in the world at large, or among a particular people, was for his mind irreferent, discontinuous, and sporadic. Not only did he fail to connect the History of the Decline and Fall of the Roman Empire with the general history of the race, or even with the general history of Rome, by exhibiting it in its relation to its antecedents and consequents, but he failed even to detect the historic principle lying at the bottom of the particular period itself. The great *moral and political causes* of the decline and fall of the Roman empire, do not stand out in bold and striking relief from the immense erudition and imposing rhetoric of that work. The reflecting reader, at the close of its perusal, feels the need of something more than a scenic representation of the period; something more than the pomp of a panorama; in order to a knowledge of the deep *ground* of all this decline and decay. He needs, in short, what Gibbon does not furnish, more of the philosophy of that organic decline, drawn from a profounder view of the nature of man and of human life, united with a deeper insight into the radical defect in the political constitution of the Roman empire; into that germ of corruption which came into existence immediately after the subjugation of the Italian tribes was completed, and in which the entire millennium of decline and decay lay coiled up.

We have thus far discussed the nature of the historic spirit on general grounds. We have mentioned only those general characteristics which are matters of interest to every cultivated mind; having reference chiefly to secular history and general education. We have now to speak of the importance of this spirit to the theologian, and must, therefore, discuss its more special nature, with a prevailing reference to Ecclesiastical History and Theological Education.

Before proceeding to the treatment of this part of the subject, it seems necessary to direct attention, for a moment, to the distinguishing difference between Secular and Church history.

Our Lord, in the most distinct manner, and repeatedly, affirms that His kingdom is not of this world. Throughout the Scriptures the church and the world are opposed to each other as direct contraries, mutually exclusive and expulsive of each other, so that "all that is in the world is not of the Father, but is of the world." There are, therefore, two kingdoms, two courses of development, two histories, in the universal history of man on the globe. There is the account of the natural and spontaneous development of human nature as left to itself, guided only by the dictates of finite reason and impelled by the determination of the free, but fallen, human will, and the impulses of human passion. And there is the history of that supernatural and gracious development of human nature which has been begun and carried forward by means of a revelation from the Divine Mind made effectual by the direct efficiency of the Divine Spirit. The fact of sin, and the fact of redemption, constitute the substance of that great historic process which is involved in the origin, growth and final triumph of the Christian church. Had there been no fall of man, there would have been but one stream of history. The spontaneou development of the human race would have been normal and perfect, and there would have been no such distinction between the church and world as is recognized in Scripture. The race would not have been broken apart; one portion being left to a merely human and entirely false development, and the other portion being renovated and started upon a spiritual and heavenward career by the electing love of God. But sin in this, as in all its aspects, is dissension and dismemberment. The original unity of the race, *so far as a common religious character and a common blessed destiny are concerned*, is destroyed, and the two halves of one being, to borrow an illustration from the Platonic myth, are now and forever separated. The original single stream of human history was parted in the garden of Eden, and became into two heads, which have flowed on, each in its own channel, and will continue to do so, forevermore. For, although the church is to encroach upon the world, in the future, to an extent far surpassing anything that appears in the present and the past, we know, from the very best authority, that sin is to be an eternal fact in the universe of God, and as such must have its own awful and isolated development; its own awful and isolated history.

In passing, therefore, from secular to church history, we pass from the domain of merely human and sinful, to that of truly divine and holy, agencies. The subject-matter becomes extraordinary. The basis of fact in the career of the church is supernatural in both senses of the word. From the expulsion from Eden down to the close of miracles in the apostolic age, a positively miraculous intervention of Divine power lies under the series of events; momentarily withdrawn and momentarily reappearing, throughout the long line of Patriarchal, Jewish and Apostolic history; the very intermittency of the action indicating, like an Icelandic Geyser, the reality and constant proximity of the power. And if we pass from external events to that inward change that was constantly brought about in human character by which the church was called out from the mass of men and made to live and grow in the midst of an ignorant or a cultivated heathenism; if we pass from the miraculous to the simply spiritual manifestation of the Divine agency as it is seen in the inward life of the church, we find that we are in a far higher sphere than that of secular history. There is now a positive intercommunication between the human and the Divine mind, and the development which results constitutes a history far profounder, far purer and holier, far more encouraging and glorious, than that of the natural man and the secular world.

It is upon the fact of this direct and supernatural communication of the Supreme mind to the human mind, and this direct agency of the Divine Spirit upon the human soul, that we would take our stand as the point of departure in the remainder of this discussion. In treating of secular history, we have regarded the unaided reason of man as the source and origin of the development. We do not find in the history of the world, as the Scriptural antithesis of the church, any evidence of any special and direct intercommunication between man and God. We find only the ordinary workings of the human mind and such products as are confessedly within its competence to originate. We can, indeed, see the hand of an overruling Providence throughout this realm, employed chiefly in restraining the wrath of man, but through the whole long course of development we see no signs or products of a supernatural and peculiar interference of God in the affairs of men. Empires rise and fall; arts and sciences bloom and decay; the poet dreams his dream of the ideal, and the philosopher develops and tasks the utmost possibility of the finite reason; and still, so far as its highest interests are concerned, the condition and history of the race remain substantially the same. It is not until a communication is established between the mind of man and the mind of God; it is not until the Creator comes down by miracle and by revelation, by incarnation and by the Holy Ghost, that a new order of ages and a new species of history begins.

The Scriptures, therefore, as the revelation of the Eternal Mind, take the place of human reason within the sphere of church history. The individual man sustains the same relation to the Bible, in the sacred historic process, that he does to natural reason in the secular. The theologian expects to find in the history of the church that same comprehensive and approximately exhaustive development and realization of Scripture truth, which the philosopher hopes to find of the finite reason in the secular history of the race. It follows, consequently, that all that has been said of the influence of historical studies upon the literary man, applies with full force, when the distinguishing difference between secular and sacred history has been taken into account, to the education and culture of the theologian. The same spirit will work with the same results in both departments of knowledge, and the theologian, like the literary man, will become, in his own intellectual domain, both reverent and vigilant; both recipient and original; both deliberate and enthusiastic; as his mind feels the influences that come off from the history of the Christian religion and the Christian church.

Without, therefore, going again over the ground which we have travelled in the first part of the discourse, let us leave the general influences and characteristics of the historic spirit, and proceed to consider some of the most important of its specific influences within the department of theology and upon theological education. And, that we may not be embarrassed by the attempt to make use of all the materials that crowd in upon the mind on all sides, and from all parts, of this encyclopaedic subject, let us leave altogether untouched the external career of the church, and keep chiefly in view that most interesting and important branch of the department which is denominated Doctrinal Church History.

I. In the first place, a historic spirit within the department of theology promotes Scripturality.

We have already mentioned that the distinctive character of church history arises from the special presence and agency of the Divine Mind in the world. Subtract that presence, and that agency, and nothing is left but the spontaneous development of the natural man; nothing is left but secular history. Divine revelation, using the term in its widest signification, to denote the entire communication of God to man in the economy of grace, is the principle and germ of church history. That shaping of human events, and that formation and moulding of human character, which has resulted from the covenant of redemption, is the substance of sacred history. The church is the concrete and realized plan of redemption; and what is the plan of redemption but the sum-total of revelations which have been made to man by the Jehovah of the Old Testament and the Incarnate Word of the New, the infallible record of which is unchangeably fixed in the Scriptures? It follows, therefore, that the true and full history of the church of God on earth will be the Scriptures in the concrete. The plant is only the unfolded germ.

There is, consequently, no surer way to fill systematic theology with a Scriptural substance than to subject it to the influence of historical studies. As the theologian passes the several ages of the church in review, and becomes acquainted with the results to which the general mind of the church has come in interpreting the Scriptures, he runs little hazard of error in regard to their real teaching and contents. As in the domain of secular history we found that there was little danger of missing the true teachings of human reason, if we collect them from the continuous and self-defeating development of ages and epochs, so in the domain of sacred history we shall find that the real mind of the Spirit, the real teaching of Scripture, comes out plainer and clearer in the general growth and development of the Christian mind. Indeed we may regard church history, so far as it is mental and inward in its nature; so far as it is the record of a mental inquiry into the nature of Christianity and the contents of the Bible; as being as near to the infallibility of the written revelation, as anything that is still imperfect and fallible can be. The church is not infallible and never can be; but it is certainly not a very bold or dangerous affirmation to say that the church, the entire body of Christ, is wiser than any one of its members, and that the whole series of ages and generations of believers have penetrated more deeply into the substance of the Christian religion and have come nearer to an approximate exhaustion of Scripture truth, than any single age or single believer has.

So far, therefore, as a theological system contains historical elements, it is likely to contain Scriptural elements. So far as its statements of doctrine coincide with those of the creeds and symbols in which the wise, the learned, and the holy, of all ages have embodied the results of their continuous and self-correcting study of the Scriptures, so far it may be expected to coincide with the substance of inspiration itself.

Again, there is no surer way to imbue the theologian himself with a Scriptural spirit than to subject his mind to the full influence of a course of study in the history of the Christian religion and church. This is one of the best means which the individual mind can employ to reach the true end of a theological education; which is to get within the circle of inspired minds and see the truth exactly as they saw it. We believe, as the church has always believed, that the inspired writers were qualified and authorized to speak upon the subject of religion as no other human minds have been. They were the subjects of an illumination clearer and brighter than that of the purest Christian experience; and of a revelation that put them in possession of truths that are absolutely beyond the ken of the wisest human mind. — Within that inspired circle, therefore, there was a body of knowledge intrinsically inaccessible to the human mind; beyond the reach of its subtlest investigation, or its purest self-development. If those supernaturally taught minds had been prevented from fixing their knowledge in a written form; or if the written revelation had perished like the lost books of Livy; the human mind of the nineteenth century would have known no more upon moral and religious subjects, for substance, than the human mind of a Plato or Aristotle knew twenty-two centuries ago. For he must have an extravagant estimate of the inherent capacities of the finite mind, who supposes that the rolling round of two millenniums, or of ten, would have witnessed in any one individual case, a more central, or a more defecated, development of the pure rationality of mere man than was witnessed in Aristotle. And he must have a very ardent belief in the omnipotence of the finite, who supposes, that, without that communication of truth and of spirit; of light and of life; which God in Christ has made to the race, ages upon ages of merely spontaneous and secular history would have produced a more beautiful development of the human imagination than appears in the Grecian Art and Literature, or a more profound development of the human reason than appears in the Grecian Philosophy and the Grecian Ethics.

The Scriptures have, accordingly, been the source of religious knowledge and progress for the Christian, as antithetic to the secular, mind, and will continue to be, until they are superseded by some other and fuller revelation in another mode of being than that of earth. It has, consequently, been the aim and endeavor of the church in all ages, to be Scriptural; to work itself into the very heart of the written revelation; to stand upon the very same point of view with the few inspired minds, and see objects precisely as they saw them. But this, though possible and a duty, is no easy task, as the whole history of Christian doctrines shows. Truth in the Scriptures is full and entire. The Scriptural idea is never defective, but contains all the elements. Hence its very perfection and completeness is an obstacle to its full apprehension. It is difficult for the human mind to take in the *whole* great thought. It is often exceedingly difficult for the human mind oppressed, first, by the vastness and mystery of the revealed truth, and, secondly, by its own singular tendency to one-sided and imperfect perception, to gather the full idea from the artless and unsystematized contents of Scripture, and then state it in the imperfect language of man. The doctrine of the Trinity, for example, is fully revealed in the Bible. *All* the elements of that great mystery; the whole truth respecting the real triune nature of God, may be found in that book. But the elements are uncombined and unexpanded, and hence one source of the heresies respecting this doctrine. Arius and Sabellius both appealed to Scripture. Neither of them took the position of the infidel. Each acknowledged the authority of the written word, and endeavored to support his position from it. — But in these instances the individual mind merely picked up Scriptural elements as they lie scattered upon the page and in the letter of Scripture, and, without combining them with others that lie just as plainly upon the very same pages, moulded them into a defective, and therefore erroneous, statement. Heresy is individual and not historic in its nature.

Now it is the characteristic of the general mind of the church; of the historic Christian mind; that it reproduces in its intuition, and in its statement, the *complex* and *complete* Scriptural idea. So far as it has any intuition at all, it sees *all* the sides; so far as it makes any statement at all, it brings into it *all* the fundamentals. By this is not meant that even the mind of the church has perfected the expansion of Scripture elements and made the fullest possible statement of the doctrine of the Trinity. There may, possibly, be a further exhaustion of the contents of revelation in this direction. There may, possibly, be a statement of this doctrine that will be yet fuller; still closer up to the Scriptural matter; than that one which the church has generally accepted since the date of the Councils of Nice and Constantinople. But there will never be a form of statement that will flatly contradict this form, or that will add any new fundamentals to it. All that is new and different must be in the way of expansion and not of addition; in the way of development and not of denial. A closer study of the teachings of Scripture, and a deeper reflection upon them, may carry the theological mind further along on the line, but will give it no diagonal or retrograde movement.

Now is it not perfectly plain that the close and thorough study of this continuous and self-correcting endeavor of the Christian church to enucleate the real meaning of Scripture; an endeavor which has been put forth by the wisest, the most reverent, and the holiest, minds in its history, tasking their own powers to the utmost, and invoking and receiving Divine illumination, during the whole of the process; an endeavor which has to a great extent formed and fixed the religious experience of ages and generations, by its results embodied in the creeds and symbols of the church: a series of mental constructions, which, even if we contemplate only their human characteristics, their scientific coherence and systematic compactness, are more than worthy to be placed side by side with the best dialectics of the secular mind is it not perfectly plain, we say, that the close and thorough study of such a strenuous endeavor, as this has been, to reach the inmost heart and fibre of Scripture, will tend irresistibly to render the theologian Scriptural in head and in heart? May we not expect that such a student will be *intensely* Scriptural? Will not this distinct and thorough knowledge of revelation be so wrought into his mental texture that he will see and judge of everything through this medium? Will he not have so thought in that same range and region in which his inspired teachers thought, that doubt and perplexity in regard to Divine revelation would be nearly as impossible for him, as for Isaiah while under the Divine afflatus, or for Paul when in the third heavens? To borrow an illustration from the kindred science of Law: if it is the effect of the continued and thoughtful study of Law Reports and Political Constitutions and Commentaries upon Political Constitutions; a body of literature which, as it originates out of the organic idea of law, breathes the purest spirit of the legal reason; if it is the effect of such study to render the individual mind legal and judicial in its tone and temper, must it not be the effect of the study of that body of symbolic literature which has come slowly but consecutively into existence through the endeavor of the theological mind to reach a perfect understanding of Scripture, to render the individual mind Scriptural in its tone and temper?

II. And this leads us to say, in the second place, that a historic spirit in the theologian, induces a correct estimate of Creeds and Systematic Theology.

One of the most interesting features in the present condition of the theological world is a revived interest in the department of church history. This interest has been slowly increasing for the last half century, and promises to become a leading interest for some time to come. In Germany, in America, and in England, scholars and thinking men are turning their attention away, somewhat, from the purely secular history of mankind, to that more solemn and momentous career which a part of the human family have been running for nearly six thousand years. They have become aware that the history of the church of God is a peculiar movement that has been silently going on in the heart of the race from the beginning of time, and which, while it has not by any means left the secular historic processes untouched and unaffected, has yet kept on in its own solitary and sublime line of direction. They are now disposed to look and see how and where

>   the sacred river ran
> Through caverns measureless to man
> Down to the sunlit sea.

But it would be an error to suppose that this interest has been awakened merely or mainly by the external history of the Christian Church. "The battles, sieges, fortunes it hath passed;" its conflicts with persecuting Paganism, Mohammedanism, and Romanism; its influence upon art, upon literature and science, upon society and government; these are not the charm which is now drawing as by a spell the best thinking of Christendom towards church history. It is not the secular and worldly elements in this history into which the mind of the time most desires to look. The great march of profane history brings to view a pomp and prodigality of such elements that has already dulled and satiated the tired sensibilities. Thinking minds now desire to look into the distinctively supernatural elements in this historic process; to see if it really has, as it claims to have, a direct connection with the Creator of the race and the Author of the human mind. It is for this reason that the revived interest in this department of knowledge has shown itself most powerfully and influentially in investigating the origin and nature of the *doctrines* of the church, as they are found speculatively in creeds and symbols, and practically in the Christian consciousness. The mind of Germany, for example, after ranging over the whole field of cultivated heathenism, and sounding the lowest depths of the finite reason, in a vain search for that absolute truth in which alone the human soul can rest, has betaken itself to the domain of Christian revelation and Christian history. Its interest in Greek and Roman culture, in Mediaeval Art, and in its own speculative systems, has given way to a deeper interest in the Christian religion; in some instances with a clear perception, in others with a dim intimation, that, if the truth which the human mind needs, is not to be found here, the last resource has failed; and that then

> The pillared firmament is rottenness
> And earth's base built on stubble.

This revived interest in church history, therefore, is in reality a search after truth, rather than after a mere dramatic scene or spectacle. The mind of the time is anxious to understand that *revealed doctrinal system*, which it now sees, has, from the beginning, been the "rock" on which the church of God has been founded, and the "quarry" out of which it has been built. Knowing this, it believes it will then have the key to the process. Knowing this, it believes it will know the whole secret; the secret of that charmed life which has borne the church of God through all the mutations and extinctions of secular history, and that unearthly life which in all ages has secured to the believer a serene or an ecstatic passage into the unknown and dreadful future.

Now this interest in a doctrinal system, which thus lies at the bottom of this general interest in church history, will be shared by the individual student. He, too, cannot stop with the scene, the spectacle, the drama. He, too, cannot stop with those characteristics which ecclesiastical history has in common with secular, but will pass on to those which are distinctive and peculiar. For him, too, the history of a single mind, like that of Augustine or Anselm; or of a single doctrine, like that of the Atonement or of the Trinity; will have a charm and fruitfulness not to be found in the entire rise of the worldly Papacy, or in centuries of merely external and earthly movement like the Crusades. The whole influence of his studies in this direction will be spiritual and spiritualizing.

But, without enlarging upon the general nature of the estimate which the historic spirit puts upon the internal as compared with the external history of the church, let us notice two particulars which fall under this head.

1. Notice, first, the interest awakened by historical studies in the creeds and symbols of the Christian church *as containing the Philosophy of Christianity.*

We have spoken of the symbolic literature of the Christian church as a growth out of Scripture soil; as a fruitage full of the flavor and juices of its germ. A Christian creed is not the product of the individual, or the general, human mind evolving out of itself those truths of natural reason and natural religion which are connate and inborn. It is not the self-development of the human mind, but the development of Scripture matter. The

Christian mind, as we have seen, is occupied, from age to age, with an endeavor to fathom the depths of Divine revelation; to make the fullest possible expression and expansion of all the truths that have been communicated from God to man. This endeavor necessarily assumes a scientific form. The practical explanation, illustration, and application, is going on continually in the popular representations of the pulpit and the sermon, but this cannot satisfy all the wants of the church. Simultaneously with this there is a constant effort to obtain a still more scientific apprehension of Scripture and make a still more full and self-consistent statement of its contents. The Christian mind, as well as the secular, is scientific; has a scientific feeling, and scientific wants. A creed is as necessary to a theologian, as a philosophical system is to the secular student.

It follows, therefore, that the philosophy, by which is meant the rationality, of the Christian religion, is to be found in these creeds and symbols. For reasonableness and self-consistence are qualities not to be carried into Christianity from without, as if they were not to be found in it, but to be brought out from within, because they belong to its intrinsic nature. The philosophy, that is, the rational necessity, of the Christian religion, is not an importation but an evolution. This religion is to be taken just as it is given in the Scriptures; just as it reappears in the close and systematic statement of the creeds; and its intrinsic truth and reasonableness evinced by what it furnishes itself. For whoever shows the *inward* necessity and reasonableness of a Doctrine of Christianity does by the very act and fact show the harmony of philosophy and religion. Whoever takes a doctrine of Christianity and without anxiously troubling himself with the tenets of this or that particular philosophical system, derives out of the very elements of the doctrine and the very terms of the statement itself, a reasonableness that irresistibly commends itself to the spontaneous reason and instinctive judgment of universal man, by this very process demonstrates the *inward, central,* unity of faith and reason. Instead, therefore, of setting the two sciences over against each other and endeavoring, by modifications upon one or both sides, to bring about the adjustment, the theologian should take the Christian system precisely as it is given in Scripture, in all its comprehension, depth, and strictness, and without being diverted by any side references to particular philosophical schools, simply exhibit the *intrinsic* truthfulness, rationality, and necessity, of the system. In this way he establishes the position, that philosophy and revelation are harmonious, in a manner that admits of no contradiction. The greater necessarily includes the less. When the theologian has demonstrated the inward necessity of Christianity, out of its own self-sufficient and independent rationality, his demonstration is perfect. For reason cannot be contrary to reason. A rational necessity anywhere, is a philosophical necessity everywhere.

The correctness of this method of finding and establishing the rationality of Christianity, is beginning to be acknowledged in that country where the conflict between reason and revelation has been hottest. It begins to be seen that the harmony between philosophy and Christianity is not to be brought about, by first assuming that the infallibility is on the side of the human reason; and that, too, as it appears in a *single* and *particular* philosophical system; and then insisting that all the adjustment, conformity, and coalescence, shall be on the side of the Divine revelation. It begins to be seen that philosophy is in reality an abstract and universal term which, by its very etymology, denotes, not that it has already attained and now possesses the truth, but that it is seeking for it.* It begins to be seen that both Aristotle and Bacon were right in calling it an *organon;* an *instrument* for getting at the truth, and neither the truth itself nor even its containing source.† It begins to be seen that philosophy is only another term for rationality, and that to exhibit the philosophy of a department, like religion, or history, or philosophy, or natural science, is simply to exhibit the real and reasonable truth that is *in* it. It begins to be seen, consequently, that each branch of knowledge, each subject of investigation, must be treated *genetically* in order to be treated philosophically; must be allowed to furnish its own matter, make its own statements, out of which, and not out of what may be carried over into it from some other quarter, its acceptance or its rejection by the human mind should be determined.

We are aware that the barrenness of those later systems of speculative philosophy, with which the German mind has been so intensely busied for the last fifty years, has been one great means of bringing it back to this moderate and true estimate of the nature and functions of philosophy; but this revived interest in the history of Christianity

---

* The *love* of wisdom, implies a present seeking for it.

† Kant, says William Humboldt, did not so much teach philosophy, as how to philosophize. Correspondence with Schiller: *Vorerinnerung.*

It is the greatest merit of Schleiermacher that he saw and asserted the independent and self-subsistent position of Christian theology in relation to philosophical systems. If he had sought the *sources* of this theology more in the objective revelation and less in the subjective Christian consciousness, he would have accomplished more than he has towards evincing the harmony of the two sciences, while his own system would have had more agreement than it now has with the general theology of the Christian church.

and profounder study of its symbols, has also contributed, greatly, to produce this disposition to let revealed religion stand or fall upon its own merits. For this study has disclosed the fact that it has philosophical and scientific merits of its own; that, in the unsystematized statements and simple but prolific teachings of the Bible, there lies the substance of a *system* deeper and wider and loftier than the whole department of philosophy, and that this substance has actually been expanded and combined by the historic mind of the church into a series of doctrines respecting the nature of God and man and the universe with their mutual relations, with which the corresponding statements upon the same subjects, of the Greek Theism or the German Pantheism cannot compare for a moment. Probably nothing has done more to exhibit the Christian system in its true nature and proportions, and thereby to render it grand and venerable to the modern scientific mind, than this history of its origin and formation. As the scientific man studies the articles of a creed, which one of the most naturally scientific minds of the race, aided by the wisdom of predecessors and contemporaries, derived from the written revelation; as the rigorous and dialectic man follows Athanasius down into those depths of the Divine nature, which yawn like a gulf of darkness before the unaided human mind; if he finds nothing to love and adore, he finds something to respect; if he finds no food for his affections, he finds some matter for his thoughts. Here, too, is science. Here, too, is the profound intuition expressed in the clear but inadequate conception; the most thorough unions, guarded against the slightest confusions; analysis and synthesis; opposite conceptions reconciled in their higher and original unities; in short, all the forms of science, filled up in this instance as in no other, with the truth of eternal necessary fact and eternal necessary being.

And this same kind of influence, only in much greater degree, is exerted by historical studies upon the mind of the theologian. As he becomes better acquainted with the history of Christian doctrines, he becomes more disposed to find his philosophy of human nature and of the Divine nature in them, rather than in human systems. As he studies the development of that great doctrine, the doctrine of sin, he becomes convinced, if he was not before, that the powers, and capacities, and possible destiny, of the human soul, have received their most profound examination within the sphere of Christian theology. As he studies the history of that other great doctrine, the doctrine of the atonement, he sees plainly that the ideas of law and justice and government, of guilt and punishment and expiation; ideas that are the life and lifeblood of the Aristotelian ethics, the best and purest ethical system which the human reason was able to construct; that these great parent ideas show truest, fullest, largest, and clearest, by far, within the consciousness of the Christian mind.

What surer method, therefore, of making his mind *grow* into the philosophy of Christianity can the theologian employ, than the historic method? In what better way can he arm himself for the contest with ignorant or with cultivated scepticism, than by getting possession, through the reproductive study of dogmatic history, of the exact contents of Scripture as expanded and systematized by the consentaneous and connected studies of the Fathers, the Reformers, and the Divines, the Councils, the Synods, and the Assemblies, of the Church universal?

2. Secondly, notice the interest awakened by histori-

cal studies in the creeds and symbols of the Christian church *as marks of development and progress in theology.*

If we have truly enunciated the idea of history, in the first part of this discourse, it follows that all *genuine* development is a *historical* development, and all *true* progress is a *historical* progress. For the *true* history of anything is the account of its development according to its true idea and necessary law. The history of a natural object, like a crystal, for example, is the account of its rigorously geometric collection and upbuilding about a nucleus. Crystallization is a *necessary* process, for it is a petrified geometry. The history of a tree is the account of its spontaneous and *inevitable* evolution out of a germ. The process itself, in both of these instances, is predetermined and fixed. The account of the process, therefore, if it is exactly conformed to the actual matter of fact, has a fixed and predetermined character also. For, if nature herself goes forward in a straight and undeviating line, the history of nature must follow on after, and tread in her very and exactest footsteps. Hence, true legitimate history, of any kind, is neither arbitrary nor capricious. It corresponds to real fact, and real fact is the process of real nature. The matter and method of nature, therefore, dictate the matter and method of the history of nature.

And the same holds true, when we pass from history in the sphere of nature, to history in the realm of mind and spirit. The matter and method of a spiritual idea dictate the matter and method of the unfolding, and, consequently, of the history, of that idea. In the case now under discussion, the real nature and inward structure of Christianity determine what does, and what does not belong to its true historical development. The *true* history of Christianity, therefore, is the history of true Christianity.* The church historian is, indeed, obliged to take into account the deviations from the true Scriptural idea, because, unlike the naturalist, he is within the sphere of freedom, and of false development, and because redemption itself is a mixed process of dying to sin and living to righteousness. But he notices the deviations not for the purpose, it should be carefully observed, of letting them make up part of the *true* and *normal* history of Scriptural Christianity. The church historian is obliged to watch the rise and growth of heresies, not surely because they constitute an integrant part of the legitimate development and true history of Scripture truth. The account of a heresy has only a negative historical value. All the positive and genuine history of Christian doctrine is to be made up out of that correct apprehension and unfolding which Scripture has received from the Catholic as antithetic to the Heretical mind. Temporary departures from the real nature of Scripture truth, and deductions from it that are illegitimate, may possibly have contributed to a return to a deeper and clearer knowledge of revelation on the part of some few minds, and have unquestionably elicited a more full and comprehensive statement and defence of Christianity on the part of others, and in this way the heresies that appear all along the line of church history, throw light upon the

* The reader will notice the value of the qualifying adjective here. The term history is used in two senses; a general and a special. In the former sense, it denotes *all* that occurred, right or wrong, normal or abnormal. In the latter sense, in which alone it is employed above, it denotes only that which *ought* to occur. It is the proper function of the philosophic historian of the Christian religion and church, to reduce the general to the special history, by throwing out of the former all that is miscellaneous and heterogeneous, and retaining only that which accords with the supernatural law and principle that constitutes the basis of sacred, as distinguished from secular, history.

true course of doctrinal development and help to bring out the true history. But these heretical processes themselves, cannot be regarded as integrant and necessary parts of the great historic process, any more than the diseases of the human body can be regarded, equally with the healthy processes of growth, as the normal development of the organism. Nosology is not a chapter in physiology.

It follows, consequently, that the *true* and *proper* history of Christianity will exhibit a *true* and *proper* theological progress. It will show that the Scripture germ implanted by God, has been slowly but correctly unfolding in the doctrine and science of the church. We cannot grant that historical theology is anti-scriptural and radically wrong; that the Bible has had no true and legitimate apprehension in the ages and generations of believers. There has been, notwithstanding all the attacks of infidelity from without, and controversies from within, a substantial agreement, and a steady advance, in understanding the written revelation. This is very plainly to be seen in the history of doctrines, and from this we may draw the most forcible proofs and illustrations. Let any one compare the first with the latest Christian creed, and he will see the development which the Scripture mustard-seed has undergone. Let any one place the Apostles' creed beside that of the Westminster Assembly, and see what a vast expansion of revealed truth has taken place. The former was all that the mind of the church in that age of infancy was able to eliminate and systematize out of the Scriptures; and this simple statement was sufficient to satisfy the imperfectly developed scientific wants of the early church. The latter creed was what the mind of the church was able to construct out of the elements of the very same written revelation, after fifteen hundred years of study and reflection upon them. The "words," the doctrinal elements, of Scripture, are "spirit and life," and hence, like all spirit and all life, are capable of expansion. Upon them the historic Christian mind, age after age, has expended its best reflection, and now the result is an enlarged and systematized statement such as the early church could not have made, and did not need.

Compare, again, the statement of the doctrine of the Trinity in the Apostles' creed with that in the Nicene creed. The erroneous and defective statements of Arius compelled the orthodox mind to a more profound reflection upon the matter of Scripture, and the result was a creed in which the implication and potentiality of revelation was so far explicated and evolved as to present a distinct and unequivocal denial of the doctrine of a created Son of God. But, besides this negative value, this systematic construction of the Scripture doctrine of the Trinity has a great positive worth. It opens before the human mind the great abyss of the Divine nature; and, though it cannot impart to the finite intelligence that absolutely full and perfect knowledge of the Godhead which only God himself can have, it yet furnishes a form of apprehension which accords with the real nature of God, and will, therefore, preserve the mind that accepts it from both the Dualistic and the Pantheistic ideas of the Supreme Being. Abstruse and dialectic as that creed has appeared to some minds and some ages in the Christian church; little connection as it has seemed to them to have with so practical a matter as vital religion; it would not be difficult to show that those councils at Nice and Constantinople, did a work in the years 325 and 381, of which the church universal will feel the salutary effects to the end of time, both in practical and scientific respects. For, if all right religious feeling towards Jesus Christ is grounded in the unassailable conviction that he is truly and verily God; " begotten, not made, being of one substance with the Father;" then this creed laid down the systematic basis of all the true worship and acceptable adoration which the church universal have paid to the Redeemer of the world.* And if a correct metaphysical conception of the Divine Being is necessary in order to all right philosophizing upon God and the universe, then this Christian doctrine of the Trinity is the only statement that is adequate to the wants of science, and the only one that can keep the philosophic mind from the Pantheistic and Dualistic deviation to which, when left to itself, it is so liable.

The importance of historical studies and the historic spirit in an age of the world that more than any other suffers from false notions regarding the nature of pro-

* By this is not meant that there can be no true worship until a creed has been systematically formed and laid down, but that all true worship is grounded in a practical belief which, when examined, is found to harmonize exactly with the speculative results reached by the Christian Scientific mind. So far as the great body of believers is concerned, their case is like that of Hilary of Poictiers, who has left one of the best of the patristic treatises upon the Trinity, but who, in his retired bishopric in Gaul, did not hear of the Nicene creed until many years after its origin. He " found in it that very same doctrine of the unity of essence in the Father and the Son, which he had, before this, ascertained to be the true doctrine, from the study of the New Testament, and had received into his Christian experience, without being aware that the faith which he bore in his heart, had been laid down in the form of a creed." — Torrey's Neander, ii. 396.

Consonant with this, Hagenbach, after speaking of the highly scientific character of the *Symbolum Quicumque*, its endeavor, namely, to express the ineffable by its series of affirmations and guarding negations, adds, that " such formulae nevertheless have their edifying no less than their scientific side, inasmuch as they testify to the struggle of the Christian mind after a satisfactory expression of that which has its full truth only in the depths of the believing heart and character." — Dogmengeschichte, third edition, p 249, note.

gress and development, cannot be exaggerated. But he who is able to see in the creeds and symbols of the Christian church so many steps of real progress; he who knows that outside of that line of symbolic literature there is nothing but deviation from the real matter of Scripture, will not be likely to be carried away with the notion of a sudden and great improvement upon all that has hitherto been accomplished in the department of theology. He will know that, as all the past development has been historic; restatement shooting out of prestatement; the fuller creed bursting out of the narrower; the expanded treatise swelling forth growth-like from the more slender; so all the present and future development in theology must be historic also. He will see, especially, that elements that have already been examined and rejected by the Christian mind, as unscriptural and foreign, can never again be rightfully introduced into creeds and symbols; that history cannot undo history; that the progress of the present and the future must be homogeneous and kindred with the progress of the past.

III. In the third place, a historic spirit in the theologian protects him from false notions respecting the nature of the visible church, and from a false church feeling.

We can devote but a moment to this branch of the discussion, unusually important just at this time.

We have seen that the most important part of the history of the church is its inward history. We have found that the external history of Christianity derives all its interest for a thoughtful mind from its connection with that dispensation of truth and of spirit which lies beneath it as its animating soul. The whole influence, consequently, of genuine and comprehensive historical study is to magnify the substance and subordinate the form to exalt truth, doctrine, and life, over rites, ceremonies, and polities.

It is undoubtedly true, that the study of ecclesiastical history, in some minds, and in some branches of the church, has strengthened a strong formalizing tendency, and promoted ecclesiasticism. The Papacy has from time immemorial appealed to tradition; and those portions of the Protestant church which have been least successful in freeing themselves from the materialism of the Papacy, have said much about the past history of the church. Hence, in some quarters in the Protestant church, there are, and always have been, apprehensions lest history should interfere with the great right of private judgment, and put a stop to all legitimate progress.

But it only needs a comprehensive idea of the nature of history to allay these apprehensions. It only needs to be remembered that the history of Christianity is something more than the history of the Nicene period or of the Scholastic age. It only needs to be recollected that the history of Christianity denotes a course of development from the beginning of the world down to the present moment; that it includes the whole of that Divine economy which began with the first promise, and which manifested itself first in the Patriarchal, next in the Jewish, and finally in the Christian, church.* The

---

* Probably the most serious defect in the construction of the history of Christianity by the school of Schleiermacher, springs from regarding the incarnation as the beginning of church history. Even if this is not always formally said, as it sometimes is, the notion itself moulds and forms the whole account. The golden position of Augustine, *Novum Testamentum in Vetere latet, Vetus in Novo patet*, is forgotten, and the Jewish religion, as it came from God, is confounded with that corruption of it which we find in the days of our Saviour, but against which the evangelical prophet Isaiah inveighs as earnestly as the evangelical apostle Paul. " He is not a Jew

influence of the study of this *whole* great process, especially if the eye is kept fastened upon the spiritual substance of it, is anything but formalizing and sectarian. — If, therefore, a papistic and anti-catholic temper has ever shown itself in connection with the study of ecclesiastical history, it was because the inward history was neglected, and even the external history was studied in sections only. He who selects a particular period merely, and neglects all that has preceded and all that has followed, will be liable to a sectarian view of the nature and history of the church of God. He who reproduces within his mind the views and feelings of a single age merely, will be individual and bigoted in his temper. — He who confines his studies, for example, as so many

which is one outwardly, neither is that circumcision which is outward in the flesh." Judaism is not Phariseeism. There is, therefore, no *inward* and *essential* difference between true Judaism and true Christianity. The former looked forward and the latter looks backward to the same central Person and the same central Cross. The manifested Jehovah of the Old Testament was the incarnate Word of the New. "The religion," says Edwards, "that the church of God has professed from the first founding of the church after the fall to this time, has always been the same. · Though the dispensations have been altered, yet the religion which the church has professed, has always, as to its essentials, been the same. The church of God, from the beginning, has been one society. The Christian church which has been since Christ's ascension, is manifestly the same society continued, with the church that was before Christ came. The Christian church is grafted on their root; they are built upon the same foundation. — The revelation upon which both have depended, is essentially the same; for, as the Christian church is built on the Holy Scriptures, so was the Jewish church, though now the Scriptures be enlarged by the addition of the New Testament; but still it is essentially the same revelation with that which was given in the Old Testament, only the subjects of Divine revelation are now more clearly recorded in the New Testament than they were in the Old. But the sum and substance of both the Old Testament and the New, is Christ and His redemption. The church of God has always been on the foundation of Divine revelation, and always on those revelations that were essentially the same, and which were summarily comprehended in the Holy Scriptures." — Edwards's Work of Redemption, i. 473

have done, and are doing, to that period from Constantine to Hildebrand, which witnessed the rise and formation of the Papacy; and, especially, he, who in this period studies merely the archaeology and the polity, without the doctrines, the morality, and the life; he, who confines himself to those tracts of Augustine which emphasize the idea of the church in opposition to ancient radicals and disorganizers, but studiously avoids those other and greater and more elaborate treatises of this earnest spiritualist, which thunder the idea of the truth, in opposition to all heretics and all formalists; he, in short, who goes to the study of ecclesiastical history with a predetermined purpose, and carries into it an antecedent interpreting idea, derived from his denomination, and not from Scripture, will undoubtedly become more and more Romish and less and less historic.

Such a disposition as this, is directly crossed and mortified by a comprehensive and philosophic conception of history. Especially will the history of doctrines destroy the belief in the infallibility, or *paramount* authority, of any particular portion of the church universal. The eye is now turned away from those external and imposing features of the history which have such a natural effect to carnalize the mind, to those simpler truths and interior living principles, which have a natural effect to spiritualize it. An interest in the theology of the church is very different from an interest in the polity of the church. It is a fact that as the one rises, the other declines; and there would be no surer method of destroying the formalism that exists in some portions of the church, than to compel their clergy to the continuous and close study of the entire history of Christian doctrines.

IV. In the fourth place, a historic spirit in theologians

promotes a profound and genial agreement on essential points, and a genial disagreement on non-essentials.

It is plain that the study of church history tends to establish and to magnify the distinction between real orthodoxy and real heterodoxy. History is discriminating and cannot be made to mingle the immiscible. In regard, therefore, to the great main currents of truth and of error, the historic mind is clear in its insight and decided in its opinions. It knows that the Christian religion has been both truly and falsely apprehended by the human mind, and that, consequently, two lines of belief can be traced down the ages and generations; that in only one of these two, is Scriptural Christianity to be found.

But its wide and catholic survey, also enables the historic mind to see as the unhistoric mind cannot, that the line of orthodoxy is not a mathematical line. It has some breadth. It is a path, upon which the church can travel, and not merely a direction in which it can look. It is a high and royal road, where Christian men may go abreast; may pass each other, and carry on the practical business of a Christian life; and not a mere hair-line down which nought can go but the one-eyed sighting of either speculative or provincial bigotry.

Hence historical studies banish both provincialism and bigotry from a theological system, and imbue it with that practical and catholic spirit which renders it interesting and influential through the whole church and world. A system of theology may be true and yet not contain the whole truth. It may have seized upon some fundamental positions, or cardinal doctrines, with a too violent energy, and have given them an exorbitant expansion, to the neglect of other equally fundamental truths. In this case, historical knowledge is one of the best correctives

A wider knowledge of the course of theological speculation; a more profound acquaintance with the origin and formation of the leading systems of the church universal; tends to produce that equilibrium of the parts and that comprehensiveness of the whole, which are so apt to be lacking in a provincial creed or system.

A similar liberalizing influence is exerted by the study of church history upon the theologian himself. He sees that men on the same side of the line which divides real orthodoxy from real heterodoxy, have differed from each other, and sometimes upon very important, though never upon vital, points. The history of Christian doctrine compels him to acknowledge that there is a theological space, within which it is safe for the theological scientific mind to expatiate and career; that this is a liberty conceded to the theologian by the unsystematized form in which the written revelation has been given to man, and a liberty, too, which, when it is not abused, greatly promotes that clearer and fuller understanding of the Scriptures, which we have seen the historic Christian mind is continually striving after.

But this scientific liberality among theologians leads directly to a more profound and genial agreement among them upon all practical and essential points. The liberality of the historic mind is very far removed from that mere indifferentism which sometimes usurps this name There *is* a truth for which the disagreeing, and perhaps (owing to imperfectly sanctified hearts) the bitterly disagreeing, theologians would both be tied to one stake and be burnt with one fire. There is a vital and necessary doctrine for which, if it were assailed by a third party, a bitter unevangelic enemy, both of the contending orthodox divines would fight under one and the same shield. That truth which history shows has been the life of the church and without which it must die; that historic truth, which is the heritage and the joy of the whole family in heaven and on earth, is dear to both hearts alike.

But what tends to make differing theologians agree, profoundly and thoroughly, upon essential points, also tends to make them differ generously and genially upon non-essentials. Those who know that, after all, they are one, in fundamental character, and in fundamental belief; that, after all their disputing, they have but one Lord, one faith and one baptism; find it more difficult to maintain a bitter tone and to employ an exasperated accent toward each other. The common Christian consciousness wells up from the lower depths of the soul, and, as in those deep inland lakes which are fed from subterranean fountains, the sweet waters neutralize and change those bitter or brackish surface currents that have in them the taint of the shores; perhaps the washings of civilization.

While, therefore, a wide acquaintance with the varieties of statement which appear in scientific orthodoxy, does not in the least render the mind indifferent to that essential truth which every man must believe or be lost eternally, it at the same time induces a generous and genial temper among differing theologians. The controversies of the Christian church have unquestionably been a benefit to systematic theology, and that mind must have a very meagre idea of the comprehensiveness and pregnancy of Divine revelation, who supposes that the Christian mind could have derived out of it that great system of doctrinal knowledge which is to outlive all the constructions of the philosophic mind, without any sharp controversy, or keen examination among theologians. That structure did not and could not rise like Thebes, at the mellifluous sound of Amphion's lute; it did not rear itself up like the Jewish temple without sound of hammer, or axe, or any tool of iron. Slowly, and with difficulty, was it upreared, by hard toil, amid opposition from foes without and foes within, and through much earnest mental conflict. And so will it continue to be reared and beautified in the ages that are to come. We cannot alter this course of things so long as the truth is infinite, and the mind is finite and sees through a glass darkly.

What is needed, therefore, is a sweet and generous temper in all parties as the work goes on. The theologian needs that great ability: *the ability to differ genially.* It has been the misery and the disgrace of the church, that too many theologians who have held the truth, and have held it, too, in its best forms, have held it, like the heathen, in unrighteousness; have held it in narrowness and bigotry. They have differed in a hard, dry, ungenial way. They have forgotten that the rich man can afford to be liberal; that the strong man need not be constantly anxious; that a scientific and rigorous orthodoxy should ever look out of a beaming, and not a sullen, eye.

Let us be thankful that some ages in the history of the church furnish examples that cheer and instruct. Look back at that most interesting period, the period of the Reformation, and contemplate the profound agreement upon essentials and the genial disagreement upon nonessentials, that prevailed among the leaders then. Martin Luther and John Calvin were two theologians who differed as greatly in mental structure, and in their spontaneous mode of contemplating and constructing doctrines, as is possible for two minds upon the same side of the great controversy between orthodoxy and heresy. No man will say that the differences between Lutheranism and Calvinism are minor or unimportant. Probably any one would say that, if those two men were able to feel the common Christian fellowship; to enjoy the communion of saints; and to realize with tenderness their common relationship to the Head of the church; there is no reason why all men who are properly within the pale of orthodoxy should not do the same.

Turn now to the letters of both of these men; written in the midst of that controversy which was going on between the two portions of the Reformed, and which resulted, not, however, through the desire or the influence of these two great men, but through the bitterness of their adherents, in their division into two distinct churches; and witness the common genial feeling that prevailed. Hear Luther in his letter to Bucer sending his cordial greeting to Calvin, whose books he has read with singular pleasure: *cum singulari voluptate.* Hear Calvin declaring his willing and glad readiness to subscribe to the Augsburg Confession, interpreting it upon the sacramental question as the Lutherans themselves authorized him to do.* Above all, turn to that burst, from Calvin, of affectionate feeling towards Melanchthon, which gives itself vent in the midst of one of his stern controversial tracts, like the music of flutes silencing for a moment the clang of war-cymbals and the blare of the trumpet: " O Philip Melanchthon, to thee I address myself, to thee who art now living in the presence of God with

* Henry's Life of Calvin, II. pp. 96, 99. It is interesting and instructive to witness the liberal feeling of the scientific and rigorously orthodox Athanasius towards the Semiarians themselves, whose statement of the doctrine of the Trinity he regarded to be inadequate. See the quotation from *Athanasius de Synodis*, § 41, in Gieseler, Chap. II. § 83, and the reference to *Hilarius de Synodis*, § 76. Says Augustine: "they who do not pertinaciously defend their opinion, false and perverse though it be, especially when it does not spring from the audacity of their own presumption, while they seek the truth with cautious solicitude, and are prepared to correct themselves when they have found it, are by no means to be ranked among heretics."—Epistle 43, Newman's Library Version.

Jesus Christ, and there awaitest us, till death shall unite us in the enjoyment of Divine peace. A hundred times hast thou said to me, when weary with so much labor and oppressed with so many burdens, thou laidst thy head upon my breast, 'God grant, God grant, that I may now die!'"*

The theology of Richard Baxter differs from the theology of John Owen by some important modifications, and each of these two types of Calvinism will probably perpetuate itself in the church to the end of time; but the confidence which both of these great men cherished towards each other, should go along down with these systems through the ages and generations of time.

But what surer method can be employed to produce and perpetuate this catholic and liberal feeling among the various types and schools of orthodox theology, than to impart to all of them the broad views of history? And what surer method than this can be taken to diminish the number and bring about more unity of opinion in the department of systematic theology? For it is one great effect of history to coalesce and harmonize. It introduces mutual modifications, by showing opponents that their predecessors were nearer together than they themselves are, by tracing the now widely separated opinions back to that point of departure where they were once very near together; and, above all, by causing all parties to remember, what all are so liable to forget in the heat of controversy, that all forms of orthodoxy took their first origin in the Scriptures, and that, therefore, all theological controversy should be carried on with a constant reference to this one infallible standard, which can teach but one infallible system.

* Henry's Life of Calvin, I. 239.

I have thus considered the nature of the historic spirit and its influence both upon the secular and theological mind, in order to indicate my own deep sense of the importance of the department in which I have been called to give instruction by the guardians of this Institution. The first instinctive feelings would have shrunk from the weight of the great burden imposed, and the extent of the very great field opened ; though in an institution where the pleasant years of professional study were all spent; though in an ancient institution, made illustrious and influential, through the land and the world, by the labors of the venerated dead and the honored living. But it does not become the individual to yield to his individuality. The stream of Divine Providence, so signally conspicuous in the life of the church, and of its members, is the stream upon which the diffident as well as the confident must alike cast themselves. And he who enters upon a new course of labor for the church of God, with just views of the greatness and glory of the kingdom and of the comparative unimportance of any individual member, will be most likely to perform a work that will best harmonize with the development and progress of the great whole.

THE IDEA OF EVOLUTION DEFINED, AND APPLIED TO HISTORY.

§ 1. The abstract idea of Evolution and of History.

In order to the successful investigation of any subject, it is necessary, first of all, to form a comprehensive and clear conception of its essential nature. Without such an antecedent general apprehension, the mind is at a loss where to begin, and which way to proceed. The true idea of any object, is a species of preparatory knowledge which throws light over the whole field of inquiry, and introduces an orderly method into the whole course of examination. It is the clue which leads through the labyrinth; the key to the problem to be solved.

It may appear strange and irrational, at first glance, to require a knowledge of the intrinsic nature of that which is to be examined, in order that it may be examined, and before the examination. At first sight, it may seem as if this perception of the true idea of a thing, should be the result, and not the antecedent, of inquiry, and that nothing of an *a priori* nature should be permitted to enter into the investigations of the human mind in any department of knowledge. To require in the outset a comprehensive idea of History, for example, and then to use this as an instrument of investigation, seems to invert the true order of things, and to convert ignorance into knowledge by some shorter method than that of study and reflection. But what is the matter of fact? Does the scientific mind start off upon its inquiries in every direction, without any preconceived ideas as to where it is going, and what it expects to find? Is the human understanding such a *tabula rasa*, that it contributes nothing of its own towards the discovery of truth, but, like the mirror, servilely reflects all that is brought before it, without regard to deflections and distortions? We have only to watch the movements of our minds to find that we carry with us into every field of investigation an antecedent idea, which gives more or less direction to our studies, and goes far to determine the result to which we come. We are not now concerned with the reasonableness or unreasonableness of this fact; we are now only alluding to it as an actual matter of fact which appears in the history of every studious and reflecting mind. Even if we deem it to be irrational and groundless, and for this reason endeavor to do away with it in our studies, we find it to be impossible. If we begin the study of Philosophy, it is with a general conception of its nature; and one that is continually reappearing in our philosophizing. If we commence the examination of Christianity itself, we find that we already have an idea of its distinctive character as a religion, which exerts a very great influence upon our inquiry into its constituent elements, and particularly upon our construction of its doctrines. This idea contains such prejudgments as, that Christianity is a *supernatural* religion; that its author is *divine;* that its truths are *mysterious*, i. e., are infinite, and therefore cannot be exhausted by the finite intelligence. These judgments are analytic and *a priori;* they flow from *the nature of the case*. For if Christianity is a religion differing in *kind* from all natural religions, then the above elements are *necessarily* involved in the conception and theory of it. The demand therefore so constantly made by the rationalist of every century, that the mind be entirely vacant of *a priori* ideas and initiating preconceptions; in his phraseology, free from "prejudices"; in order that it may make a truly scientific examination, is a demand that cannot be complied with, even if there were a disposition to do so on the part of the inquirer, and is not complied with even on the part of him who makes it. With the *origin* of such guiding ideas we have no concern at this time. It is sufficient for our purpose to indicate their actual existence in the human mind, and their actual influence and operation in all departments of its investigation. With the *correctness* of these ideas, on the contrary, we have a much closer concern; for if they exist in spite of all efforts to be rid of them, and make themselves visible in all the investigations of the student, and in all the products of his investigation, it is certainly of the first importance that they be true ideas; that is, exact correspondents to the real nature of things.

What then is the true idea of History with which we should commence our studies and reflections in this department of knowledge, and how may we know that it is the true idea, and therefore entitled to guide our inquiries, and shape our constructions?

It is very generally conceded that in its abstract and essential nature all History, be it that of matter or of mind, is Evolution, and with this we agree. The idea of an unfolding is identical with that of a history. In thinking of the one, we unavoidably think of the other, and this evinces an inward coincidence between the two conceptions. Unceasing motion, from a given point, through several stadia, to a final terminus, is a characteristic belonging inseparably to any historic process. It is seen, unquestionably, in natural History: in the progressive expansion of the vegetable seed first into the blade, then into the ear, and then into the full corn in the ear. The account of this process of evolution is the history of the seed. And this same characteristic of an evolution is equally apparent in intellectual and moral History. In bringing before our minds the passage of an intellectual or a moral idea from one degree of energy and efficiency to another, in the history of a nation or of mankind, we unavoidably construe it as a continuous and connected career. The same fact of *organic sequence* is found within the sphere of mind and of freedom that appears in the kingdom of matter and of necessity, so that terms applied to the connected events and processes of the natural world have a legitimate application in the moral, and a far more significant meaning. It is as proper to speak of the "growth" of the mind, as of the "growth" of the body; of the "development" of a nation, as of the "development" of an oak. These two growths differ, *toto genere*, in respect to the base from which each proceeds—the one being material, and the other mental; the one being necessitated by physical law, and the other being spontaneous self-determination—but they agree, in that both are alike continuous, sequacious, and evolving processes. The phrases, "principles of history," "laws of history," "ideas and forces in history," which occur so frequently in essays and treatises as to become monotonous, and which render the invention of synonymes and circumlocutions one of the most difficult of rhetorical expedients, all go to prove that the spontaneous conception of History is that of a progressive evolution from a primitive involution.

If any one doubts whether such phraseology is anything

more than the play of the fancy, and is inclined to believe that there is no actual correspondent to these terms in the truth and fact of the case, let him ask himself the question: " If History has no real and solid substance, of the nature of germs, principles, ideas, laws and forces, then what substantial matter has it at all ? If these are all unreal, the mere fictions of the fancy, with no objective correspondents in that career of man on the globe which every one concedes to be a reality, and the most solemn of all, then what is the real essence of History ? " For throwing out such deeper and more vital contents as we are speaking of, there remain only the unconnected materials of names, dates, and occurrences ; a multitudinous sea of effects without causes, an ocean of phenomena without a supporting ground, a chaos of atoms with no sort of connection or intermingling. A search after the truth and substance of the department, in this instance, as in all others, carries the mind below the surface to constituent elements and principles, so that it perceives the world of Human History to be, *after its own kind*, as full of germs, laws, and forces, as the globe beneath our feet ; and that the characteristic of reality, of forceful influential being, is as predicable of the former as of the latter.

This essential matter of Human History is continually passing through an evolution. This germ is slowly unfolding as it is the nature of all germs to do. Egyptian wheat may sleep in the swathes and foldings of a mummy through three thousand springs, but the purpose of its creation cannot be thwarted except by the destruction of its germinal substance. It was created to grow, and notwithstanding this long interval of slumbering life the development begins the instant the moist earth closes over it. In like manner an idea which originally belongs to the history of humanity may be hindered in its progress, and for ages may seem to be out of existence; yet it is none the less in being and a reality. It is all the while a factor in the earthly career of mankind, and the historian who should throw it out of the account would misconceive and misrepresent the entire historic process. An idea of human reason, like popular liberty, e. g., may make no external appearance for whole periods, but its reappearance, with an energy of operation heightened by its long suppression in the consciousness of nations, is the most impressive of all proofs that it has a necessary existence in human nature, and is destined to be developed. A doctrine of divine reason, like that of justification by Christ's atonement, is a positive truth which has been lodged in the Christian mind by divine revelation, and is destined to a universal influence, a complete development, in and through the Church, notwithstanding that some branches and ages of the Church have lost it out of their religious experience. Whatever has been *inlaid* either in matter or in mind by the Creator of both, is destined by Him and under his own superintendence to be evolved; and of all such necessary matter, be it in natural or in moral history, we may say that not a particle of it will be annihilated; it will pass through the predetermined stages of a development and obtain a full exhibition.

1. Proceeding, then, to the analytic definition of this idea of evolution, which enters so thoroughly into the theory and philosophy of History, the first characteristic that strikes our notice is the *necessary connection of parts*. Isolation is impossible. No single part can stand alone and exist by itself. The principle of interconnection binds all together, so that the part exists only in and for the whole. Atoms, in the original and strict meaning of the term, are no constituents of a process of evolution, and the atomic theory can throw no light upon such a process. The atom,

by the very etymology, is entirely disconnected from all besides itself. Matter has been cut down, ideally, to that infinitesimal point at which it constitutes the very first element, and, consequently, is now out of all connection, a single independent unit by itself. No such element as this, unassimilated and remaining so, can be a rudimental part in a development. Nothing that asserts an isolated existence, and obstinately refuses to enter into connections, can go into an evolution. The atomic particles of a heap of sand, for example, can never be part or particle of a process of growth, because each exists by and for itself. A rope of sand is the symbol of disconnection.

If now we test the history of man by this first characteristic of an evolution, do we not find exact agreement between the two conceptions? Human History is a continuous line of connections. We can no more conceive of a true break or perfect disconnection in it, than in the current of a river. Though it naturally divides into periods and ages, distinguished from each other by epochal points, yet there is no separation at these points. The epoch itself, like a living joint in the human frame, is itself a tie by which the parts are articulated together and constitute one continuous organism. It is as impossible to find a real break and absolute disconnection in the history of man, as in the history of nature. In nature, nothing but a miracle can stop the onward flow of a stream and wall up the waters on each side of a dry space in its channel; and nothing but a new fiat of creative power could now sever the human race into two halves, each of which should be entirely separate from the other, and between which there should be no more reciprocity of connection and influence than there is between the angelic hosts and the human race. As the historian follows the line backwards up toward the point of beginning, he finds the succeeding linked to the preceding, civilization joining on upon civilization, arts and inventions clinging to arts and inventions further up the line, literatures and religions tied to preceding ones; in short, he never comes to a point where there are no connected antecedents until he reaches the beginning of human history, where the basis for the whole process was laid by a fiat, supernatural and creative.*

2. The second characteristic of an evolution is the *natural connection of parts*. The sequence is not arbitrary and capricious; mere juxtaposition without any rational coherence. The two parts that are connected have a mutual adaptation to each other. The one was evidently intended to succeed the other, and the other evidently prepares for and expects the one. There is, consequently, nothing strange or whimsical in a genuine evolution, either in the sphere of nature or of spirit. Everything advances with a tranquil uniformity that precludes startling and unexpected changes, because each and every part is a preparation for that which is to come. Any movement in nature is always impressive from the perfect serenity with which it proceeds. Be it on a small, or on a large scale, be it the blowing of a rose, or the gorgeous death of the forest after the bloom and fulness of

---

* Back of the creative act there is no evolution and no history. History is in time solely, and pertains solely to the finite and created. It implies succession and changes, and therefore cannot pertain to a Being who, unlike his works, is not subject to evolving processes of any kind, but is "the same, yesterday, to-day, and forever." God has no history because He has no development. "The God of the Bible," says Guizot (Meditations, 1st series, 192), "has no biography, neither has he any personal adventures. Nothing happens to him, and nothing changes in him; he is always and invariably the same, a Being real and personal, absolutely distinct from the finite world and from humanity, identical and immutable in the bosom of the infinite diversity and movement. 'I am that I am' is the sole definition that he vouchsafes of himself."

summer, the process is as quiet as spring, as still as autumn.

Were connection in an evolution unnatural, were it whimsical and capricious, the impression made by it would be very different from what it actually is. That *fortuitous* connection of parts, of which atheism in ancient and in modern times makes so much, is incompatible with the doctrine of development. This latter requires *natural* and *adapted* connection, and hence a presiding intelligence that sees and prepares the end from the beginning. It is indeed true, that the idea of evolution which we are analyzing has been employed in an atheistic manner, and enters largely into all pantheistic methods. Of this we shall speak hereafter, and against it we shall endeavor to guard, when examining the limitations and applications of the idea. But even at this point in the discussion, it is very obvious, that provided the basis and germ of the evolution is not supposed to be *self-originated*, but is referred to the fiat of a Creator who is entirely above it, and out of it, and the absolute disposer of it; provided the germ is regarded as a pure creation from nothing, then the *naturalness* of the sequences, from that initial point, furnishes one of the most convincing arguments against the doctrine of chance. Were there merely hap-hazard connection without inward coherence, there would be no evidence of an adaptive power, and an intelligent Author of the process. But seeing, as we do, in every genuine evolution, a prophetic anticipation of the succeeding in every element of the preceding, beholding, as we do, a deliberate and intentional progress from point to point, in this "thing of life," the notion of fortuity is banished at once from the mind.

If now we test human History by this second characteristic of an evolution, we again see the coincidence and identity of the two conceptions. Nothing is more natural in its connections than the history of mankind. Symmetrical gradations, expected transitions, anticipated terminations, appear all along its course. Nothing is abrupt and saltatory in the historic movement, but one thing follows on after another with all the ease and naturalness of physical growth itself. There are convulsions and revolutions in the process, it is true, but they are always prepared for. They may indeed, and they often do, burst upon the notice of the living actors in them with the suddenness and crash of a thunderbolt from a clear sky, but it is because the living actors are unthinking actors, and give no heed to the significant premonitions. The student of History, however, the reflecting mind that is not so caught in this mighty stream of tendency as to be unable to rise above it and see the historic preparation, is never startled in this manner. He sees the awful preparation in the preceding centuries of tyranny, of poverty, of ignorance, of irreligion. Upon his mind it is no sudden shooting of a meteor from the depths of space into the totally black vault of night, but a true sunrise. For him, "far off its coming shone." Yet the student sees only what really exists. He does not make History, but finds it; and he finds it, even in its wildest and apparently most capricious sections, a genuine evolution or series of natural connections.

3. The third characteristic of an evolution is the *organic connection* of the parts. In this we reach the summit of the series, and arrive at the most significant and fruitful property. For the connection between two things may be both necessary and natural, and yet not organic. Mechanical connection is such. Take, for example, two cog wheels in a machine. Here the parts are necessarily connected; that is, they have no value except in relation

to each other. And they are naturally connected; that is, they are adapted by their construction to play into each other. But there is no higher bond than this merely external and mechanic one. There is connection, but no interconnection. The term "organic," consequently, merits fuller examination than either of the others that have been employed in the analysis.

Perhaps no better definition of an organism can be given than that of Kant. As distinguished from a mechanism, he defines it as " a product in which *each and every part is, reciprocally, means and end.*" * If we look at the human body, for example, we find that each constituent portion must be regarded, now, as the sole end for which the whole exists, and, then again, as merely the means or instrument by which the whole exists. The flesh, in one aspect of it, is the end for which the functions of respiration, circulation, secretion, digestion, and locomotion, are carried on. In one view of them, all these great processes have for their sole object this clothing of the immortal with its mortality. And yet we see again, that the production of this tissue is itself only a means whereby these systems of respiration, circulation, digestion, and secretion, are themselves kept in operation. The whole body exists for the eye, as truly as the eye exists for the whole body; for if this or any other member be maimed or mutilated, the entire vital force of the organism is at once subsidized and set to work to repair the injury. It is this *reciprocity* in the relation of the parts, that betokens the organic connection. It is this existence of the part for the whole, and of the whole for the part, that sets an organism so much higher up the scale of existence than a mechanism.

* Urtheilskraft, § 65.

An organic development, consequently, be it within the sphere of nature or of mind, is one in which all the elements and agencies mutually relate to each other, and mutually influence each other. Intercommunication, intermingling, action and reaction; these and such like, are the terms that set our thoughts upon the trail of such a constantly shifting and changing process as that of an expanding germ. For it is because the conception which we are endeavoring to define is so full of pliant, elastic, and interfusing properties, that it is so difficult to fix it in language. It is because the word "evolution" is so allied to that other most inexplicable word "life," that a writer has done the best that can be done, if, by his approximate statements, he has merely awakened the mind to an intimation of the meaning, and set it musing upon the suggestive but mysterious thought.

Again, this action and reaction, this interconnection and intermingling, implies *inward and unceasing motion* in an organism. Whenever an evolution comes to a total stop, it comes to a *dead* stop.

> "By ceaseless motion all that is subsists.
> Constant rotation of the unwearied wheel
> That Nature rides upon maintains her health,
> Her beauty, her fertility. She dreads
> An instant's pause, and lives but while she moves." *

Movement is inseparable from the conception, and hence the adjective "progressive" is always connected with the substantive, either expressly or by ellipsis. The notion of an incessant flux and reflux of elements and properties is as inseparable from the idea of an evolution, as it is incompatible with that of artificial composition. In the in-

---

* Cowper's Task, B. I. Similarly Plato (Phædrus, 245 c.) **remarks:** τὸ δὲ ὑπ' ἄλλου κινούμενον παῦλαν ἔχον κινήσεως, παῦλαν ἔχει ζωῆς.

stance of mechanical production, the motion is all *ab extra*, in the mind of the workman. His work, after all that his inventive genius has done to it, is as hard, immobile, and internally dead as it ever was. It has in it nothing of an expansion, because the living principle by which it was originated is not in *it*, but in the mind of the mechanic. This, it is true, is a living thing, a living soul, but it is unable to imbreathe itself, as a principle of growth and formation, into its rigid wooden or metallic product. The story of Pygmalion and his statue is still a fable. The " breathing " marble, and the " glowing " canvas are still and ever figures of speech. No product of finite power can be organic; for there is no pervasive moulding of the elements, no assimilation of the rudiments, no internal stir and fusion, in the work of the creature.

Again, an organic process implies *potentiality as the basis of it*. It is of importance, at this point, to direct attention to the *distinction between creation and evolution*, and thereby preclude the pantheistic employment of the latter idea. An evolution is simply the unfolding of that which has been previously folded up, and not the origination of entity from nonentity. The *growth* of a germ is not the creation of it, but is merely the expansion of a substance already existing. All attempts, therefore, to explain the *origin* of the universe by the doctrine of evolution, like the Indian Cosmogony, drive the mind back from point to point in a series of secondary processes, still leaving the inquiry after the primary origin and actual beginning of things unanswered. For it is not creation, but only emanation, when the world is regarded as the evolution of an *eternal* germ. Such a conception as this latter is, moreover, metaphysically absurd; for the idea of undeveloped being has no rational meaning except in reference to the Temporal and the Finite. Progressive development within the Divine nature would imply a career for the Deity in which He was passing from less to more perfect stages of existence, and would thus bring Him within the sphere of the relative and conditioned. Latency or potentiality is necessarily excluded from the Eternal One, by virtue of that absolute perfection and metaphysical self-completeness whereby his being is "without variableness or shadow of turning." His uncreated essence is incapable of evolving processes, and hence the created universe cannot be a part of the Divine essence, but must be another and secondary substance which is the pure make of his sheer *fiat*. To the question, therefore, which still and ever returns: "How does this potential basis come into existence? To what, or to whom, do these germs of future and unceasing processes in matter and in mind owe their origin?" the theist gives but one answer. He applies the doctrine of creation out of nothing, to all germinal substance whatsoever.*

For the Deity, though self-complete and incapable of development himself, has yet made that which is potential

---

* The whole fabric of ancient and modern Pantheism rests upon the *petitio principii* that the doctrine of evolution has the same legitimate application to the Infinite and Eternal, that it has to the Finite and Temporal. There are fatal objections to this pantheistic postulate. First, it contradicts the idea of an *Eternal* Being. For the eternal is the unchangeable; but evolution is change itself. Furthermore, the consciousness of an eternal Being must be all-comprehending and therefore simultaneous and without succession; but if, like man or angel, God is capable of an evolution, he must be conscious of the series of changes implied in it. Secondly, the pantheistic postulate contradicts the idea of an absolutely *Perfect* Being. For if all Being is only one Being, and is passing from less perfect to more perfect modes of existence, and may pass from more perfect to less perfect (since evolution may proceed in either direction), then there is no absolutely Perfect Being whatever. All Being is going on to perfection, perhaps, but as yet all Being is imperfect.

and destined to an unfolding. He has created a universe of matter and mind that is full of latent powers and agencies. The works of his hand not only display excellence in the very first moments of their existence, but reveal a still more marvellous excellence as they unfold and evolve their interior capacities. The whole progress of natural science is a gaze of admiration, and should be an anthem of adoration, towards an Architect who has *inlaid* that which is still more wonderful than what appears on the surface; who has provided in the single, instantaneous, creative, act of his omnipotence, for an evolution which is to run on under his own superintendence through all coming ages, until stopped by the same miraculous fiat.* In this property of potentiality, thus strictly defined and distinguished, we have one of the most absolute essentials of an evolution. If this conception is unreal, then is that of evolution. If we cannot conceive of, and believe in, the previous creation and deposit of a material, in order that it may be used at a future time, of the implanting of a principle which is to manifest itself, it may be, ages ahead, of the predetermination of a process and a preparation for it long before it becomes an actuality; if all such ideas as these are visionary, and all such thinking as this

---

* Theology distinguishes between substances and their modifications; that is, between what is originated from nothing, and what develops from that which is thus originated. "It is the former," says Howe (Oracles, II. ix.), "that is the proper object of creation strictly taken; the modifications of things are not properly created, in the strictest sense of creation, but are educed and brought forth out of those substantial things that were themselves created, or made out of nothing."

It is obvious to remark, here, that at no point in its history can a created substance become self-subsistent. Hence, all processes of evolution must be regarded as conducted under a sustaining energy from God, which in technical phrase is *Providence*, in distinction from Creation. The predetermination of the process, and the preparation for it, is, in the same technical phraseology, the Divine *Decree*.

has no correspondent in the world of reality; then the idea of an organic development is inconceivable and absurd. The best argument in its favor, however, would be to throw it all away, by thinking it all away, and then seriously ask the question: "What solid thing is now left either in the created universe of nature or of mind?" Expel the fact of potency, of latent powers and principles, from the sphere of the Created, in which alone, as we have remarked above, it has any application, and nothing is left but the phenomena of the instant, or a world of shadows and spectra.

Finally, an organic development implies *identity of original substance* in all the phenomenal changes that accompany the expanding process. Those who have confounded the idea which we are defining, with that of creation, have also misapprehended it at this point. The gradual advance in an evolution from something old to something new, is not a progress to something *absolutely* new; that is new in the sense of never having had any kind of existence before. An evolution can never produce anything aboriginal; it cannot create *ex nihilo*. The Creator alone can do this, and He does it when by His fiat He calls the germ with all its potentiality into being. An evolution cannot add an iota to the sum of created substance. It is confined, by the supernatural and omnipotent power that called its germ into existence, to a predetermined course and task; which is simply, and purely, and exactly, to put forth what has been put in, to evolve just what has been involved.

It follows, consequently, that the progressive advance and unfolding which is to be seen all along the line of an evolution is simply the expansion over a wider surface of that which from the instant of its creation has existed in a more invisible and metaphysical form. The progress or gain is formal and not material, external and not internal, visible and not invisible. Whether we take a seed like the acorn, or an entity like the human race, it is evident that development can create no new primary substance, or essential principle, in either. The utmost which the vivific life in each instance can do, is to assimilate already existing materials in order to its own manifestation. The last individual oak preserves its identity of substance, and sameness of essential principle, with the first acorn, and the births of individual men are not so many hundred millions of repetitions of the creative act, but only a serial exhibition of the result of the *single* fiat in Eden; of the one human species, or common substance of humanity, with the origin of which the *creation* of man, as distinguished from his *propagation*, began and ended. For if, on the one hand, there were an annihilation and subtraction of the old aboriginal matter, or, on the other, a creation and addition of a new, there would be a departure from the archetype, and the tree would be another than the oak, and the individual would not be a true specimen of humanity. But such deviations are precluded; for this potential basis, from which the evolution starts, is the involution that contains not only all the essential substance of the process, but also the law by which it is to be developed and exhibited; so that while there is unceasing change and constant variety in the outward manifestation, there is perfect identity and sameness in the inward essence.

Passing, now, from the tangled wilderness of analytic definition, into the level and open fields of application and illustration, if we test human History by this third characteristic of an evolution, we shall see more plainly than ever, that the two conceptions agree with each other. The history of man is certainly characterized by reciprocal action in its elements. Ideas, principles, laws, forces, events, and men, are constantly acting and reacting upon each other from the beginning to the end of a historic process. Everything influences everything. Everything receives influence from everything. It is impossible to make a separation between the factors, so that this interaction and intermingling shall stop at a given point. Take a single feature of Secular History, for illustration the Political Revolutions, and see how this law of reciprocal action prevails. The idea of liberty promulgated in one nation becomes the realized fact in another, and the realized fact, again, becomes the stimulating example which wakes the slumbering idea in a third. A treatise on government by Sidney in the seventeenth century and in monarchical England, finds its realization in the eighteenth century in the American Constitution. This concrete example repasses the Atlantic, and becomes the mightiest of the forces that convulse the old feudal monarchy of France, and the most influential of the agencies at work in Europe for the political elevation of the masses. But that treatise of Sidney itself was not merely the propagator of influences; it was the recipient of a most mighty influence coming down from the remote past. The currents of Greek and Roman Republicanism flowed through the English Republican. The political brain of Plato and Aristotle, of Brutus the Consul and Brutus the Patriot, was the brain in the heart of Sidney.

If we look at any of the processes in the natural world, do we find any more convincing proofs of interaction and reciprocity of agencies, than we find in the world of human society? If the terms action and reaction are not figurative in the former sphere, are they not full of the most solid meaning in the latter? And is it not the true end and aim of the student of human History, to make this play of living agencies and influences as real to his own mind and feelings, as its correspondent is to the student of nature? The scientific naturalist cannot for a moment believe that nature is a mechanism, and that organism is a fiction and metaphor in this realm. A thousand treatises, each a thousand times more ingenious than that in which Des Cartes* attempts to demonstrate that all so-called vital forces in the lower animals are in reality mechanical ones, and that the body of the brute is as much an artificial production as a watch, would not overthrow the belief of the natural philosopher that the physical world exhibits in all parts of it a process of organic development, and that natural objects are the products of a law of life and growth. The conviction that there is an internal and not merely fanciful analogy between the worlds of nature and of mind, so that the same fundamental fact of evolution prevails in both, should firmly possess the mind of the inquirer in the department of human History. The relation between the subjective principle and the outward stimuli is the same in one instance as in the other. Is there any more of vital reciprocity between the tropical Fauna or Flora, and the temperature, amount of atmospheric moisture, elevation of the land above the sea, prevailing winds, amount of sunlight, geological formation and soil, of the tropical regions, than there is of vital reciprocity between the Celtic, Gothic, and Roman components of national character, the insular isolating residence, the influence of Greek and Roman literatures, of commerce, of the Christian religion, of the intestine wars of the Roses and the wars for foreign conquest, and the historical development of England?

---

* " He denied the supermaterialism of animal life, placing it entirely under the laws of mechanics, as many are now denying the supernaturalism of Christianity."—Twesten's Dogmatik. I. 318.

Ought not the analysis and contemplation of this reciprocity of agencies to produce the same sense of organic connections, the same fresh feeling of a living process, and the same enthusiastic wonder, with which the naturalist examines material nature; with which a Gilbert White minutely surveys physical nature within the limits of his rural parish; with which a Humboldt surveys the cosmos?*

Again, is not Human History like any other organic development, characterized by an inward and unceasing motion? Is there any stagnation or immobility in it? Seize the process of human life at any point you please, and do you not find it stirring like a force and beating like a pulse? Even the most externally motionless period has its fierce passions and intense emotions. The darkest of the Dark Ages, the more it is studied, the more is it seen to have a human interest. The most stagnant stratum

---

* "Those truths are always most valuable which are most historical, that is, which tell us most about the past and future states of the object to which they belong. In a tree, for instance, it is more important to give the appearance of energy and elasticity in the limbs which is indicative of growth and life, than any particular character of leaf, or texture of bough. It is more important that we should feel that the uppermost sprays are creeping higher and higher into the sky, and be impressed with the current of life and motion which is animating every fibre, than that we should view the exact pitch of relief with which those fibres are thrown out against the sky. For the first truths tell us tales about the tree, about what it has been, and will be, while the last are characteristic of it only in its present state, and are in no way talkative about themselves. Talkative facts are always more interesting and more important than silent ones. So again the lines in a crag which mark its stratification, and how it has been washed and rounded by water, or twisted and drawn out in fire, are more important, because they tell more than the stains of the lichens which change year by year, and the accidental fissures of frost or decomposition; not but that both of these are historical, but historical in a less distinct manner and for shorter periods."—Ruskin's Modern Painters, I. chap. vi.

of the Dead Sea undulates. It has been said that the savage has no history; that there is in this form of society only a dead monotony unenlivened by the play of human feelings and the struggle of human passions. But this is not so. As, according to Dr. Johnson, the biography of the most unimportant individual on the globe, were it fully written out so that the life should appear just and fully as it was, would overflow with interest and entertainment for all men, so the real every-day life of even a savage horde would be an addition to Universal History that would waken earnest attention. Who would not eagerly peruse the history of a nomadic Tartar tribe, if it were written with the simple and minute fidelity of a chronicle of Froissart?* Who would not even spare some of the more outwardly imposing sections of General History, if in their place he could have a true unvarnished tale of the wanderings of one of those Scythian or Celtic races who were the first to come westward from Central Asia, the birthplace and cradle of mankind? What a charm and light would be thrown over the earlier history of Greece and Rome, if a veritable account of one or more branches of that great Pelasgic race; that *savage* source of " the beauty that was Greece and the grandeur that was Rome;" should be discovered among the manuscripts of a cloister?

But the secret of the interest which is thus felt in any and every section of human history, lies in the fact that there is an unceasing movement, an incessant stir and fermentation, in each and every section. The ocean itself is not more unresting than the history of man. The oceanic currents are not more distinct and unmistakable than those streams of tendency which sway eastward and westward,

* One of the most unique papers of De Quincey is " The flight of a Tartar Tribe."

northward and southward, in the migration of nations, in the rise and decline of civilizations, in the founding and fall of empires, in the alternations of national glory and decay. *Motion*, both internal and external, is the characteristic which first impresses the historical student. In passing from other domains of inquiry into this, he finds himself to be coming out from quiet vales into the region of storms; from the place of secured results and garnered products, into the place of active preparation and production. In the sphere of Poetry, there is only the still air and golden light of setting suns. In the sphere of Science, the mind is in the serene region of pure thought. But in History, the inquirer comes out into the world of agencies, actors, and actions, where everything is under motion, and, in the Baconian phrase, all "resounds like the mines."

Again, does not Human History, like any other organic process, rest upon a basis of potentiality ? Human life is the Old in the New; the old being in a new aspect. Human History does not create its wealth and variety of material as it goes along, but merely expands a varied latency that was originated primarily when the morning stars sang together, and subsequently when Adam fell. Potentiality meets us at every point, and accounts for the lights and shadows of the "pictured page." National differences and peculiarities, and consequently all that is unique and distinctive in the career of nations, must be referred to a provision made therefor in the day of man's creation. Compare the Rome of the age of Numa Pompilius with the Rome of the age of Augustus Cæsar. The latter displays elements and characteristics that had lain so entirely dormant, in preceding sections of this national history, that if Rome had gone out of political existence in the struggle with the Samnite or the Carthaginian the human mind never would have known of their existence, but would they for this reason not have been real entities? It is indeed true, that they would not have been *manifested*, but would they not just as really have been rudiments in that original political germ or basis for a nation which, whether completely unfolded or not, had a wholeness and rounded capacity of its own, because it was an integral part of the "good" and perfect creation of God, in the day that "the Lord God formed man of the dust of the ground, and breathed into his nostrils the breath of life?" The language of Ezekiel (xxviii. 13) respecting Tyre is applicable to every nation of mankind: "Thou hast been in Eden, the garden of God; the workmanship of thy tabrets, and of thy pipes was prepared in thee in the day that thou wast created." A potential existence is by no means an imaginary or fictitious one. A germ may not be permitted to run its course of evolution, and display all its marvellous inlay of elements and individuals; but it is none the less a fixed quantity by itself, and must be estimated by what it was primarily endowed with by the Creator. If a race should be stopped short in mid-career, by the same fiat that created it in the beginning, its dignity and standing in the scale of universal being would have to be determined by its created capacities; not by what had actually come forth, but by what had been originally put in; by the amount of life and the quantum of varied latency that had been primarily summed up in it.

It is by virtue of this potential basis that Human History exhibits that union of two opposite properties, permanence and progression, which is so baffling to the mind. It has a permanent identity and sameness, because it exhibits the same species of being and the same eternal truth in all its sections. It also presents a constant variety and change, because it shows this same human nature, and this same common verity, in new forms. Each age and period is as fresh and original in its appearance, as if it were the first in the series, and looked upon the new earth for the first time that it ever was looked upon, and lived the first human life that ever was lived. This co-inherence and co-working of the two factors, of the Old and the New, of the Conservatism and the Progress, is the very essence of Human History. It is difficult, we are aware, to seize and hold both conceptions at one and the same time, as the constant debate between the man of Conservatism and the man of Progress shows. It is easy and natural to separate what God has joined together, and to make choice of the one or of the other characteristic, as the key to all History and the foundation of all practical life and action. It is simpler to say that History is permanent without progress, or else that it is progressive without permanence, than to say that it is a true development and therefore *both* permanent and progressive. The extremists upon both sides have a much easier task than the one who occupies the central position between them. A simple idea is much easier to define and manage than a complex one. But it is not so fertile, so prolific, or so completely true. If simplicity and facility of management were all that the philosopher had to care for, the great comprehensive ideas of science would soon disappear; for they are neither uncomplex nor facile. "The simplest of governments," says Webster while defending the complexity of republicanism, "is a despotism." The simplest of theories is the theory of an extremist.

We have now given a theoretic answer to the question: What is the abstract idea of History? by specifying the chief characteristics of a process of evolution and pointing out their identity with those of an historical process. It is not pretended that this analysis and comparison is a complete one, and that nothing more could be said upon the subject; that it is a perfectly clear one, and could not be made more lucid. Yet no one who has ever made the attempt; an attempt much more common now than it was in the last century, when a different intellectual method prevailed; to treat a subject *physiologically*,* will be hasty to complain of the lack of thoroughness, or especially of plainness. Let any one peruse the tracts and treatises composed upon this general subject of progressive development, and observe their comparative vagueness, and he will be convinced that it is, intrinsically, one of the most difficult subjects to discuss, in the whole philosophical catalogue. For it implies the idea of *life;* one of the most familiar, and at the same time most mysterious and baffling of all ideas. It necessitates a *dynamic* method of treating the subject; a method which compels the mind, if we may so say, to a subterranean labor and examination; a method therefore that precludes that liveliness of mental movement, that perfect distinctness of statement, and especially that opulence of illustration and bright sparkling diction and style, which are characteristic of a more outward mode of investigation. To trace a law of life is a far more difficult and arduous attempt for authorship, than to draw a beautiful picture. To work the mind slowly, pertinaciously, and thoroughly, into a deep central process of development, running like a magnetic current through ages of time, winding here, thwarted there, uprearing itself and coming forth in reformations and revolutions, and then retiring down into such depths of dormancy and slumber that its reawakening seems almost an impossibility; to treat Human History in this profound and dynamic manner is far more difficult than by the aid of a versatile mind and

---

* The term is employed in its etymological meaning; to denote a method that proceeds from the intrinsic *nature* of an object.

a lively fancy to cause a series of brilliant pictures, of dazzling dissolving views, to pass with rapidity before the mind of a rapid reader. But which method is the most fruitful and fertilizing? Which is most suggestive? Which is best adapted for the foundation of a course of study and investigation? Which is capable of an unlimited expansion, and influence upon the intellect of a student? Grant that, in the beginning, both the writer and the reader feel the need of further reflection and still plainer statements, so that there is a sort of unsatisfaction in both; yet is not this very unrest a thorn and spur to still more profound and clear intuitions? This is one great benefit to be derived from the adoption, and reception into the mind, of an idea like that of evolution. Its meaning is not so entirely upon the surface, and so level to the most thoughtless comprehension, that he who runs may read it, and exhaust its whole significance in a twinkling. There is ever something in reserve, something still to be pondered over, something still to be more distinctly elucidated and stated. The idea is itself a seed sown in the mind, having an endless power of germination and fructification. A seed is not so striking or so sparkling an object as a diamond; it does not make such an instantaneous impression, and it is a thousandfold more full of mystery. But while the gem merely flickers its cold glittering flashes, generation after generation, upon the single brow of beauty or of pride, the seed is repeating itself in the harvests of a continent, in the physical comfort and thereby the general weal of a race. Easiness of immediate apprehension, distinctness and vivacity of first statement, facility of being managed, ought all to be set second to depth, comprehensiveness of scope, richness and variety of contents, and fertility of influence, when selecting an idea that is to constitute the basis of a department of knowledge, and guide the investigations of a student through its whole long and wide domain. It is for this reason, and not because a more perspicacious and facile method could not be selected, that we desire to explain so far as is possible, and to recommend, what has been termed the theory of *genetic development*, as the one which has most affinity with the real nature of History, and which consequently is the best *organon* or instrument for its investigation. The great change that has taken place, within the present century, in the way of conceiving and constructing the history of man, is owing to the adoption and use of a method that was foreign to the mind and the intellectual tendencies of the eighteenth century. One only needs to compare history like that of Dr. Robertson with history like that of Dr. Arnold, or history like that of Gibbon with history like that of Niebuhr, to see that from some cause or other a great change has come over the department. There is no improvement in respect to style. For who has excelled the clean purity of Robertson's diction, the elegant simplicity of Hume's narrative, the harmonious yet energetic pomp of Gibbon's description? Perhaps there is, in general, a falling off in respect to formal properties. But, on the other hand, is there not a vast improvement in all the material properties of historical composition? Is not the point from which men and events are now contemplated, far more central and commanding? Is not much more made of dominant ideas, general tendencies, prominent individualities, in short of the germs and dynamic forces of Human History, than was made during the last century? Are not the lessons of this science more impressive and solemn now, than they were as taught in 1750? Is not the department itself exerting an influence upon other departments far more modifying and transforming than formerly? In short, if History may have lost something of that elegance and transparency which characterizes a product of art, has it not gained far more of that vitality, and power of influential impression, which belongs to a product of nature? The cause of this change, in the spirit and influence of the department, is traceable directly to a growing disposition to regard the history of Man, as well as that of Nature, as an evolving process, and consequently as subject to a law of life and growth. Indeed it is noticeable, that this change has come in contemporaneously with a corresponding change in the method of contemplating Nature itself. As Natural Science has become more dynamic, so has History. The naturalist of the present day is not willing to regard life as the result of organization, and then to explain organization into a very curious and recondite arrangement of atomic matter. Mysterious as the principle itself may be, the investigator now prefers to assume a vital principle as the origin and cause of all organization, and of all those phenomena which some would explain by the mechanical view and theory of nature.* For though he starts with a mystery which probably he can never clear up, yet he thereby introduces a clearness, a consistency, a naturalness and vitality, into all the facts and phenomena of his science, which are never attained by the materializing naturalists. His intellectual self-denial in the beginning, is rewarded richly in the end. In like manner, the historian, by taking upon himself the severer task of regarding Human History as a process of intellectual and

* This was written in 1854, previous to the recent temporary revival of the mechanical physics. At that date, the tendency of natural science was wholly in the direction of the physics of Kepler, Newton, Linnæus, Kant, Cuvier, Blumenbach, John Hunter, Owen, and Agassiz.

moral evolution, and of penetrating into its intricate organic connections, is in the end rewarded for his disposition to be thorough and profound, by finding the subject of his investigations far more prolific and impressive than it ever was before. He is also rewarded by finding that this philosophic method, exacting as it is, in the beginning, upon the closest reflection and strictest discipline of the mind, in the end throws a clear light upon those deeper and darker portions of History, upon which not a ray of light is cast by a more superficial and easy mode of examination.

Inasmuch as the department of Church History has felt the influence of the dynamic method more thoroughly than other portions of the history of man have as yet, and the Church Historian been the most successful in applying the doctrine of development to historical materials, we shall, in the remainder of this section, draw our illustrations from this branch of the general subject.

One of the most valuable results of the application of the idea of evolution is seen in that part of Ecclesiastical History which is denominated the History of Doctrine. This may be said to have come into existence since the adoption of the physiological method. It is indeed true that the more thoughtful of the ecclesiastical historians of the eighteenth century, such as Mosheim and the elder Planck, recognize the influence of particular doctrines upon that course of external events to which they gave most attention; but they usually connect the doctrine, or the truth, with some individual of strong or passionate character, from whom, more than from the truth or doctrine, the influence upon men and things proceeds. Hence in treating of the Reformation, for example, a disproportionate weight is attached to the personal religious force and wants of a single individual like Luther, or to the personal intellectual culture and aspirations of an Erasmus; to the undervaluation of that great scripture *doctrine* of justification by faith, which, together with the general religious craving of the age in which a Luther shared so strongly and an Erasmus so feebly, was the true historic ground of the movement, the real central historic force.* It is not enough to trace the processes of history to merely individual influence. This *pragmatic* method, as it has been termed, must rest upon that *genetic* one of which we are speaking; for the individual is rooted in the general, and all this influence of historical characters has a deeper ground in historic ideas, truths, and doctrines. But this was not seen and acted upon, until the mind of the historian was led down to the doctrines themselves, as the ultimate sources and causes. The step taken by writers like Mosheim, Walch, and Planck, in sacred history, and Hume, Robertson, and Gibbon, in secular, was one in advance, but was not the ultimate one. It was something valuable, to connect the external series of events and phenomena with the characters, opinions, and acts of prominent *individuals*, but it was something invaluable, because indispensable to a truly philosophic history, to connect events, phenomena, prominent individuals themselves, together with the ages and great tendencies which they represented, with the great standing *truths* of reason and revelation, and the plans and purposes of that Supreme Being who is the author and revealer of all.

This step was taken, when the historian began to conceive and construct the facts of History on the method of a genetic development. He then began, as this term denotes, to trace the *genesis* of the process; to seize it in its very deepest source and lowest place of origin. This

---

* See Baur, Lehrbuch der Dogmengeschichte, S. 38.

necessarily compelled him to go beyond not merely the external events themselves, but also their connection with leading individuals, down to the first springs of History in the plans and purposes of God, and, in Church History especially, to the truths and doctrines which God has revealed in his written word, as the germ and measure of all true development. For it is plain that, so long as the historian confined himself to the external occurrences, and their comparatively superficial relation to individual men, he was still at a great distance from the real causes and forces of History; from the absolute centre and origin of its processes. Notwithstanding all his pretensions to a philosophic treatment of the subject, he was still at work in an upper stratum, and busied with secondary agencies. He could reach the ultimate foundation of the whole historic superstructure, only by sinking a deeper shaft, and getting below events, and individual actions, to the revealed ideas and designs of God. For here is the origin, and this is the *genesis*. There is no source more ultimate than this. The historian who starts from this point, starts from the final centre.

We cannot, perhaps, more appropriately conclude this enunciation of the abstract idea of evolution, than by directing attention, for a moment, to that Church Historian who has employed it more persistently, and successfully, than any other investigator, secular or ecclesiastical. The Church History of Neander is an embodiment of the idea of development. It is organized throughout by this single thought. And the organization is most thorough. It pervades each historic section; the external history, the history of polity, of worship, of morality, of doctrine. Each of these sections exhibits an expanding process of evolution, either upward or downward. Each of these is reciprocally related to all the others, so that the whole, eventually, are lightly but firmly bound together into a greater organism. We do not assert that the idea of the Christian Religion, as Neander conceives it in his own mind, is so exactly conformed to the New Testament representation, that the constructing principle of his history is entirely free from defective qualities. This would be saying more than can be of any uninspired mind. The most reverent admirer of this devout historian must acknowledge that his construction of Church History is affected by subjective elements, that his apprehension of Christianity is sometimes unfavorably modified by the age and country in which he lived, and especially by the type of culture into which he was born and bred. But all this can be said, and should be as we believe, without denying the substantial correctness of the idea which impelled and guided his mind in the composition of his work, or imputing to him any more material errors than the scientific mind is always liable to.

Without, therefore, entering upon any detailed criticism of Neander's conception of Christianity, which would involve a criticism of the whole work, we wish merely to allude to the remarkable perseverance, and tenacity, with which it is employed in the detection, analysis, and synthesis of the historic processes themselves. That monotony, which is complained of by a class of critics whose æsthetic feeling is stronger than their philosophic, is the monotony of organization. The types of organic life are necessarily few. Nature herself is but slightly varied and variegated within this sphere. It is only in the clothing of her few archetypal forms, that she exhibits the pomp, and prodigality, of her luxuriance. It is true that Neander's method is uniform. We know beforehand what the treatment of each section will be. We know that each subject will be handled under the same fixed number of topics and categories; that each mass of material, like iron in a rolling mill, will be run through the same number and sequence of grooves. But this very rigor in the use of one idea, and the prosecution of one plan, imparts, to the product resulting from it, an interest for the thinking mind, far higher than any merely æsthetic interest can ever be, and what is still more, renders it a far more instructive and influential work for the intellect of a student, than can be originated on the other method of historical composition. It is for this reason, therefore, that while the history of Neander has less interest for him who is attracted chiefly by the secular aspects of Christianity, it has all the more for him who knows that its spiritual aspects are its distinguishing and essential ones. He who sees in Christianity merely or mainly a religion or an institute that has exerted a most favorable influence upon literature, science, and art; upon civilization, government, and the physical improvement of mankind; will be dissatisfied with this author's account of it. For Neander was but little, too little, interested in these civilizing, and intellectual, influences. But he who sees in Christianity, first of all and last of all, a moral and spiritual power, destined by its Divine Author to regenerate the inmost heart of humanity, and hence intended to affect primarily the *eternal* interests of mankind, will find this stern æsthetic indifference, and naked but lofty spiritualism of the Historian, all the more imposing and impressive. For he passes through the pomps and splendors that thicken and trail along the march of Christianity, as St. Paul did through the temples and sculptures of Athens, or the porticos and triumphal arches of Rome; with an eye too intently fixed upon more unutterable realities and more awful splendors, to be attracted, much less dazzled, by things seen and temporal. To one who seeks to know

Christianity in its own living moral nature, with few or none of its secular adjuncts, the close and powerful method of Neander is exceedingly welcome, and exceedingly suggestive and fertile. And while the student of Church History is never to be a servile recipient of all the views of any mind, however learned or contemplative, we think it may safely be said, that, from the existing literature in this department, no single work can be selected which so well deserves as does this, to be made both a resort, and a point of departure, for his mind. While examining and pondering its contents, the inquirer will find himself, all along, in the very heart of Christianity, because the history is constructed out of the very idea of Christianity itself; that is, in its spirit and by its light.

§ 2. Evolution distinguished from Creation, and from Improvement.

In the previous section, we have confined ourselves to an analysis of the abstract idea of evolution, in order to reach the abstract nature of History. As a consequence, we have brought into view only the universal characteristics of an expanding process, paying no regard to those particular qualities which are discovered, as soon as we begin to examine the several *species* of history that fall under the generic conception. For here, as everywhere, the concrete application of a metaphysical idea is of equal importance with its abstract enunciation. An *a priori* statement requires to be completed by an *a posteriori* verification, in order to obtain scientific value and currency. An *a priori* theory is worthless whenever the thought, in the mind, is not found to correspond with the thing, in nature. In this instance the theory is no θεωρία, no seeing through and seeing around, but remains what it was in the start, an hypothesis or conjecture. The Newtonian theory of gravitation, in the moment of its first conception in the mind of the thinker, was purely hypothetical, and had not the whole subsequent course of astronomical science been a verification of it would be an hypothesis still, only an exploded one. The difference between the alchemist's theory of occult qualities, and that of a true natural philosophy, does not lie in the employment of a different mode of formation in one instance from that used in the other, but in the fact that the first does not stand the tests of observation and application, while the last does. Both are formed on the *a priori* method, but the *a posteriori* verification destroys in one case, and confirms in the other.*

The principal reason why the department of metaphysics is in such ill repute with the popular mind, on the ground of both real and imaginary deficiencies, lies in the fact that it has not in all instances been thoroughly treated. The philosopher has been content with conceptions in their abstract and universal forms. He has been averse to take the second step, and do the last work; which is, after the idea has been sufficiently enucleated by logical analysis, to bring it forth from this speculative shape, and exhibit as a concrete and working truth, or, in the phrase of Bacon, "to temper the rigor of the abstraction by the softening explanation." This is in reality more difficult to accomplish, than to merely follow the laws of logical thinking, without any regard to the refractions, and reflections, and modifications, of actual processes. To follow a pure logical sequence is no greater task for a logical mind, than it is for a vigorous body to walk up a flight of

---

* See Whewell's History of Inductive Sciences, B. V., C. iv.

stairs. The steps themselves, in both instances, perform most of the labor. The walker needs only to lift up his limbs and put them down, to be lifted upward, fifty or a hundred feet, into space, and the logician needs merely to follow the connections of an idea, to be carried through a very wide and long range of speculation. Hence the facility with which a mere logician analyzes ideas into their constituent elements, and constructs systems out of them. It is more difficult, as we have remarked, to be entirely thorough, and follow an idea out into the sphere of historical reality, and thus know it in the concrete. Had this been done more often by the metaphysical philosopher, he would have subjected truth to a more exhaustive examination, that would have precluded those misconceptions, which so often come in subsequently to an accurate *a priori* analysis and vitiate it.

The doctrine of evolution, in particular, has undergone deterioration, and lost scientific properties, by being contemplated exclusively in its abstract form. Neglecting to test and clarify it by observation, some theorists in Physics come to employ the idea in a sense that is contrary to the results of scientific analysis itself, as well as contradicted by the whole course of nature. Fastening their gaze upon the *continuity* of the process, they lose sight of its *origin*, and slide into the notion of an eternal potentiality. This necessitates the second absurd notion, of potentiality within potentiality, or evolution of heterogeneous germs out of homogeneous ones. As, upon this theory, there is but one process of evolution from one infinite and eternal germ, all the varieties of being must be accounted for by evolution. Mind must evolve from matter, life from the lifeless, the organic from the inorganic, the animal from the vegetable, the rational from the animal, the spiritual from the carnal, the holy from the sinful. The process of evolution has now lost its primitive logical simplicity and unity, and becomes a complex and fanciful scheme of emanations. The germ is no longer a transparent and pure creation from nothing, having its own qualities and no others, but an obscure and mixed product from antecedent germs, and these again from their antecedents, and so backward endlessly, with ever increasing vagueness and mixture, into the abyss of chaotic being. Now setting aside the valid objections that spring out of Ethics and Religion,* it is plain that an actual questioning of Nature for the facts in the case would have preserved these theorists from this corruption of the true idea of an evolution, and kept them upon the truly scientific position. Nature never exhibits the evolution of one specific germ from another, and the simple observation and remembrance of this matter of fact would have led the wandering theorist to retrace his steps. A verification of the abstract conception itself, by an actual reference to the organic processes actually going on in nature before his eyes, would have reminded him of the scientific truth, that mere evolution cannot account for the origin of any *new* thing; that a germ can only protrude its own latency,

* That the ancient oriental systems of emanation, and their modern counterparts the pantheistic systems, are destructive of the first principles and distinctions of Ethics and Religion, is notorious. But that these same schemes are ruinous to true Science, is not so often considered. Let any one, however, examine the stupendous system of Gnosticism, that sprung up in the 2d and 3d centuries, and he will be convinced that such a conglomerate is incompatible with logical coherence and scientific self-consistence. Starting from a false fundamental principle, and substituting emanation for creation, every new step must be an attempt at adjustment. This introduces still more troublesome and unmanageable matter, which, again, calls for new attempts at arrangement, until an amorphous mass of speculation is aggregated that is totally destitute of the homogeneity, concinnity, clearness, and nicety of Science.

and cannot inlay a foreign one. The very significant matter of fact, that one species never expands into another, would have reminded him of the truth, which is also reached by the "high priori road" of rigorous analysis, that though a process of evolution can be accounted for out of the latent potentiality at its base, this latter can be accounted for only by recurring to the creative power of God. Evolution cannot originate its own germ. The careful recognition of the fact, that in *rerum natura* the development of a vegetable seed, even if carried on through all the aeons upon aeons of the Gnostic scheme or the cycles upon cycles of the geological system, never transmutes the homogeneous into the heterogeneous, never converts the corn of wheat into the egg of animal life, would recall the attention of the speculatist to the self-evident proposition that nothing can come forth that has never been put in. The seen and acknowledged failure to discover any instance in which the passage from the animal to the rational soul, from the brute to the man, has been effected by the pure evolution of the former, would correct the vicious reasoning of the theorizer, and restore it to the strictly scientific and necessary statement, that a latency of an animal kind cannot by mere expansion be converted into one entirely heterogeneous, so as to become the basis of a moral and spiritual, as distinguished from an animal history.*

* The definition of Evolution by Herbert Spencer, as "the development of the homogeneous into the heterogeneous," is exactly wrong. It is directly contrary to the received definition. An evolution, in the historical physics, wholly *excludes* the heterogeneous. It is a process that is entirely pure, and unmixed with foreign elements. The evolution of a mustard seed, for example, is simply and only vegetable. Should anything mineral or animal, anything heterogeneous, appear in the process, the evolution would by this very fact be proved to be spurious. This definition, moreover, begs the question in dispute:

This same vitiation of true metaphysics, and misapprehension of an abstract conception, is seen also within the sphere of mind, and of human history. Theorizers here, forgetting the fact of free will, confound the idea of development with that of *improvement*. There is nothing in the logical conception of an evolving process that warrants their assertion, that all movement in the history of a self-determining moral agent must of necessity be normal and upward. All that is required by the *a priori* definition is, that the process shall be an expanding one, but of what *species*, or from what *basis*, is still undetermined. Forgetting the fact of free will, and the possibility of defection from law associated with it by the Creator, they deal with man as they do with material nature, and suppose that to say he is passing through a process of development necessarily implies that he is advancing, like "the splendor of the grass and the glory of the flower," from one degree of excellence to another.*

the question namely, whether the homogeneous ever does or can develop into the heterogeneous. To begin with defining evolution to be the very process of whose reality the opponent demands proof, is more artful than scientific.

* "Evil," says Emerson (Essay on Swedenborg), "is good in the making. That pure malignity can exist, is the extreme proposition of unbelief. It is not to be entertained by a rational agent; it is atheism; it is the last profanation. The divine effort is never relaxed; the carrion in the sun will convert itself to grass and flowers; and the man, though in brothels, or jails, or on gibbets, is on the way to all that is good and true." Extremes meet. The denial of the doctrine of human apostasy, on the ground that it is dishonorable to man, conducts to the denial of man's distinguishing and highest endowment, viz.: his free will, and results in degrading human nature to the level of "carrion," and "flowers." It is often asked, why God permitted sin? Perhaps it was to prove conclusively that man is a self-determining spirit. Certain it is, that wherever the fact of the free and guilty fall of man is acknowledged, materializing views of man's nature do not prevail, while the denial of the reality of moral evil is a characteristic of materialism of every grade and school.

Here again, the simple observation of the fact staring every inquirer in the face, of an *abuse of freedom*, and a consequent false evolution of human nature, would have impressed the lesson which a rigorous analysis also teaches, viz.: that an evolving process may be downwards, as well as upwards; one of decline and death, as well as of rise and bloom. The stubborn fact of an illegitimate development going on in the very heart of humanity, and covering the whole period of human history, compels the theorizer to notice an aspect of the doctrine of evolution that he had lost sight of. The application of the abstract idea of evolution to what he finds to be a stern matter of fact, preserves its scientific purity and precision by preventing him from surreptitiously throwing out its universality and impartiality, whereby it is capable of an application to any process, legitimate or illegitimate, so it be an organic sequence, and surreptitiously narrowing it down to a particular species of process, viz.: a normal one. For there is no more reason for regarding evolution as synonymous with improvement alone, than with degeneracy alone. Scientific definitions are wide and universal. No particular truth is told, or intended to be, when it is asserted that there is a process of development going on in the human world. This is granted upon all sides. On coming within the sphere of free agency, it is necessary, in order to any definite and valuable statement, to determine by actual observation *what* it is that is being developed; whether a primitive germ originated by the Creator, or a secondary one originated by the creature, *to either of which the abstract conception of evolution is alike applicable.*

Hence, on coming down into the sphere of the concrete, we are obliged to notice the *varieties* of evolution In endeavoring to apply the idea whose nature we have analyzed, to the actual career of man on the globe, we must take into account the *peculiarity* of this career. In specifying this, we discover the distinctive nature of Secular History, and give its definition.

The ordinary and common history of mankind, as the observer in every age sees it going on before his eyes, differs from all other histories of which he knows anything, by being contrary to the primary law of creation. All other existences, so far as he knows, are conformed to the law of their being, and their evolution is, consequently, legitimate and normal. Throughout all material nature, there is no liberty to the contrary, and consequently there is an inevitable obedience to the creative idea, and an unvarying expansion of the original germ. The few monsters, *lusus naturæ* as we call them, are very few, and do not affect the species to which they belong. A mal-formed crystal is an isolated thing, and its formation has no effect upon the law and process of crystallization. A body with two heads is entirely anomalous and uncommon, and does not in the least modify the operation of the general law of production. Material nature proceeds undeviatingly, because within this sphere there is no possibility of self-will. Evolution here is both normal and uniform. Hence, the moralist and theologian point to the perfect unfolding of the natural world, as an example to be imitated by the voluntary spirit of man. The highest authority has set the lilies of the field before us, for our deliberate imitation; and the poet, in his distich, has briefly repeated the same truth: "Seekest thou the highest, and the greatest? the plants can teach it to thee. What they are involuntarily, that be thou voluntarily." *

And if we pass from material nature into the realm of

* Schiller, Das Höchste.

spiritual existence, we find that, with the exception of man and a portion of the angelic hosts, all voluntary beings are in allegiance to law, and their development is legitimate and normal. For that catastrophe and fall in heaven was scarcely a speck upon the infinite azure of eternity. The idea of race does not apply to the angel as it does to the man. We speak of the angelic host, but never of the angelic race.* Hence the apostasy of the Son of the Morning and his followers, like the mal-formation of a crystal in the material world, was an isolated occurrence, whose effects did not extend beyond itself. Each angelic will fell for, and by, itself. Hence the general allegiance of the hierarchies continued, and continues,† so that we may say, notwithstanding this instance of deviation from the Divine law, that in the heavenly world, as in the natural, the evolution and the history are legitimate and normal.

Man then stands alone; the only unloyal *race* in the universe; the only species of being which, as a *unity* and a *whole*, has thrown itself out of the line of its true destination, and is running a false career.

With the possibility and necessary conditions of such a catastrophe, we have in this discussion no concern. It is sufficient here to postulate its occurrence through the abuse of human freedom, by the permissive will and decree of God. Had, then, the development of man pro-

---

* "Non enim sic sunt omnes angeli de uno angelo, quemadmodum omnes homines de uno homine."—Anselm, Cur Deus Homo, ii., 21, 22.

† Far the greater part have kept, I see,
Their station; heaven, yet populous, retains
Number sufficient to possess her realms,
Though wide, and this high temple to frequent
With ministeries due, and solemn rites.
Paradise Lost, vii., 145–149.

ceeded from the primary germ and original inlay given in creation, it would have been ideal and perfect. All that some theorists now say respecting the actual history of man would then have been exactly descriptive of that normal process. Human nature would then have unfolded in all the beauty, and perfect conformity to the creative idea, which we have seen to be characteristic of the crystal, or the flower. The spontaneous and the natural, in human history, would then have been the ideal and the perfect.

But we know, not by an *a priori* method, but as matter of fact, that the development of humanity did not proceed from this first and proper point of departure. The creative idea, by the Creator's permission, was not realized by the free agent. The law of man's creation was not obeyed. In the fall of Adam, the original and true historic germ was crowded out by a second false one. The first potential basis of human history, which provided for a purer progress and a grander evolution than man now can conceive of, was displaced by a second basis, which likewise provided for a false evolution, and an awful history, if not supernaturally hindered, all along through the same endless duration.

The origination of moral evil by the self-will of man, consequently, brings to view another aspect of the idea of evolution, and a different application of the doctrine of genetic development. This stubborn fact compels the speculating mind to acknowledge, what it is prone to lose sight of, viz.: that so far as the abstract definition is concerned, evolution may mean corruption and decline, as well as improvement; that the organic sequences of history may be those of decay and death, as well as those of bloom and life. For it displays, for his examination, another kind of germ, besides that one created by the

Creator, and which He pronounced "good." It shows him a very different potentiality, from that original moral perfection with which humanity was once endowed. It enables him to understand something of the meaning of free will, and yet more, something of the mystery of self-will. For that misapprehension of the abstract idea of evolution, whereby it is contracted down from its wide universality of meaning and applicability to all organic processes whatsoever, and limited to the single particular process of improvement, arises from overlooking the functions and operations of free agency, which play such a part in the history of Man, and introduce such changes and varieties into it. The philosopher, at this point, as at many others, needs the instruction of the theologian. He needs to be reminded by his scientific co-laborer, that the moral power of self-determination is totally different from a physical force, and can cause such alterations and catastrophes within the moral world as never appear in the world of material nature, and hence that when he comes into this sphere, he must not be surprised if he finds archetypes departed from, and glorious ideals unrealized. Theology reminds philosophy of the fact, that although the natural and secular man is *mentally* rational, he is not *morally* so; that though the eternal truths of right have been inlaid in his reason, by the act of his Creator, they have been expelled from his will by an act of his own. The theorist, contemplating man's mental constitution, finds him to be possessed of all the truths of reason. These truths are necessary, and, in their own nature, entitled to an universal dominion. Hence he hastily concludes, that they must, of themselves, prevail in the history of any being in whose very mental structure they are so thoroughly inwoven. The speculative maxim, "truth is mighty, and must prevail," carries him to the practical conclusion, that a rational being must inevitably act out his rationality, and be rational in all respects. But the theorist forgets that the realization of a truth, in life and conduct, can proceed only from the active and emotive side of man. The heart and will are the vitality of the human soul, and hence, the proper seat of growth and evolution within it.* We have already, by a rigorous definition, evinced that a process of evolution is an organic and consequently a thoroughly vital one. Of whichever species it be, be it development in perfection or development in corruption, be it a living life or a living death, as a connected and organic process, it must go on in the faculties of feeling and will, or not at all. Evolution, be it true or false, is the result of an *active* principle. If, therefore, the truths of reason and righteousness are not wrought into the voluntary part of man, it matters not how thoroughly they may have been elaborated by the Creator's act, into the stationary intellectual part of him. For there can be no flexible expansion of a truth of reason or revelation, unless it has been absorbed and assimilated into the moral and voluntary nature. Remaining in its rigid intellectual form, in the pure theoretic reason of man, a doctrine of natural or of revealed religion has no more power of pliantly unfolding into feeling and conduct, than a stone has of turning into vegetable matter, merely because it has been caught and held in the fork of a rapidly growing tree. The error of the theorist,

---

* It is a maxim of the lynx-eyed Aristotle, that "mere intellect *moves* nothing;" διανοιὰ δ' αὐτη οὐδεν κινεῖ. (Ethics, vi., 5). That radical movement and transformation must proceed from the practical, in distinction from the theoretic, side of human nature, is the teaching of this whole paragraph, as well as of others, in this system of ethics. The theological doctrine, that no real moral change can be brought about in humanity, but by the renewal of the *will*, will suggest itself to the reader in this connection.

who argues from the ideal to the actual, and affirms the necessary normal development of human nature, merely because it contains within itself the rule and law by which it *ought* to develop; this error of regarding evolution as the synonyme of improvement, arises from overlooking the difference between the legislative and the executive, the constitutional and the voluntary, the mental and the moral.* A very considerable degree of moral *light* may exist, without the least degree of moral *life*. The rise of a respectable system of natural theology in pagan Greece and Rome, is no more a proof of a normal, or even an improving evolution of human nature in that age and clime, than the clearest convictions of reason, and the most poignant reproaches of conscience in an individual, are proofs that his inward moral life is heavenly and heavenward. Indeed, it is only a very loose and inadequate apprehension of the idea of evolution, that can find in that wholly *speculative* movement of the ancient philosophic mind, which, moreover, even in this form, was confined to a very few of the more thoughtful sages, and never exerted any influence upon the individual and social life of the Greek and Roman populations,—it is, we say, a very meagre and narrow conception of a very pregnant and fertile idea that can find, in such a restricted phenomenon, the characteristics of a great diffusive organic process, which moulds human society internally, and from the centre. Can any candid mind say that that "moral philosophy," which, as Bacon says, "was the heathen divinity," sustained the same inward relation to heathendom that Christianity does to Christendom; that the system of Socrates was the principle of moral life for any portion of an-

---

* "Conscience," remarks Ullmann (Sinlessness of Jesus, p. 32), "is not so much productive as receptive, not so much originative as acquiescent."

tiquity, as the system of Christ has been for the Church in all ages? On the contrary, was not the truth, as St Paul affirms, held down in unrighteousness, and was not the actual spontaneous development of the old world as contrary to the doctrines of *natural* as of revealed religion?

And, so far as the individual examples of pagan virtue are concerned, we are willing to leave the decision of the question to themselves, whether the natural religion, which they apprehended in their reason and conscience, had so passed into their affections and will, and had such a vital control over their heart and character, as to constitute a normal development of human nature in their case. Read Plato, and find as full a confession, prompted by a personal consciousness, of the corruption and degeneracy of human nature, as ever came from uninstructed lips. Ask the wisest of heathen, if the principles of reason and righteousness, which lay in such clear outline before his mind's eye, constituted the life of his soul; and hear the answer, that however it may have been with him in a pre-existence of which he dreamed, and however it might be with him in a future world, of which he knew nothing with certainty, the existing inward life, the present character, and the actual on-going development, was certainly contrary to the Beautiful, the True, and the Good.

The result, then, of the investigation in this section, is the further distinction of the idea of evolution from that of *improvement*, and the definition of Secular History as an *abnormal* but organic process. We had previously distinguished evolution from creation, and now this second limitation brings us round to an exhaustive definition of an idea which is probably more potent than any other, in forming and fixing the intellectual methods of the present generation of educated men. The history of the word is instructive. The loose and unscientific use of this single term has done as much as any other single cause, to introduce error into current theories of nature, of man, and of human history. The remedy is not to be found in the rejection of either the conception or the term, but in a rigorous and scientific treatment of the idea itself, by which it is made to yield up its true and exact meaning; whereby it shall be fitted to apply equally to Sacred and to Profane History, to pure and to corrupt evolutions, to historic processes of bloom and beauty and perfection, and to historic processes of decline, decay and ruin. The downward tendencies of human nature, which constitute the substance of Secular as distinguished from Christian History; the acknowledged deterioration of languages, literatures, religions, arts, sciences, and civilizations; the slow and sure decay of national vigor, and return to barbarism; the unvarying decline from public virtue to public voluptuousness; in short, the entire history of man, so far as he is outside of supernatural influences, and unaffected by the intervention of his original Creator, though it is a self-determined and responsible process, is yet, in every part and particle, as organically connected, and as strict an evolution, as is that other upward tendency, started in the Christian Church, and ended in the eternal state, by which this same humanity is being restored to the heights whence it fell.

But while the course of evolution in Secular or Profane History presupposes a potential basis from which it proceeds, the all-important fact must be noticed, and remembered, that this is a *secondary* basis, and not a primary one, and that the originating author of this basis is the *finite*, and not the infinite will. Under and within the permissive decree of God, *sin is man's creation;* he makes it out of nothing.* For the origin of moral evil cannot be accounted for, by the evolution of something already in existence, any more than the origin of matter can be. Original righteousness, developed never so long and intensely, will never be transmuted into original sin. The passage, from one to the other, must be by an absolutely originant act of self-will, which act, subject only to the limitation and condition above-mentioned, of the permission of the Supreme Being, is strictly creative from nothing. The origin of sin is the origination of a *new* historic germ, and not the unfolding or modification of an old one; and hence the necessity of a creating, in distinction from an evolving force, such as is denoted by the *possi-*

---

*The analogy between the origination of matter or of mind from nothing, by Almighty God, and the origination of sin from nothing, by the finite will, does not, of course, hold good in every respect. No finite being can create in the strict and ordinary sense of originating a new *substance*, either material or spiritual. But sin is not a substance, and in saying that man creates sin, it is only meant that he alone is the real and true author of it. He is its first cause. He is not necessitated to originate it, he does not make it out of antecedent sin, but begins it *de novo* and absolutely. The energy of the finite will in the first act of sin resembles that of the infinite will in creation proper, in that the product resulting is in each instance *ex nihilo*. In this sense sin is man's creation. " Sin and evil," says Athanasius (Fourth Oration against the Arians)," are none of God's creatures; neither are they as old as his creatures; nor are they in all his creatures. It is the doctrine and judgment of the Christian Church, in opposition to the folly of the Manichæan hypothesis, that nothing of sin or evil is from God as its author, or in God as its subject; that it had no place among the works of the six days' creation. Unhappy man found out a way to make something (as he thought) out of nothing, when he ushered sin and disobedience into the world. He made even gods out of emptiness and nothing." Similarly Coleridge (Table Talk, May 1, 1830), remarks that " a fall of some sort or other, the *creation*, as it were, of the non-absolute, is the fundamental postulate of the moral history of man. Without this hypothesis, man is unintelligible; with it every phenomenon is explicable. The mystery itself is too profound for human insight."

8

bilitas peccandi attributed by the theologian to the will of the unfallen Adam. Supposing, then, the first origination of moral evil to be carefully referred to the abuse of human freedom, and keeping the process of its evolution within the same sphere of self-will in which it took its first start, we may then say, that moral evil undergoes a development, as truly as anything else that belongs to the history of man. If any one doubts whether this term, so often applied only in a good sense as to be for the popular mind the synonyme of normal progress, is properly applicable to a process like that of human sinfulness, he needs only to try this process by the tests that are discriminated in the metaphysical analysis of the conception. He will find that human corruption and decline has been as organic a sequence from an original centre, as is to be found in the realm of matter itself; that it exhibits all the characteristics of an evolution: the necessary and natural connection of elements and properties, their action and reaction, the sameness of generic principle in all the individual varieties, and the unceasing motion of a constant expansion.

The same rigorous application of the doctrine of evolution, moreover, compels us to the further position, that the *reversal* of this illegitimate and false process which is going on in humanity also necessitates a creative power. For no process of mere and strict evolution can go behind itself, and alter the base from which it proceeds. *Radical* changes cannot be produced in this manner. There must be an *originant* energy, in order to these. The passage from holiness to sin, we have already noticed, cannot be accounted for by the doctrine of evolution, and neither can the passage from sin to holiness be explained by it. The expulsion of the false germ, and the re-introduction of the true one, must be accomplished by an agency that is creative, in distinction from one that is merely expansive. An evolution is by its very nature and definition self-perpetuating, until an agency specifically different from its own interferes. A germ of one kind cannot originate a germ of a different kind, and consequently there is no *natural* and *germinant* passage from an illegitimate to a legitimate potentiality in human history, any more than there is from a vegetable to an animal species. The passage, if there be one, must be *supernatural :* i. e., the work of a creative, in distinction from an educing agency, and by an instantaneous act, in distinction from a gradual process.

Secular history is therefore separated from Christian by a chasm over which it cannot pass, except by the intervention of the Creator.* The abuse of human freedom

---

* The query may arise in this connection, whether this creative energy may not be in the fallen finite will itself, and thus there be no absolute necessity of the intervention of the infinite Spirit, and employment of special Divine efficiency. If the human will was possessed, before its defection from law, of a power to create moral evil, why is it not possessed, since its fall, of a power to create moral good? The objections to this are the following. (1) The affirmation of such a power rests, solely, upon an *a priori* foundation. There is no *a posteriori* test, and verification, that corroborates it. Fallen man is not conscious of such an originant energy to good, though he is at times conscious of its lack; and that he never exerted it, is a well-established fact. This power then to originate, in distinction from develop and cultivate, holiness, if attributed to the sinful will at all, must be attributed upon other grounds than psychological and practical ones. But metaphysics unsupported by psychology, we have seen, must be conjectural merely, and consequently of a spurious order. An abstract theory that is destitute of its concrete correspondent in the world of actual experience, like the Alchemist's hypothesis of occult qualities, is destitute of scientific value. Science demands a matching of the one-half with its other half; of the *a priori* with the *a posteriori*. If such be the real relation of these two intellectual methods to each other, it follows that a position like the one in question, which can get its support from only one of them, and this, the least practical of the two, should be rejected.

allows of no self-remedy. The new birth of the human spirit and the new historic process resting upon it cannot, from the very nature of the case and the very terms of the statement, be an evolution of the apostate man. To affirm this would be to confound evolution with creation. A clear and distinct conception, consequently, of the nature of Secular History, guides the mind inevitably to the doctrine and fact of Revelation, if a radical change is to be introduced. No new order of history can possibly begin, if the existing movement and evolution are simply left to themselves. An absolutely originant and creative power

(2) But in the second place, even if the position in question be held as a pure abstraction, by a dead lift of the intellect, and without any experimental corroboration, it then follows from it that the finite will can be the absolute and sole author of holiness, as it is of sin, and that, consequently, it can establish for itself an absolute meritoriousness before God, as it can and has an absolute guiltiness. It confessedly has the power of creating moral evil out of nothing, without the influence and co-operation of the Divine Spirit, so that its demerit is absolute, and its damnation eternal, in case it uses this power; and if it is capable of originating moral good, in the same unassisted manner, then a correspondent absoluteness of merit would be established upon this side. But no finite will, not even that of the unfallen angels, can take the total merit of holiness to itself, as the fallen will must take the total demerit of sinfulness. It is only on the side of moral evil, that the will of the creature can act without influence and assistance from the Creator, because it is only on this side that it can act in opposition to Him. While, therefore, man by the permission of the Supreme, and not without it, can abuse his free agency, and establish a self-derived, and therefore absolute criminality, he can never, by the use of free agency, establish a self-derived, and therefore absolute worthiness. If, then, the very relationship of all moral good to the Holy One is that of dependence, to such a degree that the doctrine of its absolute origination, or creation from nothing, is inapplicable even to the unfallen finite spirit, much more must this doctrine be excluded, in the instance of the apostate will. The theory of a strictly originant energy in the soul of man can, consequently, apply only to moral evil. All holiness in the man or angel is derived from God; but all sin is self-originated by the creature.

must be called in to reverse the process, and give it an upward instead of a downward direction.

§ 3. THE NATURE AND DEFINITION OF CHURCH HISTORY.

IN explaining and applying the idea of evolution, we have arrived at the nature of History in the abstract, and of that specific concrete form which is denominated Profane or Secular. We have now to make a third application of the idea to the history of Christianity.

Christian or Church History we define to be the restoring of the true development of the human spirit, by the supernatural agency of its Creator. The doctrine of evolution is now to be applied to that gradual process of recovery from the apostasy of his will, which regenerated man is passing through, here on earth, as a member of the spiritual kingdom of Christ. We shall find this to be a series, and sequence, as organic as any that have passed before our review, or that we can conceive of. The founder of Christianity Himself so describes it, when he says that "the kingdom of heaven is like to a grain of mustard seed which a man took, and sowed in his field; which indeed is the least of all seeds: but when it is grown it is the greatest among herbs, and becometh a tree, so that the birds of the air come and lodge in the branches thereof;" when He says, again, that "the kingdom of heaven is like unto leaven, which a woman took, and hid in three measures of meal, till the whole was leavened." * In these parables, two of the most thorough and inward processes in nature, viz.: those of germination and fermentation, are chosen by our Lord to indicate the real nature of his religion.

* Matthew xiii. 31-33.

And no one can study the illustrations which He so frequently employs in order to give a clear conception of his religion as it works in the individual soul, and in the world at large, without being convinced that it is, in its own sphere and kind, as much of the nature of a living principle as the breath of life in the nostrils. For these illustrations are almost entirely drawn from the world of animated nature, and thereby evince that the Author of nature and of grace knows that the vitality of the one best symbolizes and explains the vitality of the other.

But if it was of the first importance, in the previous sections, to direct attention to the fact that the power which *originates* the germ of any process is a creative one, it is certainly so in the present instance. This free and fresh unfolding of the Christian life, in the midst of the decadent processes of Secular History, as was indicated in the close of the last section, cannot be accounted for by any latency lying undeveloped in the heart of the secular man. Mere expansion, forever and for evermore, would only display a more thoroughly intense and concentrated corruption of human nature. We are, consequently, once more driven to the Supernatural and Divine, if any radical change in humanity, and any new species of history, is to be introduced. As Secular History is the evolution of the fallen nature of man left to its own spontaneity, so Christian History is the evolution of his regenerated nature, under the continued influence of the power that first and instantaneously effected the change. The first question, consequently, that is to be answered here, relates to this power itself. What, then, is that supernatural Power, which begins, carries forward, and perfects that new process of development in human nature which constitutes the sum and substance of Church History? In answering this question, we describe, by implication, the nature of this species of human History, and obtain a clew to the whole process itself.

Speaking generally, the power which begins, continues, and completes the restoration of the true evolution of humanity, is *Divine Revelation.* The term is taken in its most comprehensive meaning, to denote the entire *special* communication which God has made to man. In this generic form, it subdivides into two main branches: (1) The revelation of Truth; (2) The dispensation of the Spirit.

From the fall in Eden, down to the death of the last of the Apostles, God, through the medium of inspiration, at sundry times and in divers manners, has imparted to the mind of man a body of *knowledge*, the purpose of which is to enlighten his darkened understanding respecting his origin, fall, actual character, religious necessities and the divine method of meeting them. This revealed truth has been preserved by special providence, and is now, an outward, fixed, written revelation.

Again, parallel with this species of Divine communication, another has been made, viz.: a dispensation of direct *spiritual influence.* The purpose of this second form of the Divine manifestation, is to renew and sanctify the human soul. The function of the first is to enlighten, as that of the second is to enliven. These two forms of God's supernatural self-revelation are co-ordinate, and necessary to each other's success; and hence the dispensation of spiritual influence has accompanied that of truth, in all ages of the Church from the very beginning. For although the degree and extent of this influence was greatly augmented after the ascension of Christ, yet it would be as incorrect to affirm that the kind, the fact itself of direct divine efficiency upon the human soul, did not exist in the Patriarchal and Jewish churches, as it would to assert that there was no revelation of truth from God, previous to the New Testament economy, because the disclosures of this latter were so much fuller than those of its antecedent.

Revelation, then, in this generic sense, is a unity and a continuity. So far as it is a communication of Truth, it began with the promise in Eden, and ended with the glowing invitation of the beloved disciple of the Incarnate Word, who was also the Jehovah of the Patriarchs and Prophets, addressed to all men without distinction, to take the water of life freely. So far as it is a communication of the Spirit, it commenced with the regeneration of the fallen pair, and has continued, through all ages, to be the efficient agency in applying the written revelation. Unlike the communication of the Word, that of the Spirit must continue to go on until the end of the world; and yet the permanent co-ordination and mutual necessity of each will be seen in the fact, that the finished revelation of Truth, the concluded canon of Scripture, will be employed to the end of time, by the Holy Ghost, as his own and only instrument of human renovation.

We have, then, in this total *Revelation from God*, the originant creative power in Church History. The foundation of Secular History is the human mind and human power, under the merely ordinary sustaining agency of Divine Providence; that of Christian History is the Divine mind and Divine power exerting themselves with an extraordinary and creative energy. Supernatural communication from the Deity is the great objective force in this species of human History; the foundation and principle of the restored normal evolution of humanity. This revelation of Himself on the part of God, entering into the midst and mass of mankind, selects out a portion by a sovereign act, regenerates and moulds it into a body by itself, separate from the world though existing in it.* This body is therefore as truly organized, and organic, as that larger body which is denominated the race, or that smaller body which is denominated the state. It exhibits a process possessing all the properties of an expanding germ, and has a history that is vitally connected, and reciprocally related, from beginning to end.

We pass, now, to consider the characteristics of this process of restoring the true development of human nature, in order to obtain a yet fuller apprehension of the distinctive peculiarities of Church History.

1. Observe, first, that the development of regenerate man here upon earth is only *imperfectly* normal. It differs from what it would have been had human nature unfolded from the original germ, without any fall or deviation from the prescribed career, by exhibiting a mixture of true and false elements. The church on earth is not perfect. Its career contains sections of corruption, decay, decline; characteristics that cannot belong to a perfect process; elements that do not properly belong to Church History, considering the perfection of the germ from which it proceeds. For inasmuch as the creative force in this instance is the perfect Revelation of God, the evolution that proceeds should, upon abstract principles, be an entirely perfect one also. Since the inward life is supernatural and divine, the manifestation ought to be so

---

* The fall of man is generic, and hence all men are fallen; the redemption of man is individual, and electing, and consequently only a portion are saved. A catastrophe, like spiritual apostasy, occurring at a point in human history when humanity was a unit and a unity, affects the whole indiscriminately and without exception; but when man has passed out of this form of existence, into that of a series and succession of individuals, it is plain that the principle of individualism must govern his restoration, and that redemption, consequently, cannot be generic and universal.

likewise, and entirely unmixed with foreign and false elements.

But the actual history of the Church does not thus exactly conform to this its ideal. It only approximates to it, and hence the restoring of the true development of humanity is not that pure and spotless process which the history of man was originally intended to exhibit, and which it would have presented had the first divinely designed unfolding taken place. The history of the Christian Church, though vastly different from that of the secular world, though different in kind from it, is by no means that perfectly serene and beautiful evolution which is going on in the heavenly world.

Church History, consequently, as we actually find it, exhibits a complex appearance, a double movement. It is both the expansion of a true, and the destruction of a false evolution. As, in the instance of the individual Christian, the career consists of a double activity, the living unto righteousness and the dying unto sin, so in the instance of the Church, the entire history consists of the growth of the spiritual and holy, and the resistance of the natural and sinful. The fight between the flesh and the spirit, in the single believer, is both a part and a symbol of that great contest between two opposing principles which constitutes the charm of Church History, and renders it, for the contemplative mind, by far the most interesting, as it is the most important part of the Universal History of man on the globe.

Hence, although we pass into the sphere of the Supernatural, into the midst of supernatural ideas, germs, and forces, on passing from Secular to Christian History, we yet by no means go into a world of calm. We enter a world of thicker moral storm, and of hotter mental conflict, than is to be found in any section, or in the whole range of

Secular History. But there is this great difference: the storm is destined to become an eternal calm, and the conflict to end in an eternal triumph. This complexity in the process is destined to become a simple unity, and this antagonism a perfect harmony. The dualism in the now imperfectly normal history is ultimately to vanish, and God is to be all in all. But so long as the Church is militant, and until it enters upon its eternal heavenly career, it cannot exhibit that unmixed and pure process of holy life and growth which the history of man was originally intended to be. The secondary restoring of a normal development is not, like the primary unfolding, a tranquil and unhindered process; and this is the difference between the history of an unfallen, and that of a regenerate spirit.

2. Notice, in the second place, that the development in Church History is not symmetrical. We see the same lack of entire harmony in the life of the Church that we do in that of the individual believer. No Christian biography exhibits a perfect proportion in the features of the religious character, or a perfect blending of all the elements of the Christian experience. The man is either too contemplative, or too practical, too vehement, or too tranquil. There is but one individual religious life that is completely symmetrical, and that is the life of the Divine founder and exemplar of Christianity. There are, indeed, different degrees of approximation to this ideal symmetry. Some characters are much more proportionate and beautiful than others, but there is not a single one of them all that is so exactly conformed to the Divine model as to be an exact reproduction of it. Ullmann speaks of a point in religion, beyond which any further improvement is not only impossible but inconceivable. He describes it, as being that completed oneness of the human soul with God,

in which the former is determined in all its movements, and moulded in all its experiences, by the latter, and yet feels that this determination and moulding by the Divine is no pantheistic absorption, nor external compulsion, but its own most free and personal self-determination, and self-formation.* But no Christian biography discloses such a perfect Christian consciousness as this. The holiest saints on earth complain of inward conflict and an interest separate from God, mourn over a part of their experience as that of indwelling sin, and confess that even on the holy side there is too much that is ill-balanced, and disproportionate. Not one of them can apply to himself in their highest unqualified sense these words of St. Paul, "I live, and yet not I, but Christ liveth in me." Not one of them has been a perfect representative, in his earthly life, as he will be in his heavenly, of the symmetrical holiness of Jesus Christ. Precisely the same is seen in the larger sphere of the Church; for the individual life is the miniature of the general, the microcosm mirrors the macrocosm. As we trace the historic development along down the ages and generations of believers, we find the same greater or less approximation to symmetry, but never absolute proportion.

If we look at the history of Christianity upon its *practical* side, we find it an imperfectly symmetrical process. There are indications in the Apostolic epistles themselves, that the gushing love and glowing zeal of the Apostolic Church sometimes passed over into an extreme that injured the experience. The strong side of the character of the early Christians is their vivid life and feeling, and not a discriminating knowledge of the Christian system, or of human nature at large. They apprehended truth chiefly

* Studien und Kritiken, 1840. p. 48.

in the way of feeling and experience, and expected to find their own warm affection for it in every one who professed discipleship. Hence their liability to be deceived by false teachers, and their readiness to be led astray by false doctrine; traits to which the Apostolic epistles often allude, and against which they seek to guard by a more thorough instruction of this glowing love, and cautious guidance of this ardent zeal. Paul, speaking to the Roman Church of those who by good words and fair speeches would deceive the hearts of the simple (ἀκάκων, the artless and guileless good), adds, "I would have you wise unto that which is good, and simple concerning evil."* In writing to the Corinthian church, he enjoins it upon them not to be children in understanding; in malice they might be children, utterly unacquainted with any such thing, but in understanding they must be men.† The frequent warnings against false teachers and doctrine in the epistles of John we need not specify. So liable was the guileless simplicity and pure love of the Apostolic church to be imposed upon; so defective was this first form of the Christian experience on the side of knowledge; that the Head of the church made up for the deficiency, and protected his people by a special charism or miraculous gift, viz.: the power of discerning spirits, of reading the inward and real character of pretended teachers of Christianity.

When we pass from this first age to a succeeding one, like that between Constantine and Hildebrand, or, still more, like that between Hildebrand and the Reformation, we find the Christian character defective in just the opposite respect. Speaking comparatively, as we always must when comparing historic periods with each other, we may

* Romans, xvi. 18, 19.
† 1 Corinthians, xiv. 20.

say that the simplicity and love have been lost in the extreme of knowledge and discrimination. The adoption of Christianity by the temporal power secularized it, and while the first Christians were too ignorant of men and things, the Grecian-Roman and the Roman Catholic Churches knew them too well for the guilelessness and simple love of a symmetrical Christian character. They obeyed the first half of our Lord's injunction, but not the last. They were wise as serpents, but were not harmless as doves.

If again we look at the historical development of Christianity on the *theoretic* side as a system of doctrines, we find the same defect in the process. Some ages undervalue knowledge altogether, and exhibit little or no scientific interest of any kind. Others are almost exclusively speculative. It is as impossible to find an age, as it is an individual, in whom γνῶσις and πίστις, light and life, knowledge and feeling, are mingled in exact proportions. Hence the whole series of periods and ages contains more of the lineaments of a perfect symmetry than any single one of them does, and the full idea of Christianity approximates nearer to a full embodiment in the Church Universal than in any particular branch of it.

This, therefore, is a proper place to allude to the error of selecting some one ecclesiastical period as the model for all time, and some one church as the ideal for all churches. It is a false view of history that would set up the church of the two centuries preceding and the two centuries following the Nicene council, as that one particular section by which the church of the present and the future should form itself. The attempt of the Oxford party in the English church to revive Nicene Christianity as the normal type was utterly unhistoric as well as irrational. That period undoubtedly had its excellences, and just as undoubtedly its defects. Its Christianity lacked a perfect symmetry. It can, therefore, furnish only some features that are to be imitated, and perpetuated, by the church of the present, and the church of the future. Its determined opposition to heretical conceptions, and its comparatively vigorous missionary spirit, are two characteristics of this period that deserve to be reproduced in all coming time. The church, in this pantheistic and rationalistic age, should keep fast hold of those statements of the doctrine of the Trinity, and of the Person of Christ, which had their origin in this period. The church in this and in every age should retain the substance of those profound anthropological views which were the result of the great controversy between Augustine and Pelagius. But surely no mind that has any just conception of the spiritual nature of Christianity can desire that such views of prelacy and primacy, of celibacy and monasticism, of the efficacy of the sacraments in connection with the meritoriousness of good works, as prevailed in this patristic period, should be recommended to the church in all time for servile reception. He who follows the history of the Christian Religion from its beginning down to the present will not go the Nicene period for the most accurate statement of the doctrine of justification by faith, or for the most scriptural conceptions of the nature of Christian virtue, and of ecclesiastical polity. He knows of other periods whose more special and successful function it was to unfold these latter doctrines, as it was that of the Nicene period to construct the doctrines of Theology and Christology.

As really, though not equally, is it an error to set up the Apostolic Church as the model for all time. That brotherly affection, and that tender yet deathless love towards the Redeemer, must be a model for all ages, and will probably never be excelled by any generation of Christians. But the conflict which Christianity has to wage with a cultivated skepticism and a subtle heresy, and that prudent discrimination which is needed in some emergencies to protect the earthly interests of the church, call for a development of Christianity in an intellectual and scientific direction of which we see little or nothing in the Apostolic brotherhood.* The primitive Christians were in reality the pupils and children of the apostles, who answered all their questions, relieved all their doubts, and fought all their intellectual conflicts for them. But the apostles were an order of men which has not been perpetuated, to be the guardians and instructors of the church in every emergency. Their writings are left, it is true, but how often would even the didactic and thoughtful theologian, or the learned but perplexed council or assembly, after all its diligent study of these writings, have gladly betaken themselves, like the church at Corinth or Rome when in difficulty, to the inspired mind of a living apostle, for a further communication specially adapted to the case in hand. This age of pupilage could not continue, and therefore it cannot be set forth, any more than any other one, as the model to which all after ages are to be conformed in every respect.

In short, the student of the whole course of historical development will seek to make up for the want of that symmetry which is not to be found in any one section, by combining excellences that are found in each, and rejecting the defects that are found in all. For only in the

* This Church might say, in reference to scientific statements of the doctrines of Scripture, as the unlettered woman spoken of in Chalmers' memoirs did when asked some theological questions respecting the person of the Redeemer, on her examination for admission to the church: "I cannot describe him, but I would die for him."

career of the church as a whole, does he find the nearest approximation to that church "without spot or wrinkle," spoken of in Scripture, and of which Divine Revelation is the originating power and perfecting principle.

3. Notice, in the third place, that the development in Church History is not uniform in every part. This duplicity in the restoring process, of which we have spoken, hinders the movement. If there were only a single divine principle, and no remainders of a sinful human one, in the regenerated soul, the entire career of the Christian Church, would be one uninterrupted onward motion, one continual triumph of truth on the earth. But the religious life is enfeebled, and diminished, by the carnal and secular, in both the individual, and the church. In one age Christianity is vigorous, and its rapid extension into pagan regions is the consequence. A succeeding age presents the melancholy spectacle of decay and decline in these parent churches, and, perhaps, the beginning of the same process in the newly-formed societies. Northern Africa from the second to the fifth century was the seat of a very vigorous religion, both in practical and speculative respects. Tertullian, Origen, and Augustine represent a Christianity as influential as any that lies back of the Reformation. But these North African churches disappear from Christendom with the suddenness of the lost Pleiad from the sky, and from the time of the Mohammedan invasion to the present that whole region has no place in Church History. Such a phenomenon as this cannot be accounted for by external causes. Terrible as the Saracen invasion was, a civilization and culture resting upon a sound and healthy Christianity in Northern Africa would have stopped and beaten back the Saracen, as instantaneously and decisively as he was by Charles Martel and his warlike Franks. History, secular as well as sacred, shows

that no form of heathenism or of worldly power can compete with a true and genuine Christendom. But an interior process of decline and decay had gone on in the very heart of these churches and this Christian society. The moral and intellectual strength had departed along with the pure scriptural piety of the founders and first witnesses, and the whole population fell an easy prey to the fanatic zeal of the Mohammedan. Instances like this throng upon the mind, but a single one is sufficient to show that the external development of Christianity is constantly liable to interruption in parts and sections of the entire career. The same fact stares us in the face, if we look at its internal history. Compare the present condition of the Eastern church, with what it was when it took the lead of the Western; when its Athanasius was the theologian, and its golden-mouthed Chrysostom the orator, for all Christendom. If this church could, this day, be put back fifteen hundred years, it would be in advance of its present position. The development has been intermitted for this length of time, and will continue to be, until an infusion of fresh life, through the missionary efforts of Protestant churches and the Divine blessing upon them, occurs.

4. Notice, in the fourth place, as a sequence from these defects in the development which we have mentioned, that in Ecclesiastical History we can affirm a normal progress only as we view the Church as a whole. Truth and piety are unfolded in the long run of ages, though not necessarily in each and every one of them; in the general run of churches, though not necessarily in each and every one of them. Though the process is hindered, turned aside, and temporarily stopped, by the corrupt free agency of man, it is yet as a whole under the guidance and protection of God, and therefore goes on; if not in this

nation and age, yet in another. We know from the promise of the Author of Christianity that his religion is destined to a far wider extension among men than has yet been seen; and upon this we must ultimately rest, in order to maintain a confident expectation that such will be the fact. Much is sometimes said of the self-realizing power of Christianity, but unless we identity the system with its Author; unless we think of the Word and the Spirit of God as one undivided agency; we cannot read certain chapters of Church History with any firm belief that even revealed truth will continue to expand with genial life within the hearts of men, and exert a continuous and mighty influence age after age. Take away from Christianity the doctrine of the Holy Ghost, and the very life of the system disappears. Take away from Church History the actual dispensation of spiritual influences, and the vitality of the process departs. And it is because the Holy Spirit has never left the Church as a whole, while He has suspended his quickening influences in sections, that we can say with the strictest truth, that the progress of the great whole has been continuous, though sometimes interrupted in the parts.

5. Notice in the fifth place that the development of a section or an age, in Church History, is often only the reproduction of some preceding type. When Christianity has declined, in a particular branch of the Church, the reformation that takes place is really only the restoration of a previous form of vital godliness. It is not, however, the mere copy of an antecedent period, containing no more and no less elements, and in just the same proportions. History exhibits no *fac similes*. There is no copying in a living process, but there is reproduction, and a great amount of it. The Protestant Reformation was the revival of that genuine doctrine, and holy life, which had

manifested itself once before in the church of the first five centuries. And yet it was not a mere repetition of it, because those corrupt elements, in doctrine and morals, which began to come in particularly after the union of Church and State under Constantine, were expelled by the newly awakened religious life. The feeling of guilt, moreover, was more keen and poignant, and the appropriation of atonement more intelligent and cordial, than in the patristic period. Still, it was in the true sense of the word, a re-production, and it called itself a *re*-formation. The aim of Luther was to restore a piety that had once before been the glory and strength of the church, and not to invent any new style of Christian life. Probably, in the outset, his desire was merely to make the Roman Catholic church what it was in the first three centuries, before the Romish bishop had become the Romish pope. And it was not until he saw that the Romish church of 1517 was radically different, in doctrine and in practice, from the Roman church of 350, and radically different from that invisible church to which he himself belonged, in common with the holy of all ages, that he understood the true relation of the invisible to the visible, and became the instrument in the hand of God of continuing the life of the church invisible, or the true catholic church, under a new outward organization. The ecclesiastical progress which Luther desired for the age in which he lived was a return to an age that lay more than a thousand years nearer the first promulgation and spread of Christianity.

If we turn to the theology of the Reformatory period, the same fact meets us. The two theologians of this age were Melanchthon and Calvin. Examine the "Loci Communes" of the one, and the "Institutes" of the other, and see the substantial reproduction of an earlier theology. From the beginning to the end of the Institutes, in particular, there is a continual appeal to Augustine. Calvin, though of singularly strong and independent mind, and thoroughly convinced that the Scriptures are the only infallible rule of faith and practice, and thoroughly acquainted with them through a most exhaustive exegesis, nevertheless uniformly cites the exegetical and systematic opinions of the Latin father as corroborative of his own. And the relation between the two systems, is not merely that of confirmation and corroboration. So far as human influence was concerned, the one grew out of the other, and the other formed the one. Thus was it regarded as a progressive advance, by the leading spirits of the Reformation, to revive an antecedent form of faith and practice, and in the sixteenth century to return to the first five centuries.

Do we not in these facts find an incidental, but strong, corroboration of the position, that Church History is a process of organic development? Something more than mere chronological sequence, without action and reaction, is needed to account for such phenomena as we have been noticing. If the movement of Christianity in the world were merely rectilinear, straight forward in one line, we ought to find each succeeding age possessed of all that the preceding had possessed, together with something more of its own. In this case, the last must be wisest and holiest of all. But such is not the movement. The motion is circular, and spiral, rather than straight onward. The process is organic, and not mechanic, or mathematical. The line returns into itself, so that, as in the old philosophy, it is the circle, and not the right line, that symbolizes the living process.

It is from this rectilinear rather than spiral conception, this mechanical rather than organic idea of History, that the common fallacy arises of supposing that each age, as matter of course, contains all the development of the past, merely because it happens to be chronologically last in the series. This error rests upon the assumption, that juxtaposition and location determine everything in History, and that a man living in the nineteenth century is wiser of course than one living in the seventeenth, because nineteen are two more than seventeen. This would be the case, if History were not an organic process, in which a part that has come into existence last in the order of time, is very often inferior and degenerate in point of quality. The latest blossoms are not always fruit blossoms.* We have seen that in any organism whatever, the parts are reciprocally means and end. Each exists for all and all for each, so that no one part can be exalted to a supremacy over all the others. Hence, in History there is a continual inter-dependency. No one age is superior to all others. Some past periods, in the history of the church, have been in advance of the present in some particulars. The present is never in advance of all the past, in all respects. The age of the Reformation was in advance of the nineteenth century, in a profound and living apprehension of the doctrine of justification by faith. The best Soteriology is derived from the sixteenth century. The creeds of the Reformers, in connection with the practical and theoretical writings by which they defended and explained them, have been the chief human instrument in forming the

* Both Bacon and Pascal notice this oscillation in human progress. "As it happeneth sometimes," says Bacon (Advancement of Learning, B. I.), "that the grandchild, or other descendant, resembleth the ancestor more than the son doth; so, many times, occurrences of present times may sort better with ancient examples, than with those of latter or immediate times." Pascal (Miscellanies) remarks that "nature works progressively: *itus et reditus.* She passes on and returns; then recedes further, then twice the space back, then further forward than ever, and so on indefinitely."

present Protestant theory of Redemption. The present age, on the other hand, has advanced greatly beyond the sixteenth and seventeenth centuries, in respect to the application of Christianity to the wants of the world, and the exercise of a practical missionary spirit. Thus, one age is the teacher of another, the pupil of a second, the stimulator of a third. In some way or another, each of the historic sections sustains a relation of action and reaction; and in and by this interagency the total process of evolution goes forward. Looking at the parts, we find them deficient; looking at the whole, we find it approximately complete.

At this point, then, let us retrace our steps, and succinctly state the results to which we have come.

In the first division of the subject, we obtained the definition of Abstract History. We found it to be evolution in the abstract; a continuous process merely, without any qualification, in which the connection of parts and elements is necessary, natural, and organic. This is the most general idea, and is capable of being applied to each and every particular species of history, be it natural or moral; be it the history of a vegetable, or of a man. But inasmuch as it is universal and abstract, it does not of itself determine the character and value of the process. It simply indicates that it is an evolution from a potential base, but with the specific qualities of this base, the abstract conception has no concern, and hence the doctrine of evolution is applicable, indifferently, to a latency that is good, or to a latency that is evil; to a germ originated by the Creator, or to a germ originated by the creature. This rigorously abstract conception of the idea precludes that imperfect and narrow apprehension of it which insists, either expressly or tacitly, that every germ is of necessity good, and that all development is an inevitable normal process.

In the second division of the subject, we have obtained a definition of Secular History. This we have found to be a particular species of evolution: that, namely, of a false germ. The common or so-called profane history of man is an illegitimate process, but none the less an organic one, to which the idea of development applies with its fullest force. The difference between the Secular and the Christian unfolding of humanity relates not to the continuous nature of the processes themselves, but to the specific difference between their potential bases. The germ of the latter is the creation of the infinite will, while that of the former is the product of a finite faculty in its fall from God.

In the third division of the subject we found a second species of concrete history: that of the Christian Church. The foundation of this is laid by a supernatural power which is strictly creative, and as such reoriginates the lost principle of spiritual life in the apostate creature. From this germinal point, under the maintaining and educating energy of the same Divine power that established it, a new development of humanity commences, which gradually destroys and expels the relics of the false germ, and though hindered and imperfect in its stadia here below, runs its round, and becomes a perfect and serene evolution in eternity.

Neither one of these two evolutions can be or become a potential base for the other. Each can proceed only from its own germ. The origination of a false germ in the place of the expelled true one, and the restoration of the true one in the place of a dying false one, are both of them events that cannot be accounted for by the theory of development. There is no passage *in the way of evolution*, either from holiness to sin, or from sin to holiness.

§ 4. The verifying test in Christian History.

Having now determined and applied the idea of evolution, and thereby come to an understanding of the nature of both abstract and concrete history, the second question mentioned in the first section, viz.: How may we verify our *a priori* conception in any particular instance? still remains to be answered. This introduces to our notice the general subject of tests in History. To follow out this subject into all its branches would carry us beyond the limits we have prescribed for ourselves, and we shall accordingly, as in a previous instance, confine the discussion chiefly to Church History.

Lord Bacon, in both the Novum Organum and De Augmentis Scientiarum, teaches that " the sciences require a form of induction capable of explaining and separating experiments, and coming to a certain conclusion, by a proper series of rejections and exclusions." * This " form of induction " in other places he terms a " method," or " clue," by which the mind is to be led through the bewildering multitude of phenomena and experiments, without being confused by their variety, and deceived by their contrariety.† By it he means that correct *a priori* conception of a thing, in the light of which the inquirer is to detect all that properly belongs to it, and to reject

---

* Opus est ad scientias inductionis forma tali, quæ experientiam solvet, et separet, et per exclusiones ac rejectiones debitas necessario concludat. De Augmentis (Distributio operis). At inductio, quæ ad inventionem et demonstrationem scientiarum et artium erit utilis, naturam separare debet, per rejectiones et exclusiones debitas; ac deinde post negativas tot quot sufficiunt, super affirmativas concludere. Novum Organum, lib. i., § 105.

† Adhibenda est inductio legitima et vera, quæ ipsa clavis est interpretationis. Novum Organum, lib. ii., § 10.

all that does not. The reader of Bacon is struck with the frequency with which he speaks of "rejections" and "exclusions" in the investigation of nature. He everywhere assumes that there is a complexity, a mixture, and to some extent a contrariety in this domain, that renders some foregoing tests necessary, in order that the true materials for science may be discriminated from the false, It is not enough to employ the senses in a merely passive manner, and see all that is visible, and accept all that is offered; to allow the stream of facts and appearances to flow along by the mind, and simply describe what has passed. Bacon's phraseology often implies an inducing of the mind into the senses; an introducing into this complex aggregate of sensational materials, of a *mental* or *rational* principle, that is to simplify and organize; in short, an induction of a method or an idea inwards, as well as a deduction of particular conclusions outwards.*
Opposed as this sagacious and thoroughly English mind

* Ea forma inductionis, de qua dialectici loquuntur, quæ procedit per enumerationem simplicem [impressionum sensuum], puerile quiddam est, et precario concludit. Sensus ipsius informationes multis modis excutimus. Sensus enim fallunt utique. Duplex est sensus culpa : aut enim destituit nos, aut decipit. Itaque perceptioni sensus immediatæ ac propriæ non multum tribuimus : sed eo rem deducimus, ut sensus tantum de experimento, experimentum de re judicet. De Augmentis (Distributio operis). Mentis opus quod sensum subsequitur plerunque rejiciamus. Novum Organum (Præfatio). Fallunt, et incompetentes sunt eæ demonstrationes quibus utimur in universo illo processu, qui a sensu et rebus ducit ad axiomata et conclusiones. Qui quidem processus quadruplex est, et vitia ejus totidem. Primo, impressiones sensus ipsius vitiosæ sunt ; sensus enim et destituit et fallit. At destitutionibus substitutiones, fallaciis rectificationes debentur. Secundo, notiones ab impressionibus sensuum male abstrahuntur; et interminatæ et confusæ sunt, quas terminatas et bene finitas esse oportuit. Tertio, inductio mala est, quæ per enumerationem simplicem principia concludit scientiarum, non adhibites exclusionibus et solutionibus, sive separationibus naturæ debitis. Novum Organum, lib. i., § 69.

was to the unverified and mere conjectures of the fancy, such as the alchemists, e. g., employed in investigating nature, he was not opposed to the initiating ideas and preconceived methods of the contemplative scientific mind. The fictions of occult qualities and hidden spirits he rejected, but his own map of the great kingdom of nature, with his full list of *a priori* tests and capital experiments, to guide the inquirer through a region which he has not yet travelled over, and in which Bacon himself had entered only here and there by actual experiment and observation, shows that he regarded the sober and watchful employment of the *a priori* method, by the scientific mind, to be not only legitimate but necessary. *

Such a "form of induction" is needed in History, in order that the investigator may make the requisite detections, adoptions, rejections, and exclusions. For this science is not a miscellany of all that has happened. The historic spirit is not an undiscriminating one. The historian needs to reject as well as to accept; to distinguish the normal from the false development; to detect the element of error in the mass of truth, or the element of truth in the mass of error. It is not enough merely to photograph an age; to simply hold up a mirror that passively reflects all that occurred. This is the Chronicle, but not the History. It is an exceedingly interesting and dramatic manner of representing the past, and furnishes the materials for the proper history. All true history has found its stuff in this minute and passive representation of the chronicle. Grecian history took its beginning in that body of narrative poems and legends which extends from Homer to Herodotus, and though this latter is styled the father of Grecian history, yet the student feels, on

* See his "Sylva Sylvarum," and "Preparation for a Natural and Experimental History."

passing from that easy and childlike credulity which records everything with equal seriousness to the searching and philosophic criticism of Thucydides, that, with the latter, the history, as distinguished from the chronicles of Greece, begins. Roman history springs out of the legends of the monarchical period, and such annals as those of Fabius Pictor, and, we must add, such narrative as that of Livy. English history derives its matter from the prose and metrical chronicles of the monks from 600 to 1300. Now if it were the great aim of the historian to merely depicture the past exactly as it was upon its surface; to place the reader in the process as an actor, and not above it as a judge; certainly the chronicle would be the true and highest form of historic narrative. Read the chronicles of Froissart, and see with what minute fidelity everything is related, and with what dramatic vividness and interest the scenes of pacific and of warlike life are made to pass before the mind. But why are we unsatisfied with this account of the contest between France and England in those centuries, and why can we not accept it as history? It is because there is in the narrative none of that discriminating spirit which is able to elevate the important and depress the unimportant; to let the causes of events, the ideas and forces of the period, stand out with bold prominence. Because, in short, the chronicle teaches none of the lessons, and exhibits none of the philosophy, of history.*

It is plain therefore that the historian must carry an idea, a method, in the phrase of Bacon, a "form of induc-

* "In history, actions of honor and dishonor do appear plainly and distinctly, which is which; but, in the present age they are so disguised, that few there be, and those very careful, that be not grossly mistaken in them." Hobbs' Epistle Dedicatory to his Translation of Thucydides.

tion," into the world of human life, if he would exhibit its deep meaning and significance. By this he will be able to distinguish the causes from the effects, and to present them in their proper proportions and relations to each other; to refer the phenomena to their grounds, and make the latter prominent above the former; to condense minor and unimportant matter and expand what is fundamental; and especially to detect and show what belongs to the process of true historic development, and what does not.

The position which we are endeavoring to establish has been very clearly and conclusively stated by one of the most profound of English writers, and we conclude this introductory part of the discussion by an extract from him. "A very common mode of investigating a subject," he says, "is to collect the facts and trace them downward to a general conclusion. Now suppose the question is as to the true essence and character of the English Constitution. First, where will you begin your collection of facts? where will you end it? What facts will you select, and how do you know that the class of facts which you select are necessary terms, and that other classes of facts, which you neglect, are not necessary? And how do you distinguish phenomena which proceed from disease or accident, from those which are the genuine fruits of the essence of the constitution? What can be more striking, in illustration of the utter inadequacy of this line of investigation for arriving at the real truth, than the political treatises and constitutional histories which we have in every library? A Whig proves his case convincingly to the reader who knows nothing beyond his author; then comes an old Tory (Carte, for instance), and ferrets up a hamperful of conflicting documents and notices which prove *his* case *per contra*. A. takes this class of facts;

B. takes that class; each proves something true, neither proves *the* truth, or anything like *the* truth; that is, the whole truth.

We must, therefore, commence with the philosophic idea of the thing, the true nature of which we wish to find out and exhibit. We must carry our rule ready-made, if we wish to measure aright. If you ask me how I can know that this idea, my own invention and pre-conception, is the truth by which the phenomena of history are to be explained, I answer, in the same way, exactly, that you know that your eyes were made to see with; and that is, because you *do* see with them. If I propose to you an idea, or self-realizing theory of the constitution, which shall manifest itself as an existence from the earliest times to the present; which shall comprehend within it *all* the facts which history has preserved, and shall give them a meaning as interchangeably causes or effects, principles or phenomena; if I show you that such an event or reign was an obliquity to the right hand, and how produced, and such other event or reign a deviation to the left, and whence originating, that the growth was stopped here, accelerated there, that such a tendency is, and always has been, corroborative, and such other tendency destructive, of the main progress of the idea towards realization; if this idea of the English constitution, not only like a kaleidoscope shall reduce all the miscellaneous fragments into order, but shall also minister strength, and knowledge, and light, to the true patriot and statesman, for working out the bright thought, and bringing the glorious embryo to a perfect birth—then, I think, I have a right to say that the idea which led to this is not only true, but the truth, and the only truth in the case. To set up for a philosophic historian upon the knowledge of facts only, is about as wise as to set up for a musician, by the purchase of some score of flutes, fiddles, and horns. In order to make music you must know how to play; in order to make your facts speak truth, you must know what the truth is which *ought* to be proved; the ideal truth; the truth which was consciously or unconsciously, strongly or weakly, wisely or blindly, *intended* at all times." *

What then is the "form of induction" which we are to employ as our method or clew, to lead us through the mighty maze of materials in the history of the Christian Church? What is the antecedent idea, or self-verifying theory, with which we are to test and clarify the historical data in this department of inquiry, and how can we be certain that it is the true one? These are the questions now before us.

The brief and most general answer to them is, that the true idea of Christianity is the key to the history of the Christian Church, and this true idea is furnished by the Scriptures.

We have seen, in a previous section, that the foundation of Christian History is Divine Revelation; that the inmost life-power which restores the true development of humanity, and the inmost law which regulates the process, are the influences of the Divine Spirit allied with the doctrines of the Divine Word. If this is so, it follows that only revealed elements belong to the *true* history of the Church, and that all that is anti-scriptural should be detected and eliminated. The test, consequently, which the inquirer is to apply to the complex, and, as we have seen, somewhat heterogeneous materials that meet him on all sides, is the test of the written revelation. We have seen that the process of restoring a lost normal develop-

* Coleridge's Table Talk (slightly altered). Works, VI., pp. 443-444. Harper's Ed.

ment is a dual one, because the expulsion of the relics of a false germ is going on contemporaneously. The history of the Church is imperfectly normal, not entirely symmetrical, frequently interrupted, and nearer perfection as a whole than in sections. This would not be the case if the infallible and perfect revelation of God had found a full realization of itself in the Church. It follows, consequently, that this very revelation itself is to be used as the "form of induction," the antecedent norm or rule, by which conformity and agreement are to be indicated and approved, and by which deviations and contrariety are to be detected and rejected. In short, the student of Church history is to provide his mind with the Biblical idea of Christianity, and to use it rigorously, as the crucial test, while he examines the materials; while he examines the forms of polity and of worship, the varieties of orthodox and heretical doctrinal statement, the methods of defending Christianity, the modes of extending Christianity among unchristianized nations, the styles of life and morals, the specimens of individual Christian character. Through all this complex and perplexing mass of historical matter, the true Scriptural idea and theory of Christianity is to conduct the investigator, so that he may see the true meaning and worth of the facts and phenomena, and set a proper estimate upon each. That we may see the imperative need of some such guide, let us look at a single class of phenomena; a single series of facts. We find a polity, a church constitution, in all the ages of the Church. There is the Jewish church-constitution; then the exceedingly slight and almost invisible constitution of the Apostolic church of the first forty or fifty years after the death of Christ; then the more consolidated republicanism of the close of the first and the beginning of the second century; then the dim beginnings of the episcopate, followed by the established primacy of the Roman bishop in the Western church, and of the Constantinopolitan bishop in the Eastern; then the absolute monarchy of the Romish pope, and the ecclesiastical despotism of the mediæval polity; then, since the Reformation, the revival of all but the last of these forms of polity in the various branches of the Protestant church, together with the continuance of the Papacy and the Patriarchate.

Here, now, is a mass of conflicting facts and phenomena, upon which it is necessary to form a truly historic judgment. It is not enough to take the position of the annalist and chronicler, and simply exhibit the facts, without any philosophic estimate of their intrinsic and relative value. Neither is it enough to give a vivid and dramatic picture of all these features and parts of the total process, and nothing more. The historian must set a proper estimate upon each and all, and deliver a judgment regarding them. He must say and show which of these forms of ecclesiastical polity is most congruous with the spiritual nature of Christianity. He must be able to say and show which of them deviates most from the general Christian idea of church government, and which is positively contrary to it. He must be able to say and show which grew out of a false and corrupted apprehension of Christianity, and so tended to perpetuate the error in which it had its own birth.

But how can he say and show all this, in reference to this mass of historical facts and phenomena, and how can he say and show the same in reference to the whole entire mass of historical materials, if he has not clear and bright in his own mind the true idea and theory of Christianity itself; that Divine idea which is to be seen struggling for realization through all this ocean of elements; that Divine theory which is being executed feebly in this section and powerfully in that, which is resisted in this age, and cherished in that, but which, in the entire sequence of ages and the whole sweep of years, is going on conquering and to conquer? And how is he to have this idea and theory clear and bright in his mind, leading it like the Beatrice of Dante through the Hell Purgatory and Paradise of History, except as he derives it from the fixed and unchanging written revelation, in which it is distinctly enunciated and explained?

We say distinctly enunciated and explained; for notwithstanding the difficulty of interpreting certain portions of the scriptures, and the many controversies that have arisen within the church, respecting the real mind of the Spirit, the written revelation so plainly teaches one general system of religion, that its prominent and distinctive features are to be seen in each and all of the various forms of evangelical doctrine that have appeared in the Church Universal. Even when this general system is overloaded with human inventions and additions which positively contradict and nullify it, or tend to crush it to death by their materialism, there is sometimes enough of it still left to show that the original formers of a symbol were nearer the Biblical system than their successors, and found less difficulty in detecting in the Bible a common teaching and creed. The creed of the Papal church, though not evangelical upon the distinctively evangelical doctrine of justification by faith, is yet in advance of the present religious character and teaching of that body, because it still retains some of those scriptural elements that were incorporated into it in the better days of this church. And hence in modern times—since the Protestant Reformation, and undoubtedly under the influence that has radiated from the scriptural faith and purer practice of the Protestant churches—men like Pascal, and parties like the Jansenists, have endeavored to effect a reform within the Roman Catholic communion, by cutting off the excrescences of tradition, and letting the original scriptural stock, imperfect as it was, grow on by itself. All the attempts at reform within a corrupt Christianity like that of the Romish and the Greek church, are implied proofs, and tacit confessions, that the written revelation is clear and unambiguous in its general teachings. For there could be no endeavors to get back to a conformity with an original directory, like the scriptures, unless it were believed that there is such an one, and that its directions are plain to the candid and truth-seeking mind. As matter of fact the symbols of the various churches are nearer to each other than their theological tracts and treatises are, because they are derived more immediately from scripture data: the Bible being not only a unity, but unifying in its influence.

Hence we say that the idea of Christianity, which the inquirer is to take with him into Church History, can be, and must be, derived from the scriptures themselves and alone. If it were a secular historic process, the preconceived idea need not necessarily be derived from a supernatural revelation. In the instance of the English Constitution, cited above, the investigator takes a purely human idea with him, as he follows the constitutional history of England down from age to age. This idea is no other than that organic law of the realm, of which jurists speak, and which is not to be referred to a specially supernatural source, but to the spontaneous operation of the natural reason of man. The same is true of all Secular, as distinguished from Christian history. The inquirer is not in the region of the Supernatural, and hence, although the light that is thrown upon profane history by the Divine revelation is indispensable to seeing its deeper and more solemn significance, it is yet not the *sole* light in which it must be viewed.

But in Church History the light of revelation is the *sole* light by which to see, and the revealed idea and theory is the *sole* preconception by which the mind of the inquirer is to be guided. He who reads the history of the Church in the light of that Divine truth which lies at its foundation will not read amiss. He who constructs the facts, and builds up the account, by the method and plan furnished by the written word, will rear the structure in its true proportions. He who takes scriptural Christianity as the "form of induction" by which the true elements are to be discovered, and wrought into the account, and the false elements are to be detected, and expelled from it; the "form of induction" by which the tests are to be applied to all the facts and phenomena, and the corresponding adoptions and rejections of good and bad materials are to be made; he who rigorously applies this scriptural idea will investigate the history of the Church in such a manner as to convey the real lessons which it teaches. All ecclesiastical history composed in such a manner will be catholic and exactly true. It will not be made to serve the interests of any particular sect, for it will impartially, as do the scriptures themselves, expose all deviations from the truth of God, though within its own sphere, while it will faithfully report and depict all conformity to that truth, in whatever age or country it may be found.

And this brings to our notice, the necessary and natural connection between Church History and Dogmatic Theology. The two sciences are reciprocally related, and mutually influence each other. For this pre-conception, derived from the scriptures, of the nature of Christianity, whose leading Church History follows, is, for substance, that doctrinal system which the theological mind has formed by the scientific study of the written revelation. Notwithstanding all professions to the contrary, every writer of ecclesiastical history, as well as of secular, has his own stand-point and view-point. This can be inferred from the spirit and teachings of his work, as unmistakably as the position of the draughtsman can be inferred from the perspective of his picture. Who can mistake the political, philosophical, and theological ideas which Hume carried with him from the beginning to the end of his history of England? Would a Liberal theory in politics, a Platonizing instead of a Pyrrhonizing mental philosophy, and a Christian instead of a Deistic theology, have read the facts in the career of the English state and church as he has read them? Who cannot see the difference between the rationalistic and the supranaturalistic conception of the Christian religion, as he reads the ecclesiastical histories of Semler and Henke on the one hand, and those of Mosheim and Neander on the other? In all ages the written history of Christianity is very greatly affected and modified by the prevailing theological spirit and bent of the historian.

But, on the other hand, dogmatic theology is greatly affected and modified by the history of the Church. Creeds and systems that are formed without much knowledge of past symbolism, are apt to differ, sometimes in minor and sometimes in essential respects, from creeds and systems that breathe a historic spirit. Thus the relation between the two sciences of theology and history is not that of mere cause and effect, in which the activity is all on one side, and the passivity all on the other. It is rather an organic relation, of action and reaction, in which both are causes and both are effects, both are active agents and both are passive recipients.

But, in this connection, it is important to notice, that

the Scriptures stand above both theology and history, as the infallible and unchanging rule by which both are to receive their ultimate formation. We assume, and believe we are correct in so doing, that the systematic theology which the Christian mind has derived from the written word agrees with the real teaching of this unerring source of religious truth. Still, the scientific Christian mind is not infallible, and it is possible for it to deviate from the matter of Scripture. Hence the need of a continual reference and recurrence to revelation, on the part of dogmatic theology. Again, the experimental consciousness of these doctrines in the mental and moral life of the Church is not of necessity and beyond all possibility of deviation a perfect and normal experience. This historic Christian life needs the guidance, and often the rectification, of the revealed cannon. Neither dogmatic theology nor the historic movement of the Christian mind can safely be left to themselves, without any protection from the written word. Even if each should be carried along for a time by its own momentum upon the right line, the side influences of the remaining corruption and darkness of human nature would soon begin to draw it aside, and the defluction would soon be plain and great. The actual career of some branches of the Church proves that unless there is a constant recurrence to the written word, both in theoretical and practical theology, a corruption of both theory and practice is the natural result. Those who would substitute tradition and the voice of the Church for the Scriptures, as well as those who would substitute the Christian consciousness itself for them, commit the same error in common. The Romanist and the Mystic are really upon one and the same ground, and are equally exposed to that corruption of Christianity to which every human mind is liable which does not place the Scriptures above both the teachings of history and the Christian consciousness, whenever the question concerns an *ultimate* and *infallible* source of religious knowledge.

While, therefore, we believe that Ecclesiastical History, both as it occurs and as it is written, is modified by the theology which prevails, and the theology which prevails is in turn modified by the knowledge of the past history of the church, we also believe, that the two cannot safely be left to their own inter-agency, and inter-penetration, unless both are all the time feeling the influences of the infallible revelation in which they both have their origin. Two streams may mix and mingle never so thoroughly, yet, unless the fountain is constantly pouring into them, their own mere motion cannot keep them pure, any more than it can keep their volume full. The idea of Christianity is therefore to be kept full, pure, and bright, in the head of the theologian and in the heart of the Christian, by the written word, which has been preserved for the Church, in order that, amid all the grades of knowledge and consequent varieties of experience that might arise within it, there might be a rule of faith and practice which, like its Author, should be without variableness or shadow of turning ; because what is written is written.

By thus finding the Baconian " form of induction," or ultimate interpreting idea, for Church History, in the Scriptures solely, yet not refusing to employ the helps for understanding them afforded by the general theology, and the general religious experience of the Church Universal, we avoid that fault which we regard as on the whole the most serious defect in Schleiermacher and his school ; the fault, namely, of an undue subjectivity. For this school, the Christian experience, or " consciousness," has a worth and importance in both dogmatic and historic constructions to which it is not entitled. In the reaction against the dead orthodoxy of the eighteenth century, they have practically undervalued the written objective revelation. We say practically, because in theory they adopt the Protestant maxim that the Bible is the only infallible rule of faith and practice. Yet the student of a theological system like that of Schleiermacher, and a history like that of Neander, finds that the organization of the former and the construction of the latter are actually determined more by an appeal to the living consciousness of the Church than to the written word of God. The doctrinal development in the one representation, and the historical development in the other, is too much a self-determination of the Christian mind and soul with too little reference to the correcting and regulating influence of that Divine Truth in which all Christian experience must find its norm. The historian does not exhibit with sufficient fulness, the influence which the inspired canon has exerted upon the unfolding of the Christian life. The process of Sacred History is regarded, too much, as self-directed. Hence, the general undervaluation of dogmatic statements as cramping the movement of the free Christian spirit, the leniency towards certain heretical tendencies, and the occasional hesitating tone as well as vagueness of vision in respect to scientific orthodoxy, which characterize the best complete history of the Christian religion and church that has yet been written.

What is needed is, more objectivity; more moulding by that fixed Object, that unchangeable Word, whose function it is to form the changing experience by its own fixedness and immutability. Consciousness cannot be an absolute and final norm for consciousness. It is the *object* of consciousness, by which the process of consciousness is to be shaped and determined. As that subjective process of faith and of feeling which is seen in the Christian

Church owes its very existence to the objective revelation, so it must be kept pure from corruption and error by the same, and be criticised and estimated by the same. To leave the process to test itself, and to protect itself from corruption, is not safe. An individual Christian who should trust to the feelings of even a regenerate heart, and the inward light of even a renewed mind, without continually comparing this subjective feeling and knowledge with the written word, would be the victim of a deteriorating, and, probably in the end, an irrational and fanatical experience. Much more then, is it unsafe to set up the Christian experience, as the ultimate source of Christian science and the final test of Christian development, either in the particular or in the universal Church.

Hence the Church historian must guard against two extremes. He must not, with the Rationalist, magnify the individual reason and the private judgment, to the disparagement of the general reason and judgment of the Universal Church, by disregarding or despising the historic faith and the historic experience. On the other hand, he must not with the Roman Catholic seek the ultimate source of religious knowledge in a tradition theoretically co-ordinated with revelation but practically supreme over it, nor with the Mystic Theology attempt to find it in a "Christian consciousness" which, like all forms of consciousness, is fugacious and shifting, and therefore liable to deterioration. These two extremes, involving three species of subjectivity, that of Rationalism, that of Romanism, and that of Mysticism, will be avoided by him who does not regard either the individual or the general Christian mind as upon an equality, in any sense, with the Scriptures, but believes that both the individual and the Church, in all ages, are to be subjected, both in respect to doctrine and experience, to the tests of a wisdom more unerring than that of the best and wisest of human minds or of human societies: the wisdom of an infallible inspiration.

THE DOCTRINE OF ORIGINAL SIN.*

DIE CHRISTLICHE LEHRE VON DER SÜNDE, DARGESTELLT VON JULIUS MÜLLER.

WE have placed the title of this work of Müller at the head of our article, not for the purpose of entering into an analysis and criticism of it at this time, but rather, as a strong and convenient shelter under which to labor upon the much vexed and much vexing doctrine of Original Sin. We are the more inclined to connect our reflections upon this subject with this work, in even this slight and external manner, first, because they coincide substantially with what we suppose to be the general theory presented in this thorough and thoroughly elaborated treatise, though differing from it, as may be seen, on the point of the nature of the connection of the individual with Adam, and by such other modifications as would naturally result from considering the subject from other points of view, and with reference to questions current among a theological public, differing very considerably from that in the midst of which this work originated; and, secondly, because it gives us countenance in the

* Reprinted from the Christian Review, Jan. 1852.

attempt to investigate the doctrine from a metaphysical, and not merely psychological, position. For it is the misfortune of the theology in vogue for the last hundred years, as it seems to us, that sin has been contemplated in its phenomenal aspects, rather than in its hidden sources. The majority of treatises that have been written upon this subject since the middle of the eighteenth century, have been occupied principally with *conscious*, and (technically so called) *actual* transgression; while sin, in the form of a nature, deeper than consciousness, and the very fountain of all consciousness itself, on this subject, has too generally been neglected. While, therefore, the psychology of sin has been diligently investigated, and with as much success as could have been expected under the circumstances, the metaphysical side of the doctrine has made little or no progress. If we turn to the treatises of an elder day—to the doctrinal statements on this subject of Augustine or Calvin, or Turretine, or Owen, or the elder Edwards—we find the reverse to be the fact. Here the essence of sin is regarded as a nature, or state of the soul, which manifests itself in a conscious and actual transgression that derives all its malignity and guilt from this, its deeper source. With this source itself—this metaphysical ground of the psychological or conscious transgression—the profound intellect and acute speculation of these men were chiefly occupied, knowing that if all the contradiction and all the mystery on this difficult doctrine, could be cleared up at this point, the question would be settled once for all. Instead, however, of advancing in the general line of advance, marked and deeply scored into all the best theology of the past, the theological mind for the last century has stopped short, as it seems to us, and has contented itself with investigating the mere superficies of the subject—ignoring, and in some instances denying, the existence of its solid substance. The effect of this species of theologizing is every way deleterious. In the first place, the problem itself can never be solved by this method, any more than the mystery of life can be made clearer by a mere examination of the leaves and blossoms of a tree The creed statement of the doctrine of original sin has made no advance since the statement made in 1643, by the Westminster Assembly. There has been much acute and intense speculation upon the doctrine since that time,—for mysterious as it is, and repulsive as it is, to fallen human nature, it will ever charm like the serpent's eye,—but we know of no distinct and strict wording of the doctrine made since then, that contains a fuller and clearer and less contradictory statement than that of the Catechism. It is plain, that there will be no " progress in Theology " by this route. In the second place, this neglect of the sinful nature, and this fastening of the eye upon the sinful exercises only, is greatly injurious to the interests of practical religion. The attention of man is directed to the mere surface of his character. His eye is not made to penetrate into what he *is*, because he is constantly occupied with what he *does*. The standard of character itself is lowered; while, as all church history shows, the grade of character actually reached is far lower than that attained on another theory and view of sin.

Finally, less unanimity among theologians is the natural result of this neglect of the metaphysical side of the doctrine of sin. We know that it is one of the most popular of fallacies, that nothing is less settled than metaphysics,—that the brain of a thorough-bred metaphysician is as confused as his heart, according to Burke, is hard. Still, in the face of the fallacy, we re-affirm that nothing but a return to the old ground occupied by the combatants of an earlier day, will enable theologians to range themselves into two, and only two, divisions, instead of the present variety of "schools," whose name is legion. The questions that arise, and the answers that are compelled, by a metaphysical method, as distinguished from a merely empirical one, *locate* the theologian, on one side or the other of the line; because, by this method, terms are used in their strict signification, and the conceptions denoted by them are distinct.

Suppose, for example, that the term "sinful," when applied to the nature of fallen man, instead of being employed in the sense of "innocent," as it sometimes is at the present day, had but the one uniform and constant signification of "guilty,"— would not all who hold and teach the doctrine of a sinful nature see eye to eye on that point? Suppose again, that the word "imputation" were employed to denote the charge of guilt upon the absolutely guilty, and never an arbitrary charge of any sort, — would not all who hold to the imputation of a sinful nature be at one on this point? And yet the loose use of these and kindred terms, and the multiplication of schools in theology thereby, can be prevented only by that method of investigation which passes by all manifestations and phenomena, and having reached the nature itself, asks — is it innocent, or is it culpable? — is this nature as justly and properly imputable, and so, as worthy of punishment, in the case of the individual, as of Adam, or is it not? Here the subject lies in a nutshell; and while the "yea, yea," locates the theologian on one side of the line first sharply drawn in the days of Augustine, and the "nay, nay," locates him on the other side, what is still better, this strict handling of terms leads to a deeper and more satisfactory enucleation and establishment of the truth itself.

For, if a man affirm that the fallen nature is sin itself and not the mere occasion of sin; is guilt itself, and not the mere occasion of guilt; and also, that all this is as true of the posterity of Adam as of the individual Adam himself, he is not only bound to explain this on rational grounds, but he is driven to the attempt to explain it by the inevitable movement of his own mind. And this was the case with the men whom we have mentioned. They never shrank from affirming that the ultimate form of sin is a nature, that this nature is guilt, and that the wrath of God justly rests upon every individual of the human race because of it. And when pressed with the difficulties that beset this, and every other one of the "deep things of God," by as acute and able opponents as the world has ever seen, instead of relaxing the statement, or betaking themselves to a loose and equivocal use of words, they stuck to terms, and endeavored to think through, and establish, on philosophical grounds, a form of doctrine which they first and heartily adopted, on experimental and Scriptural grounds. We do not say that they completely solved the problem, but we verily believe that they were in the way of its solution, and that theological speculation must join on where they left off, and move forward in their line of advance. No one age, however wise and learned, can furnish a finished Theology for all the ages to come; but if we would have substantial advance, each and every age must be in communication with the wisdom and truth of the preceding, and form a piece of continuity with it.

Returning to this point of unanimity, consider for a moment the variety of opinions among us in regard to this subject of a sinful nature. What divisions and controversies exist among those who all alike profess to be Calvinists! How little unanimity exists upon this doctrine among those who all alike repel the charge of Arminianism! One portion or school teach, that there is a corrupt nature in man, but deny that it is really and strictly sinful. Another portion or school teach, that there is a nature in man to which the epithet "sinful" is properly applied, who yet, when pressed with the inquiry — is it *crime*, and deserving of the wrath of God? — shrink from the right answer, and return an uncertain sound, of which the substance is, that its contrariety to law, and not its voluntariness, is the essence of sin. Again, there are those who are prepared to fall back upon the ground of the elder Calvinists, up to a certain point, but who resolve the whole matter when pressed by their opponents, into the arbitrary will and sovereignty of God, and deprecate all attempts to construct the doctrine on grounds of reason and philosophy. And finally, there are some who are inclined not only to the doctrinal statement of Augustine and Owen and the elder Edwards, but also to their method of establishing and defending it, by means of the doctrine of the real oneness of Adam and his posterity, in the fall of the human soul. And yet Calvinism is one in its nature and theory. Using this term to denote not merely that particular scheme of Christian doctrine drawn up by Calvin, but that doctrinal system which had its origin in the controversy of Augustine with Pelagius, and which received a further development through the reformed theologians on the continent, and the puritan divines of England, we may say that Calvinism teaches but one thing in regard to the existence of a sinful nature in fallen man, and but one thing in regard to the meaning of the term sinful. During those ages of controversy

— the 16th and 17th centuries — those who held the doctrine of a sinful nature, and of a sinful nature that is guilt, stood upon one side, and stood all together; and those who rejected this doctrine stood upon the other side, and also stood all together.* The Christian church

* This is evident from the symbols of the three great divisions of the modern Protestant church, viz: the Lutheran, the Reformed (Calvinistic), and the Puritan.

Item docent, quod post lapsum Adae omnes homines, secundum naturam propagati, nascantur cum peccato, hoc est, sine metu Dei, sine fiducia erga Deum, et cum concupiscentia, *quodque hic morbus, seu vitium originis vere sit peccatum, damnans et afferens aeternam mortem.*

Damnant Pelagianos et alios, qui vitium originis negant esse peccatum. Confessio Augustana, Articulus II.

Est peccatum originis corruptio totius naturae, et vitium hereditarium, * * * * * estque tam foedum *atque execrabile coram Deo, ut ad universi generis humani condemnationem sufficiat.* Confessio Belgica, Articulus XV.

Peccatum originis, est vitium et depravatio naturae cuiuslibet hominis ex Adamo naturaliter propagati, qua fit ut ab originali justitia quam longissime distet, ad malum sua natura propendeat, et caro semper adversus spiritum concupiscat, *unde in unoquoque nascentium iram Dei atque damnationem meretur.* Articuli XXXIX, Articulus IX.

Qua transgressione, quae vulgo dicitur originale peccatum, prorsus deformata est illa Dei in homine imago, ipseque et ejus posteri natura facti sunt inimici Dei, mancipia Satanae, et servi peccati, *adeo ut mors aeterna habuerit et habitura est potentiam et dominium in omnes,* qui non fuerunt, non sunt coelitus regeniti. Confessio Scoticana, III.

Peccatum omne *cum originale* tum actuale, quum justae Dei legis transgressio sit eique contraria, peccatori suapte natura *reatum infert, quo ad iram Dei, ac maledictionem legis subeundam obligatur, adeoque redditur obnoxius morti simul et miseriis omnibus spiritualibus, temporalibus, ac aeternis.* Westminster Confessio fidei, Cap. VI. § 6.

Every sin, both *original* and actual, being a transgression of the righteous law of God, and contrary thereunto, doth in its own nature bring guilt upon the sinner, whereby he is bound over to the wrath of God, and curse of the law, and so made subject to death, with all miseries spiritual, temporal, and eternal. Boston Confession of Faith, Chapter VI.

Q. What are the effects of this first sin of man? A. 1. Guilt; whereby they are bound to undergo due punishment for their fault. 2. Punishment; which is the just wrath of God, with the effects of it upon them for the filth of sin. Davenport's New Haven Catechism.

was divided into two divisions, and no more. And this, because the controversy was a thorough one, owing to the profound view of sin taken by the disputants on the Augustinian side; the metaphysical, rather than merely psychological aspect of the doctrine being uppermost.

It is therefore in this connection that we rejoice at the appearance, in this age, of a work like that of Müller, which recognizes a deeper source and form of sin than particular and conscious choices, and invites the theologian to contemplate the origin and essential character of that *nature* and *state* of the human soul, from which all conscious transgression proceeds. Whether it adopt all the views of the author or not, we are confident the reflecting mind that has made itself acquainted with the history of the doctrine of original sin, will find no difficulty in deciding on which side of the great controversy this treatise is; and furthermore, that it is on the whole a substantial advance towards a complete philosophical statement of the theological statement contained germinally in the works of Augustine, and formally in all the best symbols of the church.

In commencing the investigation of the doctrine of original sin, we naturally start from one distinct and unambiguous statement of Scripture; and we know of no one at once so plain and full as the affirmation of St Paul, that man is by nature a child of wrath. The doctrine of a guilty nature in man is taught either by implication, or by an explicit detail, in other passages in Paul's Epistles, in the Psalms of David, in the Epistles of John, in the Prophecies of Isaiah and Jeremiah, and in the teachings of Christ; but perhaps no single text of Scripture enounces the doctrine so briefly and comprehensively as this. It makes specific mention of the two principal characteristics of human sinfulness: (1.) its depth, and, by implication, its universality; and (2.) its guilt. After all that may be said upon this boundless subject, in its various relations to man, to the universe, and to God, the whole substance of the doctrine may be crowded into a very narrow compass. When we have said, that man is *by nature a child of wrath* — when we have said, that sin is a nature, and that this nature is guilt — we have said in substance all that can be said. The most exhaustive investigation of the subject will not reveal any feature or element that is not contained by implication in this brief statement.

The true method of investigating the doctrine is thus prescribed by the terms in which it is stated in Scripture, and we shall endeavor to follow it rigidly. We shall endeavor to exhibit the Scriptural doctrine of original sin, not by merely reciting a series of texts, and there leaving the matter, but by seizing upon the most significant and pregnant text of all, and rigorously developing it. If we are not mistaken, the simple contents of this one proposition of St. Paul, will unfold themselves by close reflection into a detailed view, and a doctrinal statement, that will be found to harmonize also with reason and the Christian experience.

I. This passage of inspiration teaches, that sin is a *nature.* " We were φύσει — *by nature* — children of wrath." The Greek word φύσις, like the Latin, *natura,* always denotes something original and innate, in contradistinction to something acquired by practice or habit. Whenever we wish to represent an attribute or quality, as residing in a subject in the most deep and total manner possible, we say that it is in it by nature, or as a nature; and when in our investigations we are brought back to a nature, as a fundamental basis, we think we have reached the bottom.*

When we search for the essence of human sinfulness, we find it in the form of a nature in the man. Suppose we

---

* The word "nature" for some minds conveys only the meaning of "created substance," so that to assert that sin is a nature, is tantamount, for them, to the assertion that it is the substance or essence of man. This is not its use in this essay. Sin is not substance but agency: it is not the essence of the will but its action; not the constitution of this faculty but its motion. The term "nature," consequently, when applied to moral agency, is equivalent to "natural disposition."

None were more careful to guard against the Manichaean doctrine, that sin is substance, than those who have held the doctrine that man has a sinful nature and that this nature is guilt. Augustine carefully distinguishes between the work of the Creator and that of the creature. The work of the former he often designates by the term *natura*. Employed in *this* sense he denies that sin is nature, or belongs to the course and constitution of nature. Omne autem vitium *naturae nocet*, ac per hoc *contra naturam* est. (De Civ. Dei XII. 1). The entire argument in Chapter 6 of Book XII. of the De Civitate Dei, endeavors to prove that moral evil is the pure self-motion of the will of the creature.

Consonant with this, Calvin (Institutes B. II. C. I. § 11) remarks " We say, therefore, that man is corrupted by a natural depravity, but which did not originate from nature. We deny that it proceeded from nature, to signify that it is rather an adventitious quality or accident, than a *substantial property* originally innate. Yet we call it natural, that no one may suppose it to be contracted by each individual from corrupt habit." Again (Inst. B. I. C. XIV. § 3) "neither the depravity and wickedness of men and devils, nor the sins which proceed from that source, are from *mere nature*, but from a corruption of nature." Again (Inst. B. I. C. XV. § 1), " we must beware lest, in precisely pointing out the *natural* evils of man, we seem to refer them to the Author of nature." Again (Inst. B. I. C. XV. § 1), "it would redound to the dishonor of God, if nature could be proved to have had any innate depravity at its formation."

The *Formula Concordiae* is careful to assert, in opposition to the doctrine of an extreme party in the Lutheran church, " peccatum originale non esse ipsam hominis *naturam*, aut *essentiam*, hoc est, ipsius hominis *corpus* et *animam*, (quae hodie in nobis, etiam post lapsum sunt, manentque Dei opus et creatura) sed malum illud originis esse aliquid *in* ipsa hominis natura, corpore, anima, omnibusque viribus humanis." Hase's Libri Symbolici, p. 639.

arrest the sinner in the outward act, and fix our attention upon sin in this form, we are immediately compelled, by the operation of our own mind, to let go of this outward act, and to seek for the reality of his sin within him. The outward act, we see in an instant, is but an effect of a cause; and we instinctively turn our eye inward, and fasten it upon the cause. The outward act of transgression drives us, by the very laws of thought, to the power that produced it — to the particular volition that originated it. No mind that thinks at all upon sin can possibly stop with the outward act. Its own rational reflection hurries it away, almost instantaneously, from the blow of the murderer — from the momentary gleam of the knife — to the *volition* within that strung the muscle, and nerved the blow.

But the mind cannot stop here in its search for the essential reality of sin. When we have reached the sphere — the *inward* sphere — of volitions, we have by no means reached the ultimate ground and form of sin. We may suppose, that because we have gone beyond the outward act — because we are now *within* the man — we have found sin in its last form. But we are mistaken. Closer thinking, and what is still better, a deeper experience, will disclose to us a depth in our souls, lower than that in which volitions occur, and a form of sin in that depth, and to the bottom of it, very different from the sin of single volitions.

The thinking mind which cannot stop with mere effects, but seeks for first causes, and especially the heart that knows its own plague, cannot stop with that quite superficial action of the will which manifests itself in a volition. This action is too isolated — too intermittent — and, in reality, too feeble, to account for so steady and uniform a state of character as human sinfulness.

For these particular volitions, ending in particular outward actions, the mind instinctively seeks a common ground. For these innumerable volitions, occurring each by itself and separately, the mind instinctively seeks *one single indivisible nature* from which they spring. When the mind has got back to this point, it stops content, because it has reached a central point. When it has traced all these outward acts and inward volitions to one common principle and source, it stops content, because it has introduced unity into the subject of its investigation. When the human mind has attained a view that is both central and simple, it is satisfied.

It is not more certain, that we are compelled by the laws of our minds to refer properties to a substance, than that by the operation of the same laws, we are compelled to refer sinful volitions to a sinful disposition. When we see exercises of the soul, we as instinctively refer them to a natural character in that soul, as we refer the the properties of a body to the substance of that body. In both cases the human mind is seeking for unity and simplicity in its perceptions. It cannot be content with merely looking at these various properties of matter, this impenetrability, this extension in space, this form, this color, and stopping here. It wants unity of perception, and simplicity of perception, and therefore it goes farther, and *refers* all these properties to one simple substance, of which they are the manifestation. In like manner, the human mind cannot be content with merely looking at all these exercises — these unnumbered volitions of the soul. It craves unity and simplicity of perception here too, and *refers* these innumerable, sinful volitions, to a sinful *nature* in man, one and indivisible, of which they are the manifestations.

Again: the argument from the Christian experience is

as strong as that from the nature of the human mind, in favor of the position that the ultimate form — the essential reality — of sin, is a nature. Although in the first period of conviction of sin, the attention of the man may be directed mainly to actions and volitions; and although this may be the case to a considerable extent, even in the first stages of the Christian experience, it is yet safe to say, that the Christian man is troubled through the Christian life on earth, mainly, and permanently, by his sinful *nature*. The reality of sin, for every man whose experience is worth being taken as testimony, is not in particular volitions of his will, but in its abiding state — not in what he chooses to do now and then, but in that unceasing, uninterrupted determination of self to evil. This is the torment of his life — that below his volitions to sin — below his resolutions to reform — even below his deepest self-examination, and his most distinct self-knowledge — below all the conscious exercises and operations of his soul, there is a sinful *heart*, a dark ground of moral evil.

We are aware of the mysteriousness which is thrown over the subject of sin, by the assumption of a form of sin which is deeper than consciousness. But we must take things as we find them, whether they are mysterious or not; whether we can explain them or not. The contents which we are to analyze are given to our hand, and whether we succeed or not in the analysis, they have the same fixed and real nature of their own. And, we may add, the true way to arrive at the unfolding of a mystery, is to recognize in the outset, the existence of all that belongs to it. The true way to arrive at the successful solution of a dark problem, is to retain all the terms of its statement. To throw out one or more of the terms which properly belong to the problem, and in which its real nature is contained, because it seems to be a troublesome term to manage, is to utterly prevent the solution; and the attempt to unfold the deep mystery of original sin, while rejecting in the outset an element that is essential — the sin that is deeper than consciousness, or the sinful nature, as distinguished from sinful volitions — simply because it darkens a subject that is confessedly mysterious, must inevitably be a failure.

Without troubling ourselves, therefore, at this point in the investigation, about the mysteriousness of a sin of which we are not conscious, because it is the basis and explanation of consciousness, and therefore of necessity below its range and plane, let us here and now settle the fact, whether there *is* any such sin.

(1.) And, in the first place, is it not a fact, that in regard to the matter of sin, we do refer all the conscious processes of our souls to something back of these processes? The materials that make up our consciousness as sinners — the innumerable items of which it is composed — the thousands of wrong volitions, and the hundreds of thousands of wrong emotions, and the millions of wrong thoughts — do we not, as a matter of fact, refer them all to some *one* thing, out of which they spring? Can we, and as matter of fact do we, continue to chase these innumerable and constantly vanishing particulars, dropping one as soon as we have reached the next succeeding, because the mind can grasp but one thing at a time, and thus lose the mind in an endless series, instead of collecting it in one act of contemplation and reflection; or do we, with David, cease this attempt to number our iniquities, and having acknowledged that they are more than the hairs of our head, (Ps. xl. 12,) with him confess a *one* sin of heart and of nature at the bottom of them all? No man who has had any experience on this subject at all, will deny that such is the fact.— Whatever his theory may be, every man does, in his private reflections and secret confession to God, find a form of sin within him which he regards as the fountain and cause of all his particular and conscious transgressions. He finds an original sin from which these particular wrong thoughts, emotions, and volitions, proceed.

(2.) And now, in the second place, is it not a fact, that we are never conscious of this source itself of transgressions, but only of what flows from it? We are undeniably conscious of these thoughts, these emotions, these volitions — of these items which go to make up the sum of our experience — of these various materials of consciousness. But, are we, as matter of fact, ever conscious of that *principle* of evil — that sinful *nature*, to which, as we have seen, we instinctively refer all our conscious transgressions? We have only to reflect a moment to see that we are never conscious of this sinful *nature* itself, but only of what proceeds from it. The evil *principle* to which we refer all these manifestations of evil, remains ever below the plane of consciousness. These manifestations may, themselves, become more and more profound, and may carry us down into deeper and deeper regions, but we find the sinful nature ever below us; as we go down into the depths of our apostate souls, and know still more and still more of the plague of our hearts, we are all along, and at every lower point, obliged to assume the existence of a yet deeper sin than our consciousness has grasped. We never reach the bottom; we never come, in consciousness, to the lowest and ultimate form of sin; or, which is the same thing, we never see the time when we have become conscious of all our sinfulness, and there are no further discoveries for us to make. The prayer of David is the proper prayer for us to the day of our death: "Search me, O Lord, and try me, and see what evil ways are within me; cleanse Thou me from *secret* faults." A prayer, it may be remarked, that is utterly unintelligible on the hypothesis that there is no sin deeper than consciousness.

This sinful nature, as distinguished from the conscious transgressions that proceed from it, is not a part of our experience, but something which we *infer* from our experience, as the origin and explanation of it. It is the metaphysical ground of the physical — *i. e.*, psychological — phenomena. We find within consciousness, an innumerable amount of particulars — an endless series of wrong thoughts, emotions, and volitions — each occurring by itself; and this is all we do or can find in consciousness. And if we were confined merely to what we are *conscious* of — if we were shut up to the series of our *experiences* merely — we should never come to the knowledge of a sinful nature. We should be compelled to stop with the phenomenal merely. But when in reflection, and for the purposes of science, we arrest all these processes of consciousness — when we bring this ever-flowing stream of conscious transgressions to a stand-still — that we may look at them, and find the origin and first cause of them, then we are obliged to *assume* a principle below them all, to *infer* a nature back of them all.— Thus, this sinful nature is an *inference*, an *assumption*, or, to use a word borrowed from geometry, a *postulate*, which the mind is obliged to grant, in order to find a key that will unlock, and explain, its own experience.

"But granting," the objector may say, "granting that, as matter of fact, we do infer and assume, from what we find in our consciousness, the existence of a nature deeper than consciousness, to which we refer the data of experience, and by which we explain them, what evidence

THE DOCTRINE OF ORIGINAL SIN. 227

is there, that there is in reality any such thing? By your own confession, it is entirely beyond the sphere of human consciousness; and though it may be a convenien a priori postulate, under which to group and generalize the various particulars in our experience, what evidence is there, that there is an actual correspondent to it in the human soul?" We answer: The evidence in this case is precisely the same with that which exists in the case of any and every purely *metaphysical* truth. The evidence cannot of course be derived from consciousness, because we are seeking the ground and explanation of consciousness itself; and therefore must be sought for in that *normal and necessary movement of our rational intellect*, by which we are compelled to the a priori assumption.— We find ourselves *necessitated*, in every instance that we attempt to find an adequate origin for our particular transgressions, to assume the existence of a sinful nature, and this *rational necessity* in the case, is the evidence that we need. When we find that the mind is driven by the *very laws of thought* to an a priori assumption, and that it is *invariably* driven to it whenever it reflects at all upon its experience, we have all the evidence that can be had for a metaphysical truth — all the evidence that can rationally be required, that the assumption corresponds to the truth and reality in the case. Reason cannot impose upon itself, and invariably teach a truth of knowing, that is no truth of being — a truth of logic and science, that is no truth of fact; and therefore it is, that men will always believe that there is a substance in which properties inhere, and a nature from which manifestations proceed, though there is no evidence from consciousness for either. The fact, that the human mind, in the exercise of its sober reflection upon the data of consciousness, is *invariably* and *unavoidably* compelled to a given assumption, is evidence that the assumption has rational grounds, and corresponds to truth and reality.— If it is not, then a lie has been built into the very structure of the human mind, and it is not to be trusted in regard to any a priori truth. If, when following the laws of thought, and trusting to the constitution imposed upon it by the Creator, there is no certainty that the assumptions which it is compelled to make, as the sufficient ground and adequate explanation of its experimental consciousness, correspond to the truth of things, the human mind might as well stop thinking altogether.

And what shall we do in this connection with the sense of guilt? This sinful nature, as matter of fact, is the source of remorse, and the cause of the most poignant self-reproach in those whose senses have been exercised to discern good and evil. Can we suppose that there is a lie here too, and that pangs come into the human soul, and exist there, with no valid reason for them, no real ground for them to rest upon? Can we suppose that all the remorse and self-reproach that has resulted in the souls of men, from a knowledge of their *nature* and *character*, and not merely of their particular acts, was un-called for, because there is in reality no such nature? Can we suppose that He who looks on things precisely as they are, *knows* that there is no just cause for this mental distress in His creatures?

In addition to these arguments derived from the nature of the human mind, and the sense of guilt, (which latter point opens a wide and most interesting field of investigation,) we may add, that the history of Christian doctrine shows that the church has in all ages believed in a sinful nature, as distinguished from conscious transgressions. The soundest, and, as we believe, the profoundest symbols all teach the existence of a form of human sinfulness running deeper than even the most thorough and searching Christian experience — or, which is the same thing, that the Divine Eye beholds a corruption in man, more radical and more profound than has ever been seen by the eye of man himself.

II. Assuming, then, that the fact of a sinful nature has been established, we pass to the second statement of St. Paul, that man is by nature *a child of wrath*. We pass from his statement, that sin, in its ultimate form, is a nature, to his statement, that this nature is *guilt*. And we need not say, that in so doing, we are passing over into the darkest and most dangerous district in the whole domain of theological speculation. The recondite nature of the subject, the difficulty of clearly expressing one's conceptions, even when they lie distinct in one's own mind, the liability to push a point too far, the failure to guard one's statements with sufficient care, and many other causes that might be specified, conspire to render this side of the doctrine of original sin one of the most difficult of all topics of discussion. And before we venture out into this region, we wish to say beforehand, that we should regret and dread above all things, to advance any views on this important doctrine that would conflict with the Christian's experience of the plague of his heart—any views that would be in the least degree prejudicial to that profound view of sin which the soul does actually have when under the teaching and influence of the Holy Spirit. We most heartily and religiously acknowledge, that here the Practical must have preference to the Speculative; and we would immediately give up any speculative view or theory of sin that we might have formed, the moment that we saw that it would go, or tend in the least, to disparage a thoroughgoing statement of the doctrine in a creed, or to promote an imperfect and shallow experience of it in the heart.

The apostle teaches, that sinful man is a child of wrath. Now, none but a *guilty* being can be the object of the righteous and holy displeasure of God. The doctrine of the Divine Anger is tenable only on the supposition that the objects upon whom it expends itself are *really ill deserving* — are *really criminal.* It becomes necessary therefore to show, that that sinful nature of man, on account of which he becomes a child of wrath, and obnoxious to the Divine anger, is a *guilty nature.* In doing this, we shall be led to discuss sin in its relation to the human Will, and to Adam, the first man.

(1.) In regard to the first point, the position taken is, that this sinful nature is in the Will, and is the product of the Will. We say that it is in the Will, in contradistinction to the physical nature of man. One statement of the doctrine of original sin makes it to consist in the depravation of man's sensuous nature merely. In this case, the Will is conceived to be extraneous to this corrupted nature, and merely the executor of it. Original sin, in this case, is not in the voluntary part of man, but in the involuntary part of him; and guilt cleaves to him when the voluntary part executes the promptings of the involuntary part; and guilt does not cleave to him until this does take place. The adherents of this view insist, (and properly too, if this statement is correct,) that the term " sinful," in the sense of guilty or criminal, cannot be applied to this depraved physical nature — to this (so-called) original sin.

In opposition to this view, we affirm that original sin does not consist in the depravation of man's sensuous or physical nature, but in *the depravation of his Will itself.* The corruption of the physical nature of man is one of the consequences of original sin, but not original sin itself. This is a depravation of a far deeper and more central faculty than that of sense — a corruption of the voluntary power itself. It is because the human *Will* — the *governing* power in the soul — first fell away from God, that the other faculties of man are in the condition they are, that the affections are carnal, that the understanding is darkened, that the physical nature is depraved; and these effects of apostasy should never be put in the place of their cause — of that corruption of the Will which is the origin of them all.

But the examination of a single instance of the gratification of a sensuous propensity, is enough to show that sin lies elsewhere than in the physical nature. A man, we will suppose, gratifies the sensuous craving for strong drink. The sin in the case does not lie in this craving of the sensuous nature, corrupted though it be. The sin in the case lies further back, in the Will; and, be it observed, not solely in that particular volition of the Will by which the act of drinking was performed, but ultimately in that *abiding state* of the Will — that *selfishness*, or *selfish nature* in the Will — which prompted and permitted the volition. Here, as in every instance, we are led back to a sinful nature, as the essence of sin; and this nature we find in the Will itself; we find it to be a particular state of the Will itself.

But, besides saying that this sinful nature is in the Will, we have said, furthermore, that it is the product of the Will. By this we mean, that the efficient producing author of this sinful nature is the Will itself; in other words, that this nature is a *self-willed*, a *self-determined* nature. Before proceeding further with this part of the subject, we wish to premise a few remarks upon these terms, " self-willed " and " self-determined."

It is unfortunate for the cause of truth, and especially for the scientific development of the doctrine of original sin, that the term self-determination has been appropriated by the Arminian School in Theology; and still more unfortunate, that the conception denoted by it has been, and still is, such a defective and inadequate one. Both Arminians and their modern opponents have understood, and still do understand, by this term, an ability in the Will, at any moment, to choose or refuse some particular thing. The Will accordingly, both for Arminians and their opponents, is merely the faculty of single choices — the faculty of particular volitions; and self-determination for both parties denotes the ability to put forth a single volition, or not, at pleasure. The Will for both parties is simply that faculty of particular choices, by which we raise a hand or let it drop — a species of voluntary power which the horse employs, in common with man, when he chooses clover and refuses burdock.

This is the notion attached to the term self-determination in the treatise of Edwards — the ability, viz., to resolve this way or that, at any moment, and under all circumstances; and if this is the only self-determination of which we can have any conception, then Edwards was correct in denying the doctrine. So far as his work combats this defective and inadequate notion of self-determination — so far as it seeks to overthrow the *Arminian* self-determination — it is one of great value. From such a superficial view of the Will, as being merely the faculty of single isolated volitions, and from such an inadequate notion of self-determination, as being merely the ability to choose or refuse a particular thing, in a particular case, nothing but the most shallow view both of sin and of regeneration could result. The great merit of Edwards in this polemic treatise, it seems to us, consists more in his powerful and successful resistance of a false theology, in connection with a thorough view of the *fallen* and *corrupt* Will, than in his own positive statements concerning the ideal and original nature of this faculty.*

In saying, therefore, that the sinful nature of man is the product of his Will, we do not mean to teach, that it has its origin in the Will considered as the faculty of choices, or particular volitions. We no more believe that original sin was produced by a volition, than that it can be destroyed by one. And if we can have no idea of the Will except as such a faculty of single choices, and no idea of voluntary action except such as we are conscious of in our volitions and resolutions, then we grant that the sinful nature must be referred to some other producing cause than the human Will, and that the epithets, " self-determined," and " self-originated," cannot be applied to it.

But it seems to us that we can have a fuller and more adequate idea of the voluntary power in man than this comes to. It seems to us that our idea of the human Will is by no means exhausted of its contents, when we have taken into view merely that ability which a man has, to regulate his conduct in a particular instance. It seems to us that we do believe in the existence of a controlling power in the soul, that is far more central and profound than the quite superficial faculty by which we regulate the movement of our limbs outwardly, or inwardly summon up our energies to the performance of particular acts. It seems to us, that by the Will, is meant a voluntary power that lies at the very centre of the soul, and whose movements consist, not so much in

* Edwards's work on "The Affections," contains much that is of great value for the construction of a philosophic theory of the Will.

choosing or refusing, in reference to particular circumstances, as *in determining the whole man with reference to some great and ultimate end of living*. The characteristic of the Will proper, as distinguished from the volitionary faculty, is *determination of the whole being to an ultimate end*, rather than selection of means for attaining that end in a particular case.* The difference between the voluntary and the volitionary power — between the Will proper and the faculty of choices — may be seen by considering a particular instance of the exercise of the latter. Suppose that a man chooses to indulge one of his appetites in a particular instance — the appetite for alcoholic stimulus, *e. g.*—and that he actually does gratify it. In this instance, he puts forth one single volition, and performs one particular act. By an act of the faculty of choices, of which he is distinctly conscious, and over which he has arbitrary power, he drinks, and gratifies his appetite. But why does he thus choose in this particular instance? In other words, is there not a deeper ground for this single volition? Is not this particular act of the choice determined by a far deeper and pre-existing *determination of his whole inward being* to self, as an ultimate end of living? And now, if the Will should be widened out and deepened, so as to contain this whole inward state of the man — this entire *tendency* of the soul to self and sin — is it not plain that it would be a very different power from that which put forth the particular volition? Would not the Will, as thus conceived, cover a far wider surface of the soul, and reach down to a far deeper depth in it, than that faculty

---

* This distinction between the Will proper, and the faculty of choices, is marked in Latin by the two words, *Voluntas* and *Arbitrium*; and in that one of the modern tongues whose vocabulary for Philosophy is the richest of all, by the two words, *Wille* and *Willkühr*.

THE DOCTRINE OF ORIGINAL SIN. 235

of single choices which covers but a single point on the surface, and never goes below the surface? — Would not a faculty comprehensive enough to include the *whole* man, and sufficiently deep and central to be the origin and basis of a *nature, a character, a permanent moral state*, be a very different faculty from that volitionary power whose activity is merely on the surface, and whose products are single resolutions, and transient volitions?

Now, by the Will, we mean such a faculty. We mean by it a voluntary power that lies at the very foundation of the human soul, constituting its central, active principle, containing the whole moral state, and all the moral affections. We mean by it a voluntary power that carries the *whole* inward being along with it when it moves; a power, in short, which is the man himself — the *ego*, the *person*.

It will be seen from this view, that the voluntary power in man is the deepest and most central power within him. We sometimes hear the human soul spoken of as composed fundamentally of Intellect and of Feeling, and only superficially of Will; as if man were an Intellect at bottom, or a Heart at bottom, and then a Will were superinduced as the executive of these. But this cannot be so, for man is a person, and the bottom of personality is free Will. Man at bottom is a Will — a self-determining creature — and his other faculties of knowing and feeling are grafted into this stock and root; and hence he is responsible from centre to circumference.*

---

* This more capacious idea of the Will is the most common one in doctrinal history. " Voluntas est quippe in omnibus: *imo omnes nihil aliud quam voluntates sunt*. Nam quid est cupiditas, et lætitia, nisi voluntas in eorum consensionem quæ volumus? Et quid est metus atque tristitia, nisi voluntas in dissensionem ab his quæ nolumus." Aug. De civitate Dei, Lib. XIV., Cap. VI.

The Will, as thus defined, we affirm to be the responsible and guilty author of the sinful nature. *Indeed, this sinful nature is nothing more nor less than the state of the*

"The Will is in the soul like the *primum mobile* in the heavens, that doth carry all the inferior orbs away with its own motion. This is the *whole* of a man; a man is not what he knoweth, or what he remembereth, but what he *Willeth*. The Will is the Queen sitting upon its throne, exercising its dominion over the other parts of the soul. The Will is the proper seat of all our sin; and if there could be a *summum malum* as there is a *summum bonum*, this would be in the Will."—Burgess. Original Sin. Part III. chap. XIV. Sec. 1.

"In the Will we are to conceive suitable and proportionate affections to those we call passions in the sensitive part. Thus, in the Will, (as it is a rational appetite,) there are love, joy, desire, fear, and hatred. * * * So that the Will loveth, the Will rejoiceth, and the Will desireth," etc.— Burgess. Part III. chap. IV. Sec. 2.

"The heart in Scripture is variously used; sometimes for the mind and understanding; *sometimes for the Will;* sometimes for the affections; sometimes for the conscience; sometimes for the whole soul. Generally it denotes the whole soul of man, and all the faculties of it, not absolutely, *but as they are one principle of moral operations, as they all concur in our doing good or evil.*"—Owen. Indwelling Sin. Chapter III.

"And then, likewise, there is a consequent averse or transverse posture in the affections of the soul, *whereof, indeed, the Will is the seat and subject;* desires, fears, hopes, delights, anger, sorrow, all transversed in a quite contrary course and being, to what they should be."—Howe's Oracles of God. Lec. 25. Also compare pp. 1204, 1128, 891. New York Ed.

.."As to spiritual duties or acts, or any good thing in the state or immanent acts of the Will itself, or of the affections (*which are only certain modes of the exercise of the Will*), etc.—Edwards on the Will. Part III. Sec. 4.

"The Will, and the affections of the soul, are not two faculties; *the affections are not essentially distinct from the Will, nor do they differ from the mere actings of the Will, and inclination of the soul,* but only in the liveliness and sensibleness of exercise."—Edwards on the Affections. Works, III. p. 3.

Edwards everywhere dichotomizes. For example, speaking of the difference between the knowledge of the natural man and that of the regenerate, he remarks: "In the former is exercised merely the speculative faculty, or the *understanding*, strictly so called, or as spoken of in distinction from the *Will, or disposition of the soul*. In the latter, the *Will, or inclination, or heart*, is mainly concerned."—Reality of Spiritual Light. Works, IV. 442.

The terms "heart" and "will" are everywhere used as equivalents b**_y** **Calvin.** See e. g. Institutes. Book II.Chap. III. Sec. 5–11.

Will; nothing more nor less than its constant and total determination to self, as the ultimate end of living. This voluntary power lying at the bottom of the soul, as its elementary base, and carrying all the faculties and powers of the man along with it, whenever it moves, and wherever it goes, has turned away from God as an ultimate end, and this self-direction — this permanent and entire determination of itself — this *state* of the Will — is the sinful nature of man.

Here then we have a depraved nature, and a depraved nature that is guilt, because it is a self-originated nature.* Here, then, is the child of wrath. Were this nature created and put into man, as an intellectual nature, or as a particular temperament, is put into him, by the Creator of all things, it would not be a responsible and guilty nature, nor would man be a child of wrath. But it does not thus originate. It has its origin in the free and responsible use of that voluntary power which God has created and placed in the human soul, as its most central, most mysterious, and most hazardous endowment. It is a self-determined nature — *i. e., a nature originated in a Will, and by a Will.*†

---

* To use a scholastic distinction — it is peccatum *originans*, and not merely originatum.

† The Will is the principle, the next seat and cause of obedience and disobedience. Moral actions are unto us, or in us, so far good or evil as they partake of the consent of the Will. He spoke truth of old who said "Omne peccatum est adeo voluntarium, ut non sit peccatum nisi sit voluntarium"—Owen, Indwelling Sin, Chapter XII.

"I mean hereby those first acts of the soul which are thus far involuntary as that they have not the actual [i. e., deliberately conscious] consent of the Will to them; *but are voluntary, as far as sin has its residence in the Will.* I know no greater burden in the life of a believer than these involuntary surprisals of the soul; involuntary, I say, as to the actual [i. e., deliberately conscious] consent of the Will, *but not so in respect of that corruption which is in the Will, and is the principle of them.*

Owen, Indwelling Sin, Chapter **VI.**

It will be apparent, from what has been said, that we regard the Arminian idea of the Will, and of self-determination, to be altogether inadequate to the purpose intended by it. The *motive* of this school, we are charitable enough to believe, was in many instances a good one. It desired to vindicate the ways of God to man — to make man responsible for his character — but it ended in the annihilation of all sin except that of volitions; of all sin except what is technically called *actual* sin, because its view of the Will was not profound enough. And as we wish to bring out into as clear a light as possible the difference between the Arminian self-determination, and what we suppose to be the true doctrine, let us for a moment exhibit the relation of both theories to " the doctrine of inability," as it is familiarly styled.

According to the Arminian school, the Will is merely the faculty of choices; and its action consists solely in volitions. Self-determination, consequently, is the ability to put forth a volition. Now, as a volition is confessedly under the arbitrary control of a man, it follows, that he has the ability to put forth (so-called) holy or sinful volitions at pleasure; and inasmuch as no deeper action of the Will than this volitionary action is recognized in the scheme, it follows, that he has the ability to be holy or sinful at pleasure. This is the " power to the contrary," which even sinful man has, although the more

---

Owen, in the above extract plainly distinguishes between voluntary and volitionary action: between the immanent self-determination of the *Voluntas*, and the deliberate and conscious (" actual ") action of the *Arbitrium*. The old writers often denominate the disposition or nature in the Will, *activity*. Owen speaks of the Christian affections as the "*actings*" of the soul; e. g., " Christians are able to discern spiritual things, sweetly and genuinely to *act* faith, love, submission to God, and that in a high and eminent manner." (On Forgiveness Rule VI). Edwards speaks of original sin as the " leading *act*, or inclination."

thoughtful portion of the school freely acknowledge that it is never exercised, as matter of fact, except under the co-operating influence of the Holy Spirit. This view of the Will, and of self-determination, then, teaches theoretically, at all events, the doctrine of man's ability to regenerate himself. There is no other action of the Will than that of single volitions, and over these man has arbitrary power.

But the true idea of the Will, and of self-determination, while bringing man in guilty for his sinful nature and conduct, forbids the attribution to him of a self-regenerating power. According to the Arminian theory, all the action of the Will consists of volitions, and one volition being as much within the power of the man as another, a succeeding volition can at any moment reverse and undo the preceding. But, according to what we suppose to be the true view of the Will, there is an action of this voluntary power far deeper, and consequently far less easily managed than that of single choices. We have spoken of a deep and central action of the Will, which consists in the determination and tendency of the *whole* soul and of the soul as a *whole*, and which results in the origination of an inclination, a disposition, a nature, in distinction from a volition, or a resolution. We have spoken of a movement in the voluntary power that carries the whole inward being along with it. Now it is plain that such a power as this — including so much, and running so deep — cannot, from the very nature of the case, be such a facile and easily managed power, as that by which we resolve to do some particular thing in every day life. While, therefore, we affirm that the Will, using the term in the comprehensive sense in which we have defined it, is a freely self-determined power, we deny, that having once taken its direction, it can reverse its motion by a volition or resolution. If the Will were *only* the faculty of choices or volitions, this might be the case; but that deep under current, that central self-determination, that great main tendency of the Will to self and sin as an ultimate end, cannot be reversed and overcome by any power less profound and central, to say the very least, than itself. Surface action cannot reverse and overcome central action. And we have only to take the Will as thus conceived, and steadily eye it in this free process of self-determination, to see that there is no power in this *central* tendency itself, from the very nature of the case, by which the direction of its movement can be altered. Take and hold the sinful Will of man, in this steady, this inmost, this total determination of itself to self as the ultimate end of its existence, and say how the power that is to reverse all this process can possibly come out of the Will, *thus shut up, and entirely swallowed, in the process.** How is the process to destroy itself, and turn into its own contrary? How is Satan to cast out Satan? Having once set itself, with *all* its energy, in a given direction, and towards a *final* end, the human Will becomes a current that is unmanageable — a power too strong for itself to turn back — not because of any com-

---

*" The Will in the time of a *leading act or inclination* that is diverse from or opposite to the command of God, and when actually under the influence of it, *is not able to exert itself* to the contrary, to make an alteration in order to a compliance. The inclination *is unable to change itself*: and that for this plain reason that it is unable to *incline* to change itself. Present choice cannot at present choose to be otherwise: for that would be *at present* to choose something diverse from what is *at present* chosen. If the will, all things now considered, inclines or chooses to go that way, then it cannot choose, all things now considered, to go the other way, and so cannot choose to be made to go the other way. To suppose that the mind is now sincerely inclined to change itself to a different inclination, is to suppose the mind is now truly inclined otherwise than it is now inclined."

Edwards on the Will, Part III. Section 4.

pulsion or stress from without, be it observed, but simply because of its own momentum and comprehensiveness — simply because of the obstinate and all-engrossing energy with which it is perversely going in the contrary direction. For the *whole* Will is determined, if determined at all. The depravity is *total*. Consequently, when a tendency or determination, as distinguished from a volition, has been taken, there is no remainder of uncommitted power in reserve, (as it were behind the existing determination or tendency,) by which the present moral state of the Will can be reversed. For this determination or permanent state of the Will, as we have observed again and again, is something very different from a volition, which does not carry the *whole* soul along with it, and which therefore may be reversed by another volition back of it. When a determination has occurred, and a nature has been originated, the Will proper — the *whole* voluntary power — *is in for it;* and hence, in the case of sin, the bondage in the very seat of freedom — the absolute inability to be holy, springing out of, and identical with, the total determination to be evil — which is a self-determination.*

---

* This non-returning character of the will, is noticed by that subtlest and most spiritual of the Schoolmen, Anselm. Justo namque judicio Dei decretum erat, et quasi chirographo confirmatum, ut homo, qui sponte peccaverat, nec peccatum, nec poenam peccati, per se vitare posset; *est enim spiritus* (by which Anselm here means *voluntas*) *vadens, et non rediens*; et qui facit peccatum, *servus* est peccati.
Cur Deus Homo. Liber I. Cap. VII.

It may be briefly remarked here, that the whole controversy respecting original Sin has turned upon the conception of voluntary action held by the disputing parties. In the Latin anthropology, this was, simply and only, the power of *self*-determination. That which is *self*-moved is voluntary, by virtue of this bare fact of *self*-motion. Neither the presence nor the absence of a power to the contrary, can destroy the existing fact that the will is moving spontaneously and without external compulsion, and hence the

It will be seen, that according to this theory, the freedom of the Will does not consist in the ability to originate a holy or sinful nature at any instant, and according to the caprice of the individual. It does not consist in the ability to determine itself to good or evil, as an ultimate end of existence, with the same facility and agility with which single choices can be exercised. It does not consist in an ability to jerk over from one moral *state* of the will, into a contrary moral *state*, at any moment, by a violent or a resolute effort. The doctrine of the freedom of the Will does indeed require us to affirm that the Will is primarily and constantly *self*-moved — that its permanent tendency and character is not imposed upon it, as the tendency of the brute is imposed upon it, by the creative act; but the doctrine does not require us to affirm, that when the Will has once freely formed its character, and responsibly originated its nature, it can then, ad libitum, or by any power then possessed by it, form a contrary character, and originate an entirely contrary nature within itself. All that is to be claimed is, that at the initial point in the history of the human Will, a free and responsible start shall be taken, a self-determination shall begin and *continue*. It is not to be affirmed, for it contradicts the experience of every man who has had any valuable experience upon this subject, that there is power in the will to cross and re-cross from a sinful to a holy *state*, and back again, at any moment —

power to the contrary did not enter as a *sine qua non* into the Latin idea of moral agency. It might be lost, and actually had been, and the will still be a *self*-determined faculty. In the Greek anthropology, on the contrary, voluntariness was *in*determination. The will, whether fallen or unfallen at all times and in all conditions, could either choose or refuse the same object. But that it might do so, it must be itself in a state of equilibrium or indifference, and not actually *committed* or *determined* either one way or the other.

that the Will is in such an *indifferent* state in regard to the two great ultimate ends of action — God and self — that it stands affected in precisely the same way towards both, and by a volition can choose either at pleasure.

(2.) The foregoing statement, it is hoped, will be sufficient to exhibit, so far as the limits of an article will allow, what is conceived to be the true idea of the Will, and of self-determination, in distinction from the Arminian view of them. We turn now to the relation of original sin to Adam, the head and representative of the race of mankind. There is not space to examine the passages of Scripture which speak of the connection of the individual with Adam. We shall assume, that such a connection is plainly taught in Scripture, particularly in the 5th chapter of Romans; and at the same time barely call attention to the fact, that the soundest creeds of the Church, and that of the Westminster Assembly in particular, have all recognized the connection. Our object is to see if the views that have been presented will not throw some light upon one of the darkest points in speculative theology.

It will be recollected, that in the first part of this article, it was shown that the deepest and ultimate form of sin is below the sphere of consciousness — that we are not conscious of the sinful nature, but only of what proceeds from it. It will also be remembered, that this original sin, or sinful nature, has been traced to the Will as its originating cause, and thereby found to be a guilty nature. If, now, these two points have been made out, it follows as a corollary, that there is an action of the human Will deeper than the ordinary consciousness of man reaches. If man is not conscious of his sinful nature, and if, nevertheless, that nature is the product of his Will — is the very state of the Will itself — it follows, that his Will can put forth an action of which he is not conscious. And if this be so, it furthermore follows, that distinct consciousness is not an indispensable condition to the origin and existence of sin and guilt in the human soul.

We are as well aware as any body, that a statement like this seems to carry on the very face of it, not a mystery merely, but an absurdity. At first sight, it seems to be self-contradictory to affirm, that the responsible action of a free moral agent can go on in utter unconsciousness of the action — that the human Will can put forth its most important action, (action the most criminal, and the most tremendous in its consequences,) in a sphere too deep for the agent to know what he is doing. On the contrary, it seems to be plain as an axiom, that knowledge must in every instance precede action — that the Will cannot act without first distinctly knowing what it is going to do. And accordingly, this is the position laid down in the beginning of all the current treatises on the Will.

Now, without entering into any process of ratiocination to support a mere theory, we wish to raise a simple question of fact. Is it, then, a fact, that man is conscious of all the action of his will? Is it a fact, that from the commencement of his existence, on and down through every moment of his existence, he is unintermittently *self-conscious* of what he is all the while doing as a moral agent? Is it a fact, that the impenitent sinner — the *thoughtless* sinner, as we so often call him in our sermons — is *aware* every moment of what he is about? No man will pretend that such is the fact. Saying nothing in regard to that deeper action of the Will, which we have denominated its determination, no one will say that **a man** is distinctly conscious of all his volitions even. f each and every one of the millions of choices which he is exercising from the cradle to the grave. Even here, so near the surface of the soul, and with reference to its most palpable exercises, no one will be bold enough to affirm a distinct consciousness in every instance. Volition after volition, choice after choice, is exercised by the *unawakened, unanxious* sinner, with all the unconsciousness and mechanism, so to speak, with which the two thousand volitions by which he lifts his legs two thousand times in walking a single mile, are exercised.*

Take the first sinful man you meet, and say how much of his daily existence goes on within the sphere of self-consciousness. During how many moments of the day is this moral agent aware of what he is doing, as a moral agent? Of how many of the volitions which he puts forth in the attainment of his ends of living is he distinctly conscious? How many of his emotions are exercised in the clear light of self-consciousness, so that he has a distinct knowledge and sense of their moral character? Is it not safe to say, that whole days, it may be whole weeks, and it may be whole months, pass in the lives of many men, during which there is not a single instant of distinct consciousness, in regard to the nature of the agencies going on within their souls? And will it do to say, that all this while there is no action of the Will?

The truth is, we cannot lay aside pre-conceived opinions, and look at the simple facts of the case, without being compelled to the position, that there not only can be, but there actually is, action of the Will that is not

---

* That the action in this instance is voluntary, in the sense that the muscles and limbs are moved ultimately by acts of the choice, is proved by the fact, that the man can *stop* walking. If it were strictly mechanical and involuntary, the walker must go on like a clock until his ambulatory apparatus ran down.

self-conscious action, and a vast amount of it. And this too, whether the Will be regarded as the volitionary or as the voluntary faculty. If we believe the Scripture doctrine, that man is evil *continually*, we must also believe, that the Will of man is in *continual* action — absorbed in an *uninterrupted* tendency and determination to self. The motion — the κινῆσις, — is incessant. But we know from observation, and as a matter of fact, that man is not distinctly conscious of a thousandth part of this process, which is nevertheless steadily going on, whether he thinks of it or not, whether he is aware of it or not. If, now, while affirming, as we must, that there is no responsible action but action of the Will, we also affirm, as we must not, that there is no action of the Will but conscious action, we remove responsibility from the greater part of human life. Responsibility and criminality would, in this case, cleave only to that comparatively infinitesimal part of a man's life during which he sinned deliberately, and with the consciousness that he was sinning. Furthermore, it would follow, from this doctrine, that the more entire the man's absorption in evil — the more thoughtless and unconscious his life became in regard to sin — the less responsible he would be; the more depraved, the less guilty.

But in this instance again, as in a former, whatever may be our theory, we do practically acknowledge the truth of the doctrine of the responsible action of the human Will, even when there is, or has been, no distinct consciousness of it. The great aim of every awakening sermon that we preach, is to bring the sinner to the distinct perception of what he *is*, and *is doing*, as a free moral agent. And observe, the aim of the sermon is not simply to aid the memory of the sinner — to furnish him an inventory or catalogue of his past transgressions — but, in the strict meaning of the expressive phrase, *to bring him to — to bring him to himself*. The object of every awakening sermon, and the end had in view by the Holy Spirit when He sets it home, is to bring the sinner to a distinct self-consciousness in regard to sin — to make him realize the awful truth, that during his whole past life of thoughtlessness and unconsciousness of what he has been, and been about, his Will has been active, and that from the inmost centre to the outward circumference, this action has been criminal; and still more than this, to make him realize, that *now*, at this very instant, his Will is setting itself with a deep, and as yet to him, *unconscious* determination towards evil, as an ultimate end of action. The object of conviction, in short, is to impart to the sinner a conscious knowledge of that sin, the major part of which came into existence without his conscious knowledge, but by no means without his Will.

We need only take a passage that frequently occurs in the common Christian experience to see the truth of the view here presented. How often the Christian *finds* himself already in a train of thought, or of feeling, that is contrary to the divine law. Notice that he did not go into this train of thought or feeling deliberately, and with a distinct consciousness of what he was doing. The first he knows is, that he is already caught in the process. Thought and feeling in this instance have been *unconsciously* exercised in accordance with that central and abiding determination of the Will towards self, of which we have spoken; in other words, the Will has been *unconsciously* putting forth its action, in and through the powers of thought and feeling, as the self-reproach and sense of guilt consequent upon such exercises of the soul, are proof positive.* The moment the Christian man comes to distinct consciousness in regard to this action that has been going on, "without his thinking of it," (as we say in common parlance,) he acknowledges it as criminal action, responsible action, action of the Will. The fact that he was not thinking — that the Will was acting unconsciously — subtracts nothing from his sense of guilt in the case.

And if there is unconscious action of the Will in these instances, which occur in the every-day experience of the individual Christian, much more should we expect to find unconscious action in the case of that deepest and primal movement of the Will which is denominated the Fall. If, in the instance of the development or unfolding of sin, there is much of this unconscious voluntary action, much more should we expect to find it in that instance when the profound basis itself, for this development, was laid. If there is mystery in the stalk above ground, much more must we expect to find it in the dark long root under ground. The fall of the human Will unquestionably occurs back of consciousness, and in a region beyond the reach of it. Certainly no one of the posterity of Adam was ever conscious of that act whereby his Will fell from God; and even with regard to Adam himself, the remark of Augustine is true — that he had already fallen before he ate the forbidden fruit. This remark is strictly true, and characterized by those two traits in which Augustine never had a superior — depth and penetration. The act of conscious transgression in the case of Adam sprung from an evil

---

* It is evident that there may be thinking without *thinking* of thinking, as there may be acting without *thinking* of acting. In these instances there is both thought and action without self-consciousness of either.

nature that had already been unconsciously generated in his Will. He would not have eaten of the tree, if he had not in his soul already fallen from God.

We may, in this connection, add furthermore, that the other great change which occurs in the human Will — viz., its renovation by the Holy Spirit, and its determination to God as an ultimate end, consequent thereon — also occurs below the sphere of consciousness. All acknowledge that there is no consciousness of the regenerating act itself, but only of its consequences; and yet even the most careful theologian must acknowledge, that there is action of the Will of some sort in this instance; that the renovating action is in the Will and in accordance with its freedom, though by no means, as in the case of sin, to be referred solely to the Will.

Enough has been said to show, that, unless we would unclothe most of human existence of its responsibility, we must assume the possibility and reality of an action of the Will, which is unaccompanied by distinct consciousness on the part of the individual man. And this is eminently true of that deepest action of the Will, by which a nature is generated, and a character is originated. That action of the human Will, which is denominated its fall, which lies under the whole sinful history and development of the individual man — which is the ground and source of all his conscious transgression — is, without contradiction, unconscious action. The moral consciousness of man, taken at its very rise, is the consciousness of guilt — which fact shows that the responsible action, lying under it, as its just cause and valid ground, *has already occurred. If there is any guilt in falling from God, the human soul incurs that guilt in every instance, without distinct consciousness of the process by which it is brought about.* If the origination of a sinful nature — of an abiding wrong state of the Will — is a criminal procedure on the part of the soul, and justly exposes it to the Divine Anger, it is yet a procedure that occurs unconsciously to the soul itself. And in saying this, we are manufacturing no theory, but simply setting forth the simple actual facts of the case. There is no avoiding the conclusion, unless we are bold enough to affirm that only that portion of a sinner's life is responsible and guilty, during which he sins deliberately, and with the consciousness that he is sinning.

We have called attention to this fact, that the human Will can and does put forth its deepest action below the sphere of consciousness, to prepare the way for the investigation of the connection of original sin, as found in each individual, with the fall of Adam. If this hypothesis of the unconscious action of the Will has been established, the only serious objection will have been removed, that can be made to what we suppose is the Scriptural statement of the doctrine of the connection of the individual with Adam, contained in the Westminster Assembly's Catechism. According to the form of doctrine laid down by that body of profound and learned divines, each individual of the human race is supposed to have been in some way responsibly present in Adam, and responsibly sharing in his apostasy from God. The statement in the creed which they drew up, is as follows: — " The covenant being made with Adam, not only for himself but for his posterity, all mankind descending from him by ordinary generation *sinned in him and fell with him* in his first transgression." And the two strongest texts which they cite in proof of the truth of their creed, are these: " By one man's disobedience, many were made sinners." (Rom 5: 19.) " In Adam all die." (1 Cor. 15: 22.)

Now it is to be remembered, that these men were making distinct and scientific statements, and their language, consequently, is not to be regarded as merely metaphorical. It must, therefore, be understood in the same way that scientific language is always to be understood — be taken in its literal meaning, unless a palpable contradiction or absurdity is involved in so doing. In this doctrinal and scientific statement, then, it is affirmed, that all men sinned in Adam, and fell with Adam in his first transgression. This implies and teaches that all men were, in some sense, co-existent in Adam, otherwise they could not have sinned *in* him. It teaches that all men were, in some sense, co-agent in Adam, otherwise they could not have fallen *with* him. The mode of this co-existence and co-agency of the whole human race in the first man, they do not, it is true, attempt to set forth; but their language distinctly implies that they believed there was such a co-existence and co-agency, whether it could be explained or not. They regarded Adam not merely as an individual, but as a common person; as having a generic as well as individual character. They taught that he was substantially the race of mankind, and that his whole posterity existed in him. Consequently, whatever befell Adam, befell the race. In Adam's fall, the race fell. And what is to be particularly noted is, that they did not regard the fall of Adam considered as an individual, as any more guilty than the fall of each and every one of his posterity, or that original sin was any the less guilt in his posterity than it was in him. So far as responsibility was concerned, Adam and his posterity were all *alike* guilty of apostasy. They were all involved in a common condemnation, because they were all *alike* concurrent in the fall. The *race* fell in Adam, and consequently each individual of the race was in some mysterious yet real manner, existent in this common parent of all.*

* This phraseology is not to be understood as implying that the individual is in the genus *as a distinct individual.* Adam, as the generic man, was not a mere receptacle containing millions of separate individuals. The genus is not an aggregation, but a single, simple, essence. *As such,* it is not yet characterized by individuality. It, however, *becomes* varied and manifold by being individualized *in its propagation, or development into a series.* The individual consequently (with the exception of the first man, who is immediately created, and is both individual and generic) is always the result of propagation, and not of creation. In the instance of man, the creation proper is the origination of the generic species, which species is individualized in its propagation under the preserving, and providential, (but not now creating,) agency of the Creator. The individual, *as such,* is consequently only a subsequent *modus existendi;* the first and antecedent mode being the generic humanity, of which this subsequent serial mode is only another *aspect* or manifestation. Had the members of the series of human generations existed *in their proper individuality* in the progenitor, there would have been no need of the subsequent process of *individualization,* or propagation.

The doctrine of *Traducianism* is unquestionably more accordant with that of original sin than that of *Creationism,* and the only reason why Augustine, and others after him, hesitated with regard to its *formal* adoption, was its supposed incompatibility with the doctrine of the soul's immateriality and immortality. If, however, the distinction between creation and development be clearly conceived and rigorously observed, it will be seen that there is no danger of materialism in the doctrine of the soul's propagation. For development cannot change the essence of that which is being developed. It must unfold that, and only that, which is given in creation. Now, granting the creation of the generic man *in his totality of soul and body,* it is plain that his mere individualization by propagation must leave both his physical and spiritual natures as it found them, so far as this distinction between mind and matter is concerned. For matter cannot be converted into mind by mere expansion, and neither can mind be changed into matter by it. Both parts of man will, therefore, preserve their original created qualities and characteristics in this process of propagation, or individualizing of the generic, which is conducted, moreover, beneath the preserving and providential agency of the Creator. That which is flesh will be propagated *as flesh,* and that which is spirit will be propagated *as spirit,* and this because mere propagation, or development, cannot *change the kind or essence.* If, therefore, it is conceded that the *creation* of man was com-

It is on this ground that they taught that original sin is real sin — is guilt. The sinful nature they held, could be properly charged upon every child of Adam, as a nature for which he, and not his Creator, was responsible, and which rendered him obnoxious to the eternal displeasure of God — even though, as in the case of infants dying before the dawn of self-consciousness, this nature should never have manifested itself in conscious transgression. Every child of Adam fell from God, in Adam, and together with Adam, and therefore is justly chargeable with all that Adam is chargeable with, and precisely on the same ground, viz., on the ground that his fall was not necessitated, but self-determined. For the Will of Adam was not the Will of a single isolated individual merely: it was also, and besides this, the Will of the human species — the human Will generically. If he fell freely, so did his posterity — yet not one after another, and each by himself, as the series of individuals, in which the one seminal human nature manifests itself, were born into the world, but all together and all at once, in that first transgression, which stands a most awful and awfully pregnant event at the beginning of human history.

The aim of the Westminster symbol accordingly, and, it may be added, of all the creeds on the Augustinian side of the controversy, was to combine two elements, each having truth in it — to teach the fall of the human race as a unity, and, at the same time, recognize the existence, freedom, and guilt of the individual in the fall. Accordingly they locate the individual in Adam, and

plete, involving the origination from non-entity of the *entire* humanity as a synthesis of matter and mind, flesh and spirit, then it follows that mere propagation, taking him up at this point, cannot change the essence upon either side of the complex being, but can only individualize it.

make him, in some mysterious but real manner, a responsible partaker in Adam's sin — a guilty sharer, and, in some solid sense of the word, *co-agent* in a common apostasy. As proof of this assertion, we shall quote from a few of the leading authors on this side of the great controversy.

Augustine, although the first to philosophize upon this difficult point, in order to bring it within the limits of a doctrinal system, has, nevertheless, as it seems to us, not been excelled by any of his successors in the profundity and comprehensiveness of his views. He is explicit in teaching the oneness of the human race in Adam, and of the fall of Adam and his posterity in the first transgression. In his work on the desert and remission of sin, he says: " All men at that time sinned in Adam, since, in his nature, all men were as yet that one man." * And the sentiment is repeated still more distinctly in that most elaborate of his treatises — De Civitate Dei; a work which was the fruit of mature reason, and ripe Christian experience, and which, notwithstanding the crudity of some of its speculations on subjects pertaining to the sensuous nature of man, and to the physical nature generally, is unrivalled for the depth and clearness of its insight into all that is distinctively and purely spiritual. " We were all *in* that one man, since we *were* all that one man, who lapsed into sin through that woman, who was made from him previous to transgression. *The form in which we were to live as individuals had not been created and assigned to us, man by man,* but that seminal nature was in existence, from which we were to be propagated." † In the words of Neander,

---

* In Adamo omnes tunc peccaverunt, quando in ejus natura adhuc omnes ille unus fuerunt. — De pec. mer. et rem. III. 7.

† Omnes enim fuimus in illo uno, quando omnes fuimus ille unus, qui

"Augustine, supposed not only that that bondage, under the principle of sin, by which sin is its own punishment, was transmitted by the progenitor of the human race to his posterity; but also that the first transgression, as an act, was to be imputed to the whole human race — that the guilt and the penalty were propagated from one to all. This participation of all in Adam's transgression, Augustine made clear to his own mind in this way: Adam was the representative of the whole race, and bore in himself the entire human nature and kind, in germ, since it was from him that it unfolded itself. And this theory would easily blend with Augustine's speculative form of thought, as he had appropriated to himself the Platonico-Aristotelian realism, in the doctrine of general conceptions, *and conceived of general conceptions as the original types of the kind realized in individual things.*"*

Calvin, though not so explicit as his predecessor Augustine, or as some of his successors, in regard to the precise nature of the individual's connection with Adam, yet leaves no doubt in the mind of the reader that he believed in the original oneness of Adam and his posterity, in the act of apostasy. He says: "It is certain that Adam was not only the progenitor, but, as it were, the root of mankind, and therefore all the race were necessarily vitiated in his corruption." Again he says: "He who pronounces that we were all dead in Adam, does also, at the same time, plainly declare that we were implicated in the guilt of his sin. For no condemnation could

---

per feminam lapsus est in peccatum, quæ de illo facta est ante peccatum. Nondum erat nobis singillatim creata et distributa forma, in qua singuli viveremus; sed jam natura erat seminalis ex qua propagaremur.—De Civ Dei. XIII. 14.

* Torrey's Neander, II. 609.

reach those who were perfectly clear from all charge of iniquity," [as Adam's posterity would be, were each and every man merely a distinct and isolated individual, existing entirely by himself.] Again he says: "No other explanation, therefore, can be given of our being said to be in Adam, than that his transgression not only procured misery and ruin for himself, but also precipitated our nature into similar destruction; and that not by his personal guilt as an individual, which pertains not to us, but because he infected all his descendants with the corruption into which he had fallen."*

John Owen is more explicit still, and he unquestionably reflects the views of the Westminster divines, to say nothing of his general profundity and clearness on all points of systematic theology. In his treatise, entitled "A Display of Arminianism,"† in connection with some other answers to the objection that original sin is not voluntary, and therefore cannot be sin in the sense of guilt, he expressly affirms that it *is* voluntary, in some sense of that word — that it has the element of free self-determination in it. "But, thirdly," he says, "in respect to our wills, we are not thus innocent neither, for we all sinned in Adam, as the apostle affirmeth. Now all sin is voluntary, say the remonstrants, [the party whom Owen was opposing, but whose statement in this case he was willing to grant,] and therefore Adam's transgression was our voluntary sin also, and that in divers respects; *first*, in that his voluntary act is imputed to us as ours, by reason of the covenant which was made with him in our behalf; but because this consisting in an imputation, must needs be extrinsical to us; therefore, *secondly*, we

---

* Institutes, Book II. Chapter 1. Allen's Trans.

†.Works, V. 127. Russell's Ed.

say that Adam, being the root and head of all human kind, and we all branches from that root, all parts of that body whereof he was the head, his will may be said to be ours; we were then all that one man, (omnes eramus unus ille homo, Aug.,) we were all in him, and had no other will but his; so that though that (viz., Adam's will) be extrinsical unto us, considered as particular persons, yet it (viz., Adam's will) is intrinsical, as we are all parts of one common nature; as in him we sinned, so in him we had a will of sinning." In a passage in his "Vindiciæ Evangelicæ,"* he also says, "By Adam sin entered into the world, so that all sinned in him, and are made sinners thereby — so that also his sin is called the 'sin of the world;' in him all mankind sinned, and his sin is imputed to them." †

* Works, VIII. p. 222. Russell's Ed.

† This same reasoning, from the basis of realism, is seen in John Robinson, the pastor of the Plymouth Pilgrims. In his "Defence of the doctrine of the Synod of Dort," he answers the question, Did infants sin in Adam? — in the affirmative, on the ground that they "had being in Adam after a sort, namely, so far as they were in him. If they had being in Adam any way, they had life also in him; for nothing in Adam was dead, but all living; their being, therefore, so far as it was in him, was a living being." This 'being,' Robinson goes on to argue, was that of a rational existence composed of understanding and will. — Robinson's Works, I. 404 et seq. Congregational Board's Ed.

Leigh, a graduate of Magdalen Hall, Oxford, published a system of divinity in 1654, which has the *imprimatur* of Edmund Calamy. In it we find the following:

"The first Adam represented all mankind, and the second all the elect *God might as well ground an imputation on a natural, as on a mystical, union Omnes eramus unus ille homo,* (Augustine); therefore the sin of that one man is the sin of us all.

"*Objection.* This sin of Adam, being but one, could not defile the universal nature. *Socinus.*

"*Answer.* Adam had in him the whole nature of mankind, 1 Cor. 15: 47; by one offence the whole nature of man was defiled, Rom. 5: 12, 17.

"*Objection.* Adam's sin was not voluntary in us, we never gave consent to it.

"*Answer.* There is a two-fold will. 1. *Voluntas naturae,* the whole nature

One more quotation shall suffice, in corroboration of the view presented of the oneness of Adam and his posterity, in respect both to the act and the guilt of apostasy, and this shall be from Jonathan Edwards. In his treatise upon original sin, after citing the passage, " By one man sin entered into the world," he adds, " this passage implies that sin became *universal* in the world, and not merely (which would be a trifling insignificant assertion) that one man, who was made first, sinned first, be-

---

of man was represented in Adam, therefore the will of nature was sufficient to convey the sin of nature. 2. *Voluntas personae,* by every actual sin we justify Adam's breach of covenant. Rom. 5 : 12, 19 seems clear for the imputation of Adam's sin. All were in Adam, and sinned in him, as, after Augustine, Beza doth interpret ἐφ' ᾧ in Rom. 5 : 12; and so our last translators in the margent. And though it be rendered, 'for that all have sinned,' by us, the Syriac, Erasmus, Vatablus, Calvin, and Piscatorius, *yet must it be so understood that all have sinned in Adam. For otherwise, it is not true that all upon whom death hath passed have sinned, as namely infants newly born.* It is not said *all are sinners,* but, all *have sinned,* which imports an imputation of Adam's *act* unto his posterity.

" Some divines do not differ so much *re* as *modo loquendi* about this point. They grant the imputation of Adam's sin to his posterity, in some sense, so as that there is a communication of it with them, and the guilt is charged upon them, yet they deny the imputation of it to posterity as it was Adams's personal sin. But it is not to be considered as Adam's personal sin, but as the sin of all mankind, whose person Adam did then represent. Adam's personal sin did infect the whole nature, and ever since the nature hath infected the personal actions."—Leigh's Body of Divinity, Book IV. Chap. 1.

" The whole history of the first man evinces, that he was not looked upon as an individual person, but that the whole human nature was considered in him. For it was not said to our first parents only, *Increase and multiply;* by virtue of which words the propagation of the human race is still continued; nor is it true of Adam only, *It is not good that man should be alone;* nor does that conjugal law concern him alone, *Therefore shall a man leave his father and his mother, and these two shall be one flesh;* which Christ still urges (Mt. 19: 5); nor did the penalty, which God threatened to Adam in case of sin, affect him alone, *Dying thou shalt die;* but *death passed upon all men,* as the Apostle observes. All which loudly proclaim, that Adam was here considered as the head of mankind." — Witsius on the Covenants, II. 14.

fore other men sinned; or that it did not so happen that many men began to sin just together at the same moment." "The latter part of the verse" (he goes on to say) 'and death by sin, and so death passed upon all men, for that all have sinned,' shows that in the eye of the Judge of the world, in Adam's first sin *all* sinned; not only *in some sort*, but all sinned *so* as to be exposed to that *death* and final destruction, which is the proper *wages of sin*."* In another chapter of this treatise he combats the objection made against the imputation of Adam's sin to his posterity "that such imputation is unjust and unreasonable, inasmuch as Adam and his posterity are not one and the same," (one of the principal objections to the doctrine, and a fatal one, if it can maintained). He combats it by denying the truth of the affirmation, that Adam and his posterity are not one and the same, and by establishing the contrary position by as profound and truthful a course of speculation as ever emanated from his mind. " I think," (he says) " it would go far towards directing us to the more clear and distinct conceiving and right stating of this affair, (of original sin,) were we steadily to bear this in mind: that God, in each step of his proceeding with Adam, in relation to the covenant or constitution established with him, looked on his posterity as being *one with him.* * * * Therefore, I am humbly of opinion, that if any have supposed the children of Adam to come into the world with a *double guilt:* one, the guilt of Adam's sin; another, the guilt arising from their having a corrupt heart, they have not so well conceived of the matter. The *guilt* a man has on his soul at his first existence is one and simple, viz., the guilt of the original apostasy, the guilt of the sin by

---

* The italics are Edwards's, and the italics of Edwards are always significant.

which the species first rebelled from God. * * The *first existing* of a corrupt disposition in the hearts of Adam's posterity is not to be looked upon as sin belonging to them, *distinct* from their participation of Adam's first sin: it is, as it were, the *extended pollution* of that sin, through the whole tree, by virtue of the constituted *union* of the branches with the root; or the *inherence* of the sin of that head of the species in the members, in the consent and concurrence of the hearts of the members, with the head in that first act." Edwards also quotes with approbation the following from Stapfer: " It is objected against the imputation of Adam's sin, that we never committed the same sin with Adam, neither in number nor in kind. I answer, we should distinguish here between the physical act itself, which Adam committed, and the morality of the action and consent to it. If we have respect only to the external act, to be sure it must be confessed that Adam's posterity did not put forth their hands to the forbidden fruit: in which sense that act of transgression, and that fall of Adam, cannot be physically one with the sin of his posterity. But if we consider the morality of the action, [*i. e.* the voluntary ground of it,] and what consent there is to it, it is altogether to be maintained that his posterity committed the same sin both in number and in kind, inasmuch as they are to be looked upon as consenting to it: for where there is a consent to a sin, there the same sin is committed. Seeing, therefore, that Adam, with all his posterity, constitute but one moral person, and are united in the same covenant, and are transgressors of the same law, they are also to be looked upon as having, in a moral estimation, committed the same transgression of the law both in manner and in kind." Edwards finally remarks, that all the objections that can be brought against the doctrine of the imputation of Adam's sin to his posterity, are summed up in this assumption and assertion — viz., that Adam and his posterity are *not originally one*, but are from first to last entirely *distinct and individual agents :* this assumption he earnestly denies, and enters into a long and subtle investigation, well worthy any man's study, of what is meant by personal identity, to show that there is no absurdity or contradiction in the hypothesis, that, by the divine establishment and constitution, all of Adam's posterity were, in some real and important sense, in him and one with him.*

Any one who will take the pains to study the history of the doctrine of original sin, and to trace its development, will find that the more profound minds in the Christian church have ever sought to relieve the subject of those difficulties which encompass it, by this doctrine of the oneness of Adam with his posterity. A mystery overhangs, and, perhaps, ever must overhang the nature and possibility of this oneness; but this mystery being once waived, or put up with by the mind, the principal difficulties that beset the doctrine of a sinful nature originated antecedently to all consciousness, and beginning to manifest itself in the case of every individual with the first dawn of self-consciousness, disappear. Granting the possibility and the fact of the individual's fall in Adam and with Adam, then it is easy to see how this fall can be charged as guilt upon the individual, and the sinful nature be truly and really a self-determined and responsible nature, deserving and incurring the wrath of God. Original sin, by this hypothesis, is seen to be the work of the creature, and not the Creator, the chief peculiarity in this case being, that it was originated by the

* Edwards on Original Sin. Part IV. Chap. 3.

whole race, and for the whole race, *not as it exists in the historical series of its individual members, but as it existed a seminal and common nature in the first man.*

With regard to the possibility of such a co-existence of Adam and his posterity, little can be said, although the more the mind reflects upon the subject, the less surprising does it seem. One thing is certain, that the mysteriousness of the subject has not deterred the human mind from receiving the doctrine. We see the clearest and deepest minds of the church, men of unquestioned intellectual power, and of profound insight into their own hearts, drawn, as by a spell, to this hypothesis, as the best theory by which to free the doctrine of original sin from its principal difficulties : and this fact of itself constitutes a strong ground for the belief that the truth lies in this direction.

1. We would merely call attention, however, to the fact, that the doctrine of the oneness and co-existence of the race in the first man, by no means contradicts what we know from physiology, but rather finds a corroboration from it. When the first individuals of a new species are created out of nothing by the Creator of all things, the *species*, as well as these individuals, is created. The remaining individuals of the species — the posterity of the first pair — do not come into existence each by a new fiat, like that which called the first into being, but by a propagation. The primordial elements of all the individuals of the series are created, when the first pair of the species is created, and then are developed into a series of individuals. Any catastrophe, therefore, any radical change that befalls these first individuals, affects the whole species, and in precisely the same way. If that science, whose business it is to investigate the nature and mutual relations of the species and the individual

and to give an account of the development of the creation of God, teaches anything, it teaches this.

2. The other principal objection — that the individual was never conscious of this fall in Adam — has been removed by what has been advanced in regard to the possibility of a voluntary action that is deeper than consciousness. If there can be, and actually is, action of the human Will, unaccompanied by self-consciousness, then it is not absurd or self-contradictory to affirm that the Will of the whole species, generically including the Will of every individual within it, fell in the first man.

The doctrine of original sin, then, as stated in the Westminster Catechism taken in its strict and literal acceptation, we deem to be in accordance with the teaching of Scripture on this subject. Only put up with the inexplicability of the oneness, and co-existence, of Adam and his posterity — only grant this assumption, which all the analogies in the world of physical nature, and all the investigations of physiology, yet seem to corroborate — and we can hold to a sinful nature, and a sinful nature that is guilt. We know of no other theory that does not in the end, either reduce sin to a minimum, by recognizing no sin but that of single volitions, or else, while asserting a sinful nature, does it at the expense of human freedom and responsibility. And surely a theory which removes the real and honest difficulties that cling to one of the most vexed questions in theology, ought not to be rejected merely on the ground of a mystery that attaches to one of its parts. Manifest absurdity and self-contradiction would be the only valid grounds for rejecting it; and these, we think, cannot be fixed upon it.

In conclusion, we would say, that we cannot think, with some, that such speculations into a difficult doctrine like that of original sin, are valueless — that they merely baffle the mind and harden the heart. We rise from this investigation with a more profound belief than ever, in the doctrine of the innate and total depravity of man — of his bondage to evil, and his guilt in this bondage. It is only when we turn away our eye from the particular exhibitions of sin to that evil nature that lies under them all, and lies under them all the while — it is only when we turn away from what we *do* to what we *are* — that we become filled with that deep sense of guilt, that profound self-abasement, before the infinite purity of God, and that utter self-despair, which alone fit us to be the subjects of renewing and sanctifying grace. If the church and the ministry of the present day need any one thing more than another, it is profound views of sin; and if the current theology of the day is lacking in any one thing, it is in that thorough-going, that truly philosophic, and, at the same time, truly edifying theory of sin, which runs like a strong muscular cord through all the soundest theology of the church.

THE ATONEMENT, A SATISFACTION FOR THE ETHICAL NATURE OF BOTH GOD AND MAN.*

It is a very important question whether, in the reconciliation of man with God, the change of feeling and relationship that confessedly occurs between the parties, is solely upon the side of man, or whether that method which proposes to bring about peace and harmony between the sinner and his Judge, contains a provision that refers immediately to the being and ethical nature of God. Is the Divine Essence absolutely passive, and entirely unaffected by the propitiatory death of Christ, and is all the movement and affection that occurs confined to human nature; or is there in the Godhead itself, by virtue of its essential nature and quality, something that requires a judicial satisfaction for sin, and which, when satisfied, produces the specific *sense* of satisfaction, or, to use a biblical term, of "propitiation," in the Deity himself? In short, is the reconciliation of man with God merely and wholly subjective, an occurrence in the human soul but no real event and fact in the Divine Mind? Is the sinner merely reconciled to God, God remaining precisely the same towards him that He is irrespective of the work of Christ, and antecedent to his appropriation of that work; or does God first, by and

* Reprinted from the Bibliotheca Sacra, Oct. 1859.

through a judicial infliction of his own providing, and his own enduring in the person of the Son, — Himself the judge, Himself the priest, Himself the sacrifice, — conciliate his own holy justice towards the guilty, and thereby lay the foundation for the *consciousness* of reconciliation in the penitent?*

The phraseology of scripture teaches, beyond a doubt, that the transaction of reconciliation is not confined exclusively to human nature. We are told, for example, by the apostle John, that "Jesus Christ the righteous is the *propitiation* for our sins." † Propitiation is the strong word employed to denote the real nature of Christ's work by that mild and loving apostle whose intuition of Christianity some biblical critics would array against that of Paul, and in whose writings they profess to find only the doctrine of spiritual life and sanctification, and not that of expiation and justification. But this term certainly implies two parties, — an offending and an

---

* That God, in the work of atonement, is both the first cause and last end, or, in other words, at once the propitiating and the offended party, is plainly taught in such texts as 2 Cor. v. 18, and Coloss. i. 20: "God hath reconciled us to *Himself*, by Jesus Christ. It pleased God . . . by Christ to reconcile all things to *Himself*, having made peace through the blood of his cross." *Augustine* notices this fact in the following manner: "How hast Thou loved us, for whom He that thought it no robbery to be equal with Thee, was made subject even to the death of the cross, He alone, free among the dead, having power to lay down His life, and power to take it again; for us, to Thee, *both victor and victim*, and therefore victor because the victim; for us, to Thee, *both priest and sacrifice*, and therefore priest because the sacrifice." — Confessions, X. xliii. 69. The same thought is expressed in a very dense and comprehensive form by *John Wessel*, one of the forerunners of the Reformation: "Ipse deus, ipse sacerdos, ipse hostia, pro se, de se, sibi satisfecit." — De causis incarnationis, c. 17. And *Pascal* makes a similar remark in his fragmentary reflections: "Agnus occisus est ab origine mundi. The judge himself is the sacrifice." — Thoughts, London Ed. by Pearce, p. 255.

† 1 John ii. 2.

offended one. "A mediator," argues Paul, in his Epistle to the Galatians, "is not a mediator of one;" that is, in order to mediation, there must be two persons between whom to mediate. In like manner, propitiation implies that one being has wakened the just displeasure of another being, and that the latter needs to be placated by some valid and satisfactory method. Propitiation, therefore, — an idea that weaves the warp and weaves the woof of the entire scriptures, — if it has any solid signification, looks Godward.* God, and not man, is the party primarily offended by sin. It is *his* nature which requires the propitiatory sacrifice, and he himself provides it. " Since, in his crucifixion," says John Howe, " Christ was a sacrifice, that is, was placatory and reconciling, and since reconciliations are always mutual, of both the contending parties to one another, it must have the proper influence of a sacrifice immediately upon *both*, and as well mollify men's hearts towards God, as *procure that he should express favorable inclinations towards them.*" †

Another very pointed scripture text, from which we

---

* This is very apparent when we analyze those words in different languages which bring to view the relation of sinful man to the Supreme Being. The primary meaning always implies that the *Deity* is displacent, and it is only the secondary signification that refers to the creature. The word ἱλάσκομαι, for example, in Homer, is always objective in its signification when applied to the gods. Ἱλάσκεσθαι θεόν primarily means to appease God, to produce a favorable feeling or affection in God, and then in a secondary sense to reconcile oneself to him, to attain a peaceful feeling subjectively. The Saxon *bot* (whence the modern *boot*) signifies a compensation paid to an *injured* party, a redressing, recompense, amends, satisfaction, offering; then a remedy or cure, effected by such compensation; and *lastly*, a *repentance, renewing, restoring*, wrought out by means of boot or satisfaction given. In this way repentance is inseparable from atonement; and its genuineness is evinced by the cordiality with which judicial satisfaction is rendered, if it can be, or appropriated as rendered by a substitute, in case it cannot be.

† *Living Temple*, Pt. II. c. 5. (Vol. I. p. 81. New York Ed.).

cannot deduce anything but the doctrine of a real satisfaction of the Divine Nature by the work of Christ, is the declaration of Paul, that " if while we were yet [impenitent] sinners Christ died for us, much more, then, being now justified by his blood we shall be *saved from wrath* through him."* *Whose* wrath is this, from which, the apostle teaches, we are saved by the propitiatory death of Christ? Is it the wrath of man, and not the wrath of God? Most certainly it is not from that selfish and wicked passion in the human heart, which we most commonly associate with the term *anger*, that we are delivered by the blood of redemption. But may it not be our own moral indignation *merely*, and not that of our Creator and Judge, to which the apostle refers? May not the appeasing effect of Christ's blood of expiation be confined to the human conscience solely, and there be no actual pacification of any attribute or feeling in the Deity? But this is only a part of the truth. We do, indeed, need to be saved from the terrible wrath and remorse of our own consciences, as they bite back (*remordere*) upon us after the commission of sin, — and of this we shall speak in its place, — but we need primarily to be saved from the judicial displeasure of that immaculate SPIRIT, in whose character and ethical feeling towards sin the human conscience itself has its eternal ground and authority, and of which it is the most sensitive index and measure.

The natural teaching, then, of these and similar passages of scripture is, that the atoning sacrifice of the God-man renders, "*propitious*" towards the transgressor, that particular side of the Divine Nature, and that one specific emotion of the living God, which other-

---

* Romans, v. 8, 9.

wise and without it is displacent and unappeased. This atonement is a satisfaction for the ethical nature of God as well as man. This propitiation sustains an immediate relation to an attribute and quality in the Divine Essence, and exerts a specific influence upon it. By it God's holy justice and moral anger against sin are conciliated to guilty man, that man's remorseful conscience may, as a consequence of this pacification in the Divine Essence, experience the peace that passeth all understanding. It will therefore be the purpose of this Essay to evince that the piacular work of the incarnate Deity sustains relations to *both* the nature of God and the nature of man ; and more particularly to show that the pacification of the human conscience itself is possible only in case there has been an antecedent propitiation and satisfaction of that side of the Divine Nature which is the deep and eternal ground of conscience.

Before commencing the discussion, we would in the very outset guard against a misconception, which almost uniformly arises in a certain class of minds, and which is not only incompatible with any just understanding of the doctrine of atonement, but prevents even a dispassionate and candid attention to it. When it is asserted that "God requires to be propitiated," and that " his wrath needs to be averted by a judicial infliction upon the sinner's substitute," the image immediately arises before such minds of an enraged and ugly demon, whose wrath is *wrong*, and who must be pacified by some *other* being than himself. Such minds labor under a twofold error, of which they ought to be disabused. Their first fatal misconception is, that the Divine anger is selfish and vindictive, instead of just and vindicative of law. And their second consists in their assumption that the placation issues from some other source than the offended One himself. Assuming, as they do, that anger in God is illegitimate, the attribution of this emotion to him, of course undeifies him. And assuming, still further, that wrath against the sinner's *sin* cannot exist at the same instant with compassion towards the sinner's *soul*, they find no pity in the Deity as thus defined. His sole emotion must be that of wrath, because, as they imagine, He can have but one feeling at a time, and therefore the creature who has incurred God's displeasure must look elsewhere than to God for the source of hope and peace.

Now this whole view overlooks the complex nature, the infinite plenitude, of the Godhead. For at the very instant when the immaculate holiness of God is burning with intensity, and reacting by an organic recoil against sin,* the infinite pity of God is yearning with a fathomless desire to save the transgressor from *the effects of this very displeasure*. The emotion of anger against sin is constitutional to the Deity, and is irrepressible at the sight of sin. But this is entirely compatible with the existence and exercise of another and opposite feeling, at the very same moment, in reference, not indeed to the sin, but to the *soul* of the sinner.† Mercy and

---

* The inspired words that express the emotion of displacency in the Divine Being are startling from their energy and vividness. The primary sensuous meaning, or the visual image called up by them, illustrates this. The verb זעם, employed in Ps. vii. 11, signifies *to foam at the mouth;* the verb קצף means to *cut up,* or *break up, into pieces;* the verb אנף signifies *to breathe hard through the distended nostrils;* etc. Does not the application of such words as these to the emotions of the Deity imply an inspiration that includes phraseology as well as ideas? Would an uninspired writer venture upon such diction in such a connection?

† The two emotions of which we are speaking, are clearly discriminated from each other by the fact that one of them is constitutional, and the other

truth meet *together*, righteousness and peace kiss each other, in the Divine Essence; and it is a mutilated and meagre conception of the Godhead that can grasp but one of these opposites at once. Even within the narrow and imperfect sphere of human life there may be, and were man holier, there often would be, the most holy and unselfish indignation at wrong doing, united with the utmost readiness to suffer and die if need be for the eternal welfare of the wrong doer.

Such being the actual relation of indignation to com-

voluntary. The Divine wrath (ὀργὴ Θεοῦ, Rom. i. 18), issues from the necessary antagonism between the pure essence of the Godhead, and moral evil. It is, therefore, natural, organic, necessary, and eternal. The logical idea of the Holy implies it. But the love of benevolence, or the Divine compassion, issues from the voluntary disposition of God, — from his heart and affections. It is good-*will*. It is, consequently, easy to see that the existence of the constitutional emotion is perfectly compatible with that of the voluntary, in one and the same being, and at one and the same moment; and, in God, from all eternity, since he is unchangeable. Says *Augustine* (Tractatus in Joannem, 110) : "It is written, 'God commendeth his love towards us, in that, while we were yet sinners, Christ died for us' (Rom. v. 8). He loved us, therefore, even when, in the exercise of enmity against him, we were working iniquity. And yet it is said with perfect truth: 'Thou hatest, O Lord, all workers of iniquity' (Ps. v. 5). Wherefore, in a wonderful and divine manner, *he both hated and loved us at the same time.* He hated us, as being different from what he had made us ; but as our iniquity had not entirely destroyed his work in us, he could at the same time, in every one of us, hate what we had *done* and love what he had *created* In every instance it is truly said of God : 'Thou hatest nothing which thou hast made ; for never wouldest thou have made anything, if thou hadst hated it' (Wisdom xi. 24)." *Calvin*, after quoting the above from Augustine, remarks (Institutes II. xvi. 3) : " God, who is the perfection of righteousness, cannot love iniquity, which he beholds in us all. We all, therefore, have in us that which deserves God's hatred. Wherefore, in respect to our corrupt nature, and the succeeding depravity of our lives, we are all really offensive to God, guilty in his sight, and born to the damnation of hell. But because the Lord will not lose in us that which is his own, he yet discovers something that his goodness may love. For notwithstanding we are *sinners* through our own fault, yet we are still his *creatures ;* notwithstanding we have brought death upon ourselves, yet he had created us for life."

passion in the Divine Essence, it is plain that it is God himself that propitiates himself to the transgressor. In the *incarnate* person of the Son, God voluntarily endures the weight of his own judicial displeasure, in order that the real criminal may be spared. The Divine compassion itself bears the inflictions of the Divine indignation, in the place of the transgressor.* That ethical emotion in the being of God, which from the nature and necessity of the case is incensed against sin, God himself placates by a personal self-sacrifice that inures to the benefit of the creature. The "propitiation" spoken of by the apostle John is, therefore, no oblation *ab extra*, no device of a third party, or even of man himself, to render God placable towards man. It is wholly *ab intra*, a *self*-oblation upon the part of Deity itself, by which to satisfy those immanent and eternal imperatives of the Divine Nature which without it must find their satisfaction in the punishment of the transgressor, or else be outraged. Neither does the purpose to employ this method of salvation, to provide this satisfaction of ethical and judicial claims, originate outside of the Divine Nature. God is inherently inclined to forgive; and there is no proof of this so strong as the fact, that he does not shrink from this amazing *self*-sacrifice which forgiveness necessitates. The desire to save his transgressing and guilty creature wells up and overflows from the depths of his own compassionate

---

* In all these statements we would be understood as making them in harmony with, and subject to, all the limitations of the catholic doctrine of the two natures in the one Person of Christ. The Divine Nature, in itself, is impassible; but we have scriptural warrant in Acts xx. 28, for saying that God *incarnate*, or the *God-Man*, is passible, and suffers and dies. Hence, while there can be no transfer of predicates from one *nature* to the other, the predicates of both natures alike belong to the *Person*, and that Person is God as well as man.

heart, and needs no soliciting or prompting from without. Side by side in the Godhead, then, there dwell the impulse to punish and the desire to pardon; but the desire to pardon is realized in act, by *carrying out* the impulse to punish, not indeed upon the person of the criminal, but upon that of his substitute. And the substitute is the Punisher Himself! Side by side in the Godhead there reside the emotion of moral wrath and the feeling of pity; but the feeling of pity is manifested, not by denying, but by asserting, the entire legitimacy of the emotion of moral wrath, and "propitiating" its holy intensity by a sufficient oblation. And that oblation is incarnate Deity Itself!

Viewed from this central point, and under this focal light, how impossible it is not to recognize *both* love and wrath in the Godhead,* and how impossible it is to conceive of a schism in the Divine Being, and separate his justice from his mercy. It is a real "propitiation" of the Divine anger against sin that is effected, but it is a propitiation that is effected by the Deity himself, out of his own self-sacrificing and principled compassion.

Turning now to the discussion of the theme proposed, the first step requires us to consider the relation which the ethical nature of man sustains to the ethical nature of God. For if both alike are to be satisfied by one and the same atoning work of one and the same

* The inspired assertion that "God is a consuming fire" (Heb. xi. 29), is just as categorical and unqualified as the inspired assertion that "God is love" (1 John iv. 8), or the inspired assertion that "God is light" (1 John i. 5). Hence it is as inaccurate to resolve all the Divine emotions into love, as it would be to resolve them all into wrath. The truth is, that it is the Divine *Essence* alone, and not any one particular attribute, that can be logically regarded as the unity in which all the characteristic qualities of the Deity centre and inhere.

Person, the Lord Jesus Christ, it is plain that there must be some common kindredness and sympathy between them. What then is the actual relation that exists between conscience in man and the attribute of justice in God? Do they give differing judgments with respect to the demerit of sin, and do they require different methods of satisfaction for it? Is the human conscience clamorous for an atonement, while the Divine Nature is wholly indifferent? Or, does the judicial sentiment in the Deity demand the infliction of penalty upon crime, while that of man is opposed to such an infliction? Is there, or is there not, an entire and perfect agreement between the finite faculty and the infinite attribute, upon these points, so that in reference to sin and guilt, what God requires, man's moral nature also insists upon, and what an awakened conscience craves, eternal Justice also demands?

The moral reason, as containing for its substance and inlay the moral law of God, and the conscience as the faculty that testifies with respect to the harmony or the hostility of the will with this law, — this side of human nature is a part of that "image and likeness of God," after which man was originally created. These faculties have to do with what is religious, ethical, eternal; and, notwithstanding the apostasy and corruption of man's heart and will, they still constitute a point of connection and communication between the being of man and the being of God. The moral reason and conscience are the intellectual media whereby, if we may so speak, man and his Maker are put *en rapport*. When the Eternal Judge addresses the creature upon the subject of religion, upon the duties which he owes, and the liabilities under which he stands, he speaks first of all, not to his imagination, or his taste, or his hostile heart, or his perverse will, but to his moral sense and sentiment. When God begins the work of conviction, and in order to this throws in an influence from his own holy and immaculate Essence, He first shoots a pang through this part of man's complex being. This, like Darien, is the isthmus of volcanic fire that both divides and joins the oceans.

Here, then, if anywhere in the being of man, we are to look for views of the Deity that correspond to his real nature and character. And here, in particular, we are to find the true index of his *judicial emotions* towards sin, and the clue to what his ethical nature and feeling demands in order to its remission. We must not ask the sinful heart, or the taste, or the mere understanding, what God thinks of sin, and what is his feeling respecting it. Upon these points we must take counsel of the conscience. For the God of the selfish heart is the deity of sentimentalism; the God of the imagination and the taste is the beautiful Grecian Apollo; the God of the understanding merely is the cold and unemotional abstraction of the deist and the pantheist; but the God of the conscience is the living and holy God of Israel, — the God of punishments and atonements. This ethical part of man's being, then, has a closer affinity than any other part with the Divine Essence, and consequently its phenomena, its pangs and its pacification, have a more intimate connection than those of any other of his powers, with the processes of the Eternal Mind. This is the finite contacting point in man that corresponds with the infinite surface in God. The moral reason and conscience, thus having their counterpart and antithesis in the Deity, must, therefore, be regarded as indexes of him, and particularly of what goes on in his being in relation to human sin and guilt. The calm condemnation of man's ethical nature, and the unselfish organic remorse of his conscience, which are consequent upon his transgression of law, are effluences from that Being whose eyes " devour all iniquity." The righteous indignation into which the judicial part of the human soul is stirred by sin, is the finite but *homogeneous* expression of that anger against moral evil which burns with an eternal intensity in the purity of the Divine Essence.

Hence it follows that a careful examination of what we find in the workings of this part of the human constitution, instead of deterring, will compel us to transfer in the same species to God, what exists in man in only a finite degree. In other words, the emotion of the human conscience towards sin will be found to be the same in *kind* with the emotion of God towards sin. The analysis must, indeed, be very careful. We must eliminate from the indignation of the moral sense all elements of selfish passion that have become mixed with it, owing to that corruption of human nature which prevents even as serious a power as conscience from working with a perfectly normal action.* We must clarify remorse until the residuum left is pure spiritual wrath against pure wickedness. We must do our utmost, under the illumination of divine truth and the actuation of the Holy Spirit, to have conscience do its

---

* *Trench* remarks upon Eph. iv. 26, that " St. Paul is not, as so many understand him, condescending to human infirmity, and saying : 'Your anger shall not be imputed to you as a sin, if you put it away before nightfall ; ' but rather, ' Be ye angry, yet in this anger of yours suffer no sinful element to mingle ; ' there is that which may cleave even to a righteous anger, the παροργισμός, the irritation, the exasperation, which must be dismissed at once ; that so, being defeated of this impurer element which mingled with it, that only which ought to remain, may remain." — *Synonymes of N. T*, § 37.

perfect, unmixed work; and then we need not shrink from asserting, that this righteous displacency of the moral sense, against the voluntary wickedness, is precisely the same emotion *in specie* with the wrath of God.*

It will aid us if at this point we direct attention to the distinction between the human conscience and the human heart; and particularly to the difference between *emotion in conscience* and *emotion in the heart*.† The feelings and passions of the corrupt human heart we cannot, in any form, attribute to God. Envy, pride, malice, shame, selfish love, and selfish hatred, cannot possibly exist in that pure and blessed Nature. Hence it is that we are so apt to shrink from those portions of scripture which clothe the Deity with indignant and

---

* Hence the Divine injunction in Ps. xcvii. 18: "Ye that love the Lord, *hate evil*;" and in Rom. xii. 9: "*Abhor* that which is evil." This pure and spiritual displacency towards moral evil, unmixed with any elements of sinful and human passion, is one of the last accomplishments of the Christian life. Hear the following low and sad refrain from the spirit of the intensely earnest and ethical Master of Rugby, as he muses under the dark chestnut-trees, and beside the limpid waters, and beneath the cerulean sky of Lake Como: "It is almost awful to look at the overwhelming beauty around me, and then think of moral evil; it seems as if heaven and hell, instead of being separated by a great gulf from one another, were absolutely on each other's confines, and indeed not far from every one of us. Might the sense of moral evil be as strong in me as my delight in external beauty; *for in a deep sense of moral evil, more perhaps than in anything else, abides a saving knowledge of God!* It is not so much to admire moral good; that we may do, and yet not be ourselves conformed to it; but if we really do *abhor* that which is evil, not the persons in whom evil resides, but the evil that dwelleth in them, and much more manifestly and certainly to our own knowledge, in our own hearts, — this is to have the feeling of God and of Christ, and to have our spirit in sympathy with the spirit of God. Alas! how easy to see this and say it, — how hard to do it and to feel it!" — *Arnold's Life and Correspondence.* Appendix D.

† For some further explanation, and illustration, of the important distinction between the mental and the moral, the constitutional and the voluntary, see pp. 164—167.

condemnatory feelings, because this class of emotions are those in and by which the depravity of the human heart is most wont to display itself. But the emotion of which we are speaking is not a passion of the human *heart*. The heart of man *loves* sin; but we are describing *remorse*, which is the wrath of the conscience *against* sin. We are delineating the operations and processes of a very different part of the human constitution from that which is the source and seat of earthly passions and sinful emotions. We have passed beyond the hot and passionate heart of man to the cool and silent *judicial* centre of his being; and here we find feelings and processes of an altogether different and higher order. Indignation in conscience is a totally different emotion from indignation in the heart. A man's moral displeasure at his own sin is an entirely different mental exercise from his selfish displeasure towards his neighbor. The former is an ethical and impartial emotion, totally independent of the will and affections, and called out involuntarily from the conscience by the mere sheer contact between it and the heart's iniquity. Hence a man never condemns himself for the existence of such a species of displeasure within his breast. He may be angry in this style and sin not.* The sun may go down upon this kind of wrath. And yet it is not a virtue for which he can take credit to himself; for it is no product of his. It is not an emotion of his heart or his will, but is simply an involuntary and irrepressible efflux from his rational nature. He may only give glory to his Creator for it, as the only relic left him, in his total

---

* "I further read: '*Be angry and sin not.*' And how was I moved, O my God, who had now learned to be angry at myself, for things past, that I might not sin in time to come! Yea to be *justly* angry." — *Augustine's Confessions*, IX. iv. 10.

alienation of heart and will from God, of his primitive and constitutional kindredness with the First Perfect and the First Fair.

Again, this judicial emotion, this *conscientious* wrath of which we are speaking, differs from the selfish and partial emotions of the human heart, in that it is not intrinsically an unhappy feeling. It does not, like the latter, of necessity render the being in whom it exists miserable. Envy, hatred, malice, shame, pride, are each and all of them unhappy exercises in themselves, as well as in their consequences. They cannot exist in any being without mental suffering. But it is not so with the moral displeasure of the moral sense. Whether this just and legitimate emotion be a torment or not, depends altogether upon the state of the heart and will, upon the moral character. It is indeed true that it causes unhappiness in a *sinful* being, because in this instance the emotions of the heart are in antagonism with the emotion of conscience; because the executive faculty is not in harmony with the judicial faculty. But where there is no personal sin, both the wrath of conscience and the wrath of God are as innocuous as fire upon asbestos. Hence this very same emotion of moral indignation and abhorrence exists in an intense degree in the angels and the seraphim, but is productive of no disquietude in them, because there is nothing evil in their *own* character upon which it can wreak its force. There is a perfect harmony within them, between the emotions of the heart and the judicial emotion, between the character and the conscience. And, in like manner, this same feeling of ethical displeasure exists in an infinite degree in the being of God, without disturbing, in the least, the ineffable peace and blessedness of that pure nature which is the paradise and elysium of all who are conformed to it. For this judicial sentiment is a *legitimate* one, and nothing that is legitimate can be intrinsically miserable. And therefore it is that the saints and the seraphim, as they look down from the crystal battlements with holy abhorrence and indignation upon the sorceries and murders and uncleanness of the fallen Babylon, are not distressed by their emotion, but, on the contrary, rejoice with a holy joy at the final triumph of justice in the universe of God, and say, Alleluia, as the smoke of that just torment rises up for ever and ever.* And therefore it is that God himself carries eternally, in his own blessed nature, a righteous indignation against moral evil, that is no source of disquietude to. him, because there is no moral evil in him, nor to the angels and saints and seraphim, because there is none in them; but only to those rebellious and wicked spirits into whom it does fall like lightning from the sky.

For if the emotion of moral indignation were intrinsically one of unhappiness, then the existence of evil would be the destruction of the Divine blessedness; because God " cannot look upon evil with allowance," †

---

* "And after these things, I heard a great voice of much people in heaven, saying, Alleluia: Salvation, and glory, and honor, and power unto the Lord our God: for *true and righteous are his judgments*, for he hath judged the great whore which did corrupt the earth with her fornication, and hath avenged the blood of his servants at her hand. And again they said, Alleluia : *and her smoke rose up forever and ever.* And the four and twenty elders, and the four beasts fell down, and worshipped God that sat on the throne, saying, *Amen, Alleluia.*" — Rev. xix. 1—4.

† " Thou art not a God that hath pleasure in wickedness. Thou hatest all workers of iniquity" (Ps. v. 5, 6). " God is angry with the wicked every day" (Ps. vii. 11). " Who may stand in thy sight when once thou art angry" (Ps. lxxvi. 7). " Who knoweth the power of thine anger? Even according to thy fear so is thy wrath" (Ps. xc. 11). " He that believeth not the Son, shall not see life; but the wrath of God abideth on him" (John iii. 36).

and yet he is constantly looking upon it. But it is not so. On the contrary, the Deity is *blessed* in his displacency at that which is vile and hateful. For pleasure is the coincidence between a feeling and its correlated object. It implies intrinsic congruity and fitness. It would therefore be unhappiness in any being to hate what is lovely, or to love what is hateful; to be pleased with what is wrong, and displeased with what is right; because the proper coincidence between the emotion and the object would not obtain. But when God, or any being, hates what is hateful, and is angry at that which *merits* wrath, the true nature and fitness of things is observed, and that inward harmony which is the substance of mental happiness is maintained. Anger and hatred are almost indissolubly connected in our minds with mental wretchedness, because we behold their exercise only in an abnormal and sinful sphere. In an apostate world, as such, there is no proper and fitting coincidence between emotions and their objects. A sinner hates holiness, which he ought to love; and loves sin, which he ought to hate. The anger of his heart is not legitimate, but passionate and selfish. The love of his heart is illicit; and therefore, as it is styled in the scripture, is mere lust or evil concupiscence ($\epsilon\pi\iota\vartheta\upsilon\mu\iota\alpha$). In a sinful world, as such, all the true relations and correlations are reversed. Love and hatred are expended upon exactly the wrong objects. But when these emotions are contemplated within the sphere of the Holy and the Eternal; when they are beheld in God, exercised only upon their appropriate and deserving objects; when the wrath falls only upon the sin and uncleanness of hell, and burns up nothing but filth in its pure celestial flame; the emotion is not merely legitimate, but beautiful with an august beauty, and is no source of pain either to the Divine Mind or to any minds in sympathy with it. It is only upon this principle that we can explain the blessedness of the Deity, in connection with his omniscience and omnipresence. We know that sin and the punishment of sin are ever before him. The smoke of torment is perpetually rolling up in the presence of the Omnipresent. And yet he is supremely blessed. But he can be so only because there is a just and proper correlationship between his wrath and the object upon which it falls; only because he condemns that which is intrinsically damnable.* The least disturbance of this coincidence, the slightest love for the hateful, or hatred for the lovely, would indeed render God a wretched being. But the perfect harmony of it makes him "God over *all*," hell as well as heaven, "blessed forever."† Were this ethical feeling once to be outraged by the final triumph of iniquity over righteousness; were the smoke of torment to ascend eter-

---

* It is at this point that the metaphysical necessity of endless punishment appears. For if sin be intrinsically damnable, it is intrinsically punishable. If then the question be asked: How *long* is it intrinsically damnable and punishable? there is but one answer. There is, in fact, no logical mean between no punishment at all of sin as an *intrinsic* evil, and an absolute, that is, an endless punishment of it.

† It is a standing objection of infidelity to the Biblical idea and representation of the Deity, that it conflicts with the natural intuitions of the human mind. It is asserted that the instinctive sentiments of the soul repel the doctrine of anger against sin. The ethics of nature, say these theorizers, are contrary to the ethics of scripture upon this point, and hence mankind must make a choice between the two. But a careful study of the most profound systems of natural religion does not corroborate this assertion. Probably no mind, outside of the pale of Christianity, has made a more discriminating and truthful representation of the natural sentiments of the human mind, than Aristotle. But this dispassionate thinker asserts that "He who feels anger on proper occasions, at proper persons, and in a proper manner, and for a proper length of time, is an object of praise." — *Nicomachean Ethics*, Book IV. c. 5.

nally from pure and innocent spirits, and were the revelry of joy to steam up everlastingly from the souls of the vile and the worthless; were the great relations of right and wrong, sin and penalty, happiness and misery, once to be reversed in the universe, and under the government of God, then indeed this quick sense of justice, and this holy indignation at sin, would be a grief and a sorrow to its possessor. And therefore it is, that, in all the Divine administration, and in the entire plan of redemption, the utmost possible pains is taken to justify, and legitimate, and satisfy this judicial sentiment, and to see that its demands are fully met.

There must be this correspondence between the judicial nature of man and the judicial nature of God, or religion is impossible. How can man even know what is meant by justice in the Deity, if there is absolutely nothing of the same species in his own rational constitution, which if realized in his own character as it is in that of God, would make him just as God is just? How can he know what is meant by moral perfection in God, if in his own rational spirit there is absolutely no ideal of moral excellence, which if realized in himself as it is in the Creator, would make him excellent as he is excellent? Without some mental correspondent, to which to appeal and commend themselves, the teachings of revelation could not be apprehended. A body of knowledge alone is not the whole; there must be an inlet for it, an organ of apprehension. But if there is no such particular part of the human constitution as has been described, and these calm judgments of the moral sense, and this righteous displeasure of the conscience, are to be put upon a level with the workings of the fancy and imagination, or the selfish passions of the human heart, then there is no point of contact and communication between the nature of man and the being of God. There is no part of his own complex being upon which man may fall back, with the certainty of not being mistaken in judgments of ethics and religion. Both anchor and anchoring-ground are gone, and he is afloat upon the boundless, starless ocean of ignorance and scepticism. Even if revelations are made, they cannot enter his mind. There is no contacting surface through which they can approach and take hold of his being. They cannot be seen to be what they really are, the absolute truth of God, because there is no eye with which to see them.

Assuming, then, that there is this correspondence and correlationship between the moral constitution of man and the Divine Nature, we proceed, in the light of the fact, to evince the doctrine, taught in the scripture texts which we have cited, that the atonement of Christ is a real satisfaction both on the part of God and man. The death of incarnate Deity has always been regarded, by those who have believed that the Deity became incarnate in Jesus Christ, as *expiatory*. As such, it relates immediately to the attribute of justice in the Creator, and to the faculty of conscience in the creature. And the position taken here, is that it sustains the *same* relation to both. It satisfies that which would be dissatisfied both in God and man if the penalty of sin were merely set aside and abolished by an act of will. It placates an ethical feeling which is manifesting itself in the form of remorse in the conscience of the transgressor, only because it has first existed in the nature of God in the form of a judicial displeasure towards moral evil.

A fundamental attribute of Deity is justice. This comes first into view, and continues in sight to the very last, in all inquiries into the Divine Nature. No attribute can be conceived of that is more ultimate and central than this one. This is proved by the fact that the operation of all the other Divine attributes, love itself not excepted, is *conditioned* and *limited* by justice. For whatever else God may be, or may not be, he must be just. It is not optional with him to exercise this attribute, or not to exercise it, as it is in the instance of that class of attributes which are antithetic to it. We can say: " God may be merciful or not, as he pleases;" but we cannot say : " God may be just or not, as he pleases." It cannot be asserted that God is inexorably obligated to show pity ; but it can be categorically affirmed that God is inexorably obligated to do justly.* For the characteristic of justice is necessary exaction; while, if we may accommodate a Shaksperean phrase, " the quality of mercy is not *strained.*" Hence the exercise of justice can be demonstrated upon *à priori* grounds, while that of mercy is known only by a declaration or *promise* upon the part of God. It is for this reason that man can have no *certainty* that the

* *Owen* (Dissertation on Divine Justice, Chap. II.), notices the self-contradiction there is, in conceding that justice is an essential attribute in God, and yet that it can be set aside by an act of arbitrary omnipotence, in the following terms : " To me, these arguments are altogether astonishing, viz.: ' That sin-punishing justice should be natural to God, and yet that God, sin being supposed to exist, *may either exercise it, or not exercise it.*' They may also say, and with as much propriety, that truth is natural to God, but upon a supposition that he were to converse with man, *he might either use it, or not;* or, that omnipotence is natural to God, but upon a supposition that he were inclined to do any work without (extra) himself, that *it were free to him to act omnipotently or not;* or, finally, that sin-punishing justice is among the primary causes of the death of Christ, and that Christ was set forth as a propitiation, to declare his righteousness, and yet that that justice required not the punishment of sin. For if it should require it, how is it possible that it should not *necessarily* require it, since God would be unjust, if he should not inflict punishment."

Deity is a merciful being, except as he obtains it from a special revelation. When the thoughtful pagan looked up into the pure heavens above him, or into the deep recesses within him, he had no doubt that the Infinite One is just, and a punisher of evil doing, because he *must* be such. Hence he trembled; and hence he offered a propitiatory sacrifice. But neither from the heavens, nor from anything in his own moral constitution, could he obtain certainty in regard to the attribute of mercy; because there is nothing of a *necessary* nature in the exercise of this attribute. God might or might not be merciful to him. Man may dare to hope that there is pity in the Deity; but whether there actually is, he cannot know with certainty until the heavens are opened, and a voice issues from the lips of the Supreme himself, saying: "I *will* show mercy, and this is my beloved Son in whom I am well pleased." The light of nature is sufficient for man's damnation; but it casts not a ray in the direction of his salvation. There is ample evidence from natural religion that the Deity is holy and impartial; but it is only from revealed religion that the human mind obtains its warrant for believing in the Divine clemency. From the position of natural ethics alone, man is merely condemned to retribution; and, as matter of fact, while standing only upon this position, his conscience accuses him, and fills him with fears and forebodings of judgment. Nothing but a *promise* of forgiveness, from the mouth of God, can remove these fears; but a promise to pardon is not *à priori*, and necessary, like a threatening to punish.

The absolute and indefeasible nature of justice is seen, again, by considering the nature of law. If we regard the moral law as the efflux of the Divine Nature, and not, as in the Grotian theory, a positive statute which may be relaxed in part, or wholly abrogated, by the law-making power,* we find this same stark necessity existing. The law is *obligated* to punish the transgressor, as much as the transgressor is obligated to obey the law. Human society, for instance, has claim upon law for penalty, as really as law has claim upon human society for obedience. Law has no option. Justice has but one function. The necessity of penalty is as great as the necessity of obligation. The law itself is under law; that is, it is under the necessity of its own nature; and therefore the only possible way whereby a transgressor can escape the penalty of law, is for a substitute to endure it for him. The language of Milton respecting the transgressor is metaphysically true:

---

* "All positive laws," says *Grotius* (Defensio Fidei, Caput. III. p. 310, Ed. Amstelaedemi, 1679), "are relaxable. Those who fear that if we concede this, we do an injury to God because we thereby represent him as mutable, are much deceived. For law is not something internal in God, or in the will itself of God, but it is *a particular effect or product* of his will (voluntatis quidam effectus). But that the effects, or products of the Divine will are mutable, is very certain. Moreover, in promulgating a positive law, which he might wish to relax at some future time, God does not exhibit any fickleness of will. For God seriously indicated that he desired that his law should be valid, and obligatory; *while yet he reserved the right of relaxing it, if he saw fit*, because this right pertains to a positive law, from the very nature of the case, and cannot be abdicated by the Deity. Nay more, the Deity does not abdicate the right of even abrogating law altogether, as is apparent from the instance of the ceremonial law." Grotius then proceeds to apply this principle to the moral law, and the penalty accompanying it, and though intending to counteract the Socinian theory, lays down positions which in the judgment of dogmatic historians logically lead to it. — See *Baumgarten — Crusius* (Dogmengeschichte, II. 274); *Münscher — Von Cölln — Neudecker* (Dogmengeschichte, III. 508); *Baur* (Versöhnungslehre, 414—435, — translated in Bibliotheca Sacra, IX. 259—272); *Hagenbach*, (Dogmengeschichte, 3 Aufl. § 268); *Ersch und Gruber's Encyclopädie* (Art. Acceptilatio); *Hengstenberg's Kirchen-Zeitung* for 1834.

> " He, with all his posterity, must die:
> Die he, or justice must; unless for him
> Some other able, and as willing, pay
> The rigid satisfaction, death for death."*

And *the mercy of God consists in substituting Himself incarnate for his creature, for purposes of atonement.* Analyzed to its ultimate elements, God's pity towards the soul of man is God's satisfying his own eternal attribute of justice for it. It does not consist in outraging his own law, and the guilt-smitten conscience itself, by simply snatching the criminal away from their retributions, in the exercise of an unprincipled and an unbridled almightiness, or in substituting a partial for a complete atonement; but in enduring the full and entire penal infliction by which both are satisfied.†

---

* *Paradise Lost*, III. 209—212.

† It was one of the objections of Socinus to the theory of plenary satisfaction, that if God has received a full equivalent for the punishment due to man, then he does not exercise any mercy in remitting his sin. But this objection overlooks the fact that the equivalent is not furnished by man, but by God. Were the atonement the *creature's* oblation to justice, Socinus's objection would have force. But it is *God*, and not man, who satisfies justice for the sinner. It is indeed a *self*-satisfaction upon the part of God, yet none the less a self-*sacrifice;* and self-sacrifice is confessedly the highest form of love. The truth is, that this objection of Socinus begs the question in dispute, by defining mercy in its own way. It assumes (as Socinus expressly argues, *Bib. Frat. Pol.* I. 566 sq.) that the ideas of satisfaction and mercy mutually exclude each other; that mercy consists in *relaxing* and *waiving* justice, and not in *vicariously satisfying* it. From this premiss it follows, of course, that where there is any satisfaction of justice there is no mercy, and where there is any waiving of justice there is mercy. A complete atonement, consequently, would exclude mercy altogether; a partial atonement would allow some room for mercy, in partially waiving legal claims; and no atonement at all would afford full play for the attribute, by the entire nullification of all judicial demands. According to the catholic view, on the contrary, the ideas of satisfaction and mercy are combined and harmonized in a *vicarious* atonement, or the *assumption* of penalty by a competent person. If the sinner himself should suffer the penalty, there

Still another proof of the primary nature of justice is found in the fact of human accountability. The most distinguishing characteristic of man is evidence of the most distinguishing characteristic of God; and thus the correspondence between the Divine and the human meets us again. Man is not a link in the necessary chain of material nature. He is by creation a free creature; capable of continuing holy as he was created, or of turning to sin. Now, over against this freedom and responsibility on the part of man, there stands justice on the part of God. This great divine attribute presupposes the hazardous human endowment of *will*, and holds the possessor of it accountable for its use or abuse. Without such a characteristic, man could not stand in any sort of relationship to such solemn realities as law and justice. There would be nothing in his constitution that could feel the tremendous swing and blow of penal infliction. For justice smites a transgressor as one who has illegitimately assumed a centre of his own, and who is wickedly standing upon that centre, in hostility to the being and government of God. In a certain sense, though not that which excludes the permissive decree and the preventive power of the Supreme Being, justice supposes the sinner to be sustaining something of the isolated and self-asserting relation to God that the principle of evil in the system of dualism sustains to the principle of good; and when the accountable self-will of a creature attempts to set itself up as an independent and hostile agent in the doing

would be no vicariousness in the suffering, and there would be the execution of justice merely, without any mercy. But when the incarnate Son of God, as the sinner's substitute, endures the penalty due to sin, justice is satisfied by the suffering which is undergone; and the Son of God, surely, shows the height of compassion in undergoing it.

of evil, it then feels the full force of the avenging, vindicating stroke of law, as if it were a single disconnected atom, all alone and by itself, in the middle of creation.

Any just view of sin as *guilt*, as the product of *will*, is, consequently, corroborative of the position that the attribute of which we are speaking is an immanent and necessary one in the Divine Nature. We might conceive of the same amount of evil consequences as those which flow from human transgression; but if this latter were not the real work and agency of a responsible creature, Eternal Justice could take no cognizance of it. Unless sin is *crime*, penalty has no more relation to it than it has to the disease and corruption in the material world about us; and the fall of man could no more be visited by the infliction of judicial suffering, than could that process of decay which is continually going on in the forests, by means of which a more luxuriant vegetation springs up, and a more glorious forest waves in the breeze.

It has been a query among those who have speculated upon the nature of the Deity: What is the base or substrate of His being? The inquiry has too often been so answered as to bring in a subtle pantheism, because there was more reference to the natural than the ethical attributes of the Godhead. Whether the question in such a reference can be answered by the finite mind, we do not pretend to decide here; but with reference to God's *moral* constitution, with reference to that congeries of *ethical* attributes which belongs to him as a personal being, it is as certain as anything can be, that the deep substrate and base of them all, is eternal law and impartial justice. This pervades all the rest, keeps them in equilibrium, and constitutes, as it were, the very divinity of the Deity. And this view of the primary nature of justice coincides with the convictions of men in all ages. In all time, justice has been the one particular divine attribute that has pressed most heavily upon the human race. This always comes first into man's mind, when the idea of the Deity overshadows him. He trembles when he remembers that God is just; and he remembers this when he remembers nothing else. Nor let it be objected that this is owing to the fact that man is sinful, and that this quality in the Supreme Being would not be so prominent in the mind of an unfallen creature who has nothing to fear from it. The utterance of the pure burning seraphim is: *Holy, Holy, Holy.* That which comes first into the minds of the spotless and unfearing worshippers in God's immediate presence, — they whose spirits, in the phrase of Jeremy Taylor, "are becalmed, and made even as the brow of Jesus, and smooth like the heart of God," — is that particular characteristic in the Divine Being, by virtue of which he has a right to sit on the eternal throne; that specific attribute upon which the moral administration of the universe must be established.

Now, if this be a correct statement of the necessary nature and the capital position of Divine Justice, it is plain that any plan or method that has to do with sin and guilt, must have primary reference to it, and must give *plenary satisfaction* to it as it exists in God himself. Inasmuch as justice, and not mercy, is the *limiting* and *conditioning* attribute, its demands must be acknowledged and met in order that mercy may make even the first advances towards the transgressor. Compassion cannot, by mere arbitrary will and might, stride forward to reach its own private ends, and trample down justice by sheer force ; but must come forth, as she does in the bleeding Lamb of God, as the voluntary servant and victim of Law, doing all its behests, and bearing all its burdens, and enduring its sharp, inexorable pains, *in the place of* (*vice, vicarie*) the helpless object whom vengeance suffereth not to live. The cup must be put to the lips of him who has volunteered to be the Atoner, and he must drink it to the bottom, for the guilty transgressor whose law-place he has taken. The God-man having, out of his own free will and affection, become the sinner's *Substitute*, must now receive a sinner's treatment, and be "numbered with the transgressors" (Isa. liii. 12). He cannot therefore escape the agony and passion, the hour and the power of darkness. He may give expression to his spontaneous shrinking from the awful self-oblation, as the hour darkens and draws on, in the utterance : "O my Father, if it be possible, let this cup pass from me ;" but having taken the place of the *guilty*, it is not possible, and he must sweat the bloody sweat, he must cry : "My God, my God, why hast thou forsaken me?" that his voice may then ring through the universe and down the ages : "It is finished, — the atonement is made."*

For the Deity cannot, by an arbitrary and unprincipled procedure, release the transgressor's Substitute from the penal suffering, and inflict a wound upon that holy judicial nature, which is vital in every part with

---

* "The *justice* of God is exceedingly glorified in this work. God is so strictly and immutably just, that he would not spare his beloved Son when he took upon him the guilt of men's sins, and was substituted in the room of sinners. He would not abate him the least mite of that debt which justice demanded. Justice should take place, though it cost his infinitely dear Son his precious blood ; and his enduring such extraordinary reproach, and pain, and death in its most dreadful form." — *Edwards's Works*, IV. 140.

the breath of law and the life of justice. By reason of an immanent necessity, he cannot disturb his own eternal sense of righteousness and ethical tranquillity, by doing damage to one whole side of his Godhead.

He has not. In the voluntary, the cordially offered, sacrifice of the incarnate Son, the judicial nature of God, which by a constitutional necessity requires the punishment of sin, finds its righteous requirement fully met. Plenary punishment is inflicted upon One who is infinite, and therefore competent; upon One who is finite, and therefore passible; upon One who is innocent, and therefore can suffer for others; upon One who is voluntary, and therefore uncompelled. By this theanthropic oblation, the ethical feeling, the organic emotion of displeasure in the Deity is, in the scripture phrase, made "propitious" towards the guilty, because it has been placated by it. Thus God is immutably just while he justifies (Rom. iii. 26), and his mercy is, in the last analysis, one with his truth and his law.

We turn, now, to the other half of the proposition derived from the scripture texts that have been cited, and proceed to show that the atonement of Christ effects a real satisfaction upon the part of man. We have seen that the propitiatory death of the God-man meets the immanent ethical necessities of the Divine Nature. We have now the easier task of evincing that it meets the moral wants of human nature.

In discussing the fact of a divinely-established correspondence between the judicial nature of man and that of God, we have already observed that the attribute of justice naturally selects this judicial part of man as the inlet of approach to him. Eternal law has, in all ages, poured itself down through the human *conscience*, like a fountain through the channel it has worn for itself, and in this instance like hot lava down a mountain gorge. Hence by watching its workings within this particular faculty, we are enabled to determine what man's judicial nature requires, and also incidentally to throw back some more light upon the relations of the atonement to the Divine Nature. It is indeed true that Divine Justice manifests itself in other modes than this. There are revelations of it in the written word, and in the course of providence and human history. But we are endeavoring to establish the position that the atonement has an *internal* necessity grounded in the very moral being of man. It is necessary, therefore, to look at the principle of law in its vital and felt manifestation within the soul of the criminal himself. By the analysis of the contents of a remorseful conscience, especially if it has been made unusually living and poignant by the truth and Spirit of God, we may discover much of the real quality of Eternal Justice. As this august attribute acts and reacts within the breast of man upon his violation of law, we may obtain some clear and *conscious* knowledge of its nature and operations; and also of what the human conscience itself demands, and with what it is satisfied.

The commission of sin is either attended or succeeded by the sensation of *guilt*,—one of the most distinct and unique of all the sensations that emerge within the horizon of self-consciousness. Provided conscience does its unmixed work, the transgressor is conscious, not merely of unhappiness, which is a very low form of feeling, but of *criminality*, which is a very high form. Nay, the more profound and thorough the operation of the moral faculty becomes, the more does the sense of mere wretchedness retreat into the background, and the sense of ill-desert come forth into the foreground of consciousness. It is possible for this latter element to drive out, for a time, the particular feeling of misery, and to absorb the mind in the sense of *horror* and *amazement* at the past transgression. The guilty, in the final day, are represented as calling upon the rocks and the mountains to fall upon them, as inviting new forms of suffering, in the vain hope that the awful consciousness of crime may be drowned thereby.

Now, seizing and holding the experience of the transgressor at this point, let us examine it more closely. Notice that this consciousness of guilt, pure and simple, is wholly *involuntary*. It comes in upon the criminal, not only without his will, but in spite of it. He would keep it out, if he could. He would drive it out, if he could. His experience at this stage, then, is the result of no voluntary effort upon his part, but of the simple *reaction of law*, the most dispassionate and unselfish of all realities, against its violator. In the conscience, that part of the human constitution which we have seen to be the proper seat and organ for such an operation, the commandment is making itself felt again, not as at first in the form of command, but of condemnation. The free agent has responsibly disobeyed the holy, just, and good statute, and is now feeling the tremendous reaction of it in his own moral being. This remorse, or damnatory emotion, therefore, is the work of God's law, and not of man's will. There is, consequently, very little of the selfish and the earthly, but much of the unearthly and the eternal, in the transgressor's experience held at this point. He can take no merit to himself, because it is of such an intensely ethical and spiritual character, since the entire process, so far as he is concerned, is involuntary and organic. It is provided for in his judicial constitution, and as an operation within himself it is to be regarded, not as the working of his corrupt heart, but as the *infliction* of Divine retribution and justice, in and through the judicial faculty. Man can take no merit to himself because he possesses a power that condemns evil, and distresses therefor. For this is the workmanship of the Creator, and it exists in hell as well as heaven. The workings of conscience are as much beyond the control of the will, are as truly organic, as those of the sympathetic nerve, and therefore are worthy of neither praise nor blame. Given conscience and sin, within one and the same soul, and remorse must follow as a matter of necessity. Hence remorse is never made the subject of a command. Man is commanded to melt down in godly sorrow, but never to be filled with remorse; for this is provided for in the moral constitution given by Him who makes it the fiery chariot by which he himself rides into man's being, in majesty, to judgment.

Hence this sense of ill-desert, though its sensorium is the human conscience, must be traced back for its first cause, to a yet deeper ground, and a yet higher origin. For if it were a fact, that remorse had nothing but a human source, though that source were the highest and most venerable of the human faculties, and the transgressor should know it, he could overcome and suppress it. Nothing that has a merely finite origin can be a permanent source of misery; and if the victim of remorse could but be certain that the just and holy God has had nothing to do with the origin of the distress within him, he could ultimately expel it from his breast. If he could be assured that the terrible emotion which follows the commission of evil, though welling up from the lowest springs of his own nature, yet has no connection with the nether fountains of the Divine Essence, he could put an end to his torment. For no man is afraid of himself alone, and irrespective of his Maker and Judge. That which renders a portion of our common and finite humanity terrible to us, is the fact, that it is grounded in and supported by that which is more than human. In the instance before us, the highest part of the human constitution supports itself by striking its deep roots into the holiness and justice of the Godhead; and therefore it is that conscience makes cowards of us all, and its remorse is a feeling that is invincible by the strongest finite will, and requires, in order to its extinction, the blood of atonement.

We are, therefore, compelled back into the being and character of God, for the ultimate origin of this sense of guilt, and this "fearful looking-for of judgment and fiery indignation." And why should we not be? If Justice is living and sensitive anywhere, it must be so in its eternal seat and home. If law is jealous for its own authority and maintenance anywhere, it must be in that Being to whom all eyes in the universe are turned with the inquiry: "Shall not the Judge of all the earth do right?" What, therefore, conscience affirms, in the transgressor's case, God affirms, and is the first to affirm. What, therefore, conscience feels in respect to the sinner's transgression, God feels, and is the first to feel. What, therefore, conscience requires in order that it may cease to punish the guilty spirit, God requires and is the first to require. In fine, all that is requisite in order to the satisfaction and pacification of conscience towards the sinful soul in which it dwells, is also requisite in order to the satisfaction and "propitiation" of God the Just; and it is requisite in the former case only because it is first requisite in the latter. The subjective in man is shaped by the objective in God, and not the objective in God by the subjective in man. The consciousness of the conscience is the reflex of the consciousness of God.

But what, now, does conscience require, in order that it may become pacified with respect to past transgression? We answer, simply and solely an *atonement* for that past transgression; simply and solely that just *infliction* which is due to guilt. That is a powerful, because profoundly truthful, passage in Coleridge's play of " Remorse," in which the guilty and guilt-smitten Ordonio is stabbed by Alhadra, the wife of the murdered Isidore. As the steel drinks his own heart's blood, he utters the one single word "*Atonement!*" His self-accusing spirit, which is wrung with its remorseful recollections, and which the warm and hearty forgiveness of his injured brother has not been able to soothe in the least, actually feels its first gush of relief only as the avenging knife enters, and crime meets penalty.* And how often, in the annals of guilt, is this principle illustrated! The criminal has wandered up and down the earth, vainly seeking repose of conscience, but finds none until he surrenders himself to the penalty of law. Those are the only hopeful executions, in which the guilty goes to his death *justifying* the judicial sentence that condemns him, and, as a completing act of the solemn mental process, appropriating that yet more august and transcendent expiation which has been made for man by a higher Being than man. A guilty conscience, when it

---

* *Remorse*, Act V. Scene 1. *Coleridge's Works*, VII. p. 401. — The psychology of crime, or the analysis of the consciousness of guilt (Schuldbewusztseyn), is a portion of mental philosophy that has been generally neglected. The only treatise specifically devoted to it, that we have met with, is the *Criminal-Psychologie* of Heinroth.

has come to a clear consciousness, *wants* its guilt expiated by the infliction of punishment. It feels that strange unearthly thirst of which Christ speaks, and for which he asserts that his blood of atonement is "drink *indeed.*" It cannot be made peaceful except through the medium of a judicial infliction; that is to say, of a particular species of suffering that will *expiate* its guilt. The mere offer of kindness, or good-humor, to remit the sin without any regard to that eternal law of retribution which is now distressing the soul by its righteous claim, does not meet the ethical wants. The moral sense, when in normal action, feels the *necessity* that crime be punished. Hence the human conscience is a faculty that is unappeased, and gnaws like a blind worm, until it hears of the Lamb, the *Atonement*, of God, that taketh away the *guilt* of the world. Hence, however much the selfish heart may desire to escape at the expense of right and justice, the impartial conscience can do no such thing. Before this judicial faculty can be pacified, crime must incur penalty, transgression must receive an exact recompense of reward. When this is done, there is entire pacification; there is great peace, such as death, and Satan the accuser, and the day of judgment, and the bar of justice, and the final doom, cannot disturb with a single ripple.

For the correlate to guilt is punishment; and nothing but the correlate itself can perform the function of a correlate. A liquid, for example, is the correlative to thirst, and nothing that is not liquid, however nutritious, and necessary to human life in other relations, it may be, can be a substitute for it. There may be the "fat kidneys of wheat," in superabundance, but if there be not also the "brook in the way," the human body must die of thirst. In like manner, a judicial infliction, or *suffering for purposes of justice*, is the only means by which culpability can be extinguished. Sanctification, or holiness, in this reference, is powerless, because there is nothing penal, nothing correlated to guilt, in it. The Tridentine method of justification by sanctification, is not an adaptation of means to ends. So far as the guilt of an act, — in other words, its obligation to punishment, — is concerned, if the transgressor, or his *accepted* substitute,* has endured the infliction that is set

---

* Accepted by the law and lawgiver. The primal source of law has no power to abolish penalty any more than to abolish law, but it has full power to *substitute* penalty. In case of a substitution, however, it must be a *strict* equivalent, and not a fictitious or nominal one. It would contravene the attribute of justice, instead of satisfying it, should God, for instance, by an arbitrary act of will, substitute the sacrifice of bulls and goats for the penalty due to man; or if he should offset any *finite* oblation against the infinite demerit of moral evil. The inquiry whether the satisfaction of justice by Christ's atonement was a strict and literal one, has a practical and not merely theoretical importance. A guilt-smitten conscience is exceedingly timorous, and hence, if there be room for doubting the strict adequacy of the judicial provision that has been made for satisfying the claims of law, a perfect peace, the "peace of God," is impossible. Hence the doctrine of a plenary satisfaction by an infinite substitute is the only one that ministers to evangelical repose. The dispute upon this point has sometimes, at least, resulted from a confusion of ideas and terms. Strict equivalency has been confounded with *identity*. The assertion that Christ's death is a literal equivalent for the punishment due to mankind, has been supposed to be the same as the assertion, that it is identical with it; and a punishment identical with that due to man would involve remorse, and endless duration. But identity of punishment is ruled out by the principle of *substitution* or *vicariousness*, — a principle that is conceded by all who hold the doctrine of atonement. The penalty endured by Christ, therefore, must be a *substituted*, and not an identical one. And the only question that remains is, whether that which is to be substituted shall be of a *strictly equal value* with that, the place of which it takes, or whether it may be of an inferior value, — and it must be one or the other. When a loan of one hundred dollars in silver is repaid by one hundred dollars in gold, there is a substitution of one metal for another. It is not an identical payment; for this would require the return of the very identical hundred pieces of silver, the *ipsissima pecunia*, that had been loaned. But it is a *strictly* and *literally*

over against it, the law is satisfied, and the obligation to punishment is discharged. And so far as guilt, or obligation to punishment is concerned, until the affixed penalty has been endured, by himself or his accepted substitute, he is a guilty man, do what else he may. Even if he should be renewed and sanctified by the Spirit of God, this sanctification has in it nothing *expiatory*, or correlative to guilt, and therefore could not remove his remorse. Food is good and necessary, but it cannot slake thirst. Personal holiness is excellent and indispensable, but it cannot perform the function of atonement. Hence sanctification is wrought by spiritual influences, but justification by expiating blood. The former is the work of the third Person in the Trinity; the latter is that of the second. Hence, when the convicted man is distressed because of what the Psalmist denominates the "*iniquity* of sin," its intrinsic guilty quality, in distinction from its miserable consequences, he craves expiation sometimes with a hunger like that of famine. And hence his desperate endeavor to atone for the past, until he discovers that it is impossible. Then he cries with David: "Thou desirest not sacrifice"—such atonement as I can render is inadequate—"*else would I give it.*"* Taking him at this

---

equivalent payment. *All* claims are cancelled by it. In like manner, when the suffering and death of God incarnate is substituted for that of the creature, the satisfaction rendered to law is strictly plenary, though not identical with that which is exacted from the transgressor. It contains the element of infinitude, which is the element of value in the case, with even greater precision than the satisfaction of the creature does; because it is the suffering of a strictly infinite Person in a finite time, while the latter is only the suffering of a finite person in an endless but not strictly infinite time. A strictly infinite duration would be without beginning, as well as without end.

* The true and accurate rendering of Psalm li. 7, is not "*purge* me with hyssop," but "*atone* me (תְּחַטְּאֵנִי) with hyssop." David, in the poignancy

point in his experience, his desire is for *justification*. He wants, first of all, to be *pardoned;* and, be it observed, *to be pardoned upon those just and eternal principles that will not give way in the great judicial emergencies of this life and the life to come.* Then he will commence the good fight of faith. Then he will run in the way of obedience with an exulting heart, because he is no longer under condemnation. " Whom he justifies, them he glorifies."

Such, it is conceived, is the general doctrine of atonement, to be deduced from the sharp and pointed texts of scripture cited in the outset of this discussion. The Christian atonement possesses both an objective and a subjective validity; it is a satisfaction for the ethical nature of both God and man.

Having thus contemplated the inward and metaphysical nature of that atoning work of incarnate Deity, which is the most stupendous fact in the history of the world, and one upon which all its religious hopes and welfare hang, we naturally turn, in conclusion, to the more external and practical aspects of the great theme. And the application of the doctrine will be found to be all the more acceptable to the Christian heart, and profitable for Christian edification, if the principles and theory from which it flows are profound and thorough. The cup of cold water is all the more grateful to the thirsty soul, if it has been drawn up from the deep wells; and it is certain that divine truth gains, rather than loses, in popular and practical efficiency, upon both the mind and heart, if it be sought for in its purest and most central sources. That view of the work of Christ which represents it as meeting all the ethical

of his consciousness of guilt, prays, not for a cleansing merely but, for an *expiatory* cleansing.

necessities of both the divine and the human natures, is well fitted to inspire belief and trust in it, and to draw out the heart towards its Blessed Author.

1. One of the first and obvious inferences, then, from the subject as it has been unfolded, is, that an atonement for sin is no arbitrary requirement on the part of God. If the positions taken in this discussion are correct, the doctrine of expiation contains a *metaphysique*, and is defensible at the bar of philosophic reason.

One great obstacle to the reception of the evangelical system lies in the fact, that very many are of opinion that the scripture method of forgiving sin is needlessly embarrassed by a sacrificial expiation. " Why should not God," they ask, " forgive the creature of his footstool in the same manner that an earthly father does his child? Why does he not, at once, and without any of this apparatus of atonement, bid the erring one go his way, with the assurance that the past is forgotten? Is not this expiation, even though made by the Deity himself, after all, a hinderance rather than an encouragement to an approach to the eternal throne? Is it not, at least, something that is not *strictly* necessary, and might have been dispensed with?" This lurking or open doubt, with regard to the rationality and intrinsic necessity of an atonement for sin, cuts the root of all evangelical faith in a large class of men.

Indeed, it may be a question whether the preacher in Christian lands has not a more difficult task to perform for a certain class of minds, in reference to the doctrine of Christ crucified, than the missionary in pagan lands has; and whether Christian theology itself would not have an easier labor than it now has, to vindicate the ways of God to man, in the respect of which we are speaking, if the Old-Ethnic, or what is far better, the

Old-Jewish ideas respecting guilt and retribution were more current than they are in a certain class in nominal Christendom. Taking a portion of men in the modern civilized world as a sample, it would seem as if the unregenerate Christian world does not possess such a spontaneous and irrepressible conviction that guilt must be punished, as did the old unsophisticated Pagan world.* The system of bloody sacrifices, an emphatic acknowledgment of this great truth, was almost universal among them; and the doctrine that mere sorrow for transgression is a sufficient ground for its forgiveness, had little force. The Grecian Nemesis, or personification of vindicative justice, was a divinity to whom even Jove himself was subject. The ancient religious institutions and ceremonials, fanciful and irrational as they were in most of their elements, yet distinctly recognized, through their sacrificial cultus, the amenability of man to law, and his culpability. Add to this, the workings of natural conscience, and we have, even in the midst of polytheism, quite a strong influence at work to keep the pagan mind healthy and sound upon the relations of guilt to justice. Men could not well deny the need

---

* The barbarians of Melita, when they saw the venomous beast hanging upon the hand of Paul, said among themselves : " No doubt this man is a murderer, whom though he hath escaped the sea, *yet vengeance* ($\Delta\iota\kappa\eta$) *suffereth not to live."* Their ethical instinct was sound and healthy, though their knowledge of the facts in the case was inaccurate. But when, in the middle of the nineteenth century, and upon a spot where the edifices and emblems of government cast their solemn shadows, a human being, in the heat and fury of his heart, slays his foe to mutilation in the illegal redress of his own wrongs, and the public conscience is found to be so debauched that only one in one hundred of the resident population condemns the deed, the comparison between Christendom and Paganism is humiliating. Such occurrences illustrate the difference between private revenge and public justice, and prove that the only security which society has against the former, is in the rigid and impartial execution of the latter.

of sin-expiation before whose eyes the blood of the piacular victim was constantly smoking, in accordance with a custom that had come down from their ancestors, and which fell in so accordantly with the workings of a remorseful conscience.

But a portion of the modern world have made use of Christianity itself to undermine the very foundations of Christianity. The Christian religion, by *furnishing* that one great sacrifice and real atonement, to which all other sacrifices look and point, has of course abolished the system of external sacrifices, and now that class of minds who live under its outward and civilizing influences without appropriating its inward and spiritual blessings, reject the legal and judicial elements which it contains, and deny the necessity of satisfying justice in the plan of redemption. There is nothing in the religious rites and customs under which they live to elicit the sense of guilt; and hence, from an inadequate knowledge of their own consciences and a defective apprehension of Christianity, they strenuously combat that fundamental truth, " without the shedding of blood there is no remission," upon which Christianity itself is founded, and in reference to which alone it has any worth or preciousness for a guilt-smitten soul.

The same tendency to underestimate the fact of human criminality, and the value of the piacular provision for it in the gospel, is seen also in the individual. How difficult it is to bring the person, for whose spiritual interests we are anxious, to see himself in the light of law and condemnation! How we ourselves shrink from the clear, solemn assertion of his culpability, and turn aside to enlarge upon the unworthiness or the unhappiness of his sin! When we make the attempt to charge home guilt upon him, how lacking we are in that tender solemnity, and earnest truthfulness of tone, which make the impression! And, even if we have succeeded in wakening his conscience to a somewhat normal action in this respect, how swiftly does he elude the terrible but righteous feeling, which alone can prepare him for the sprinkling of the blood of Jesus!

When we pass up into the Christian experience, we discover the same fact in a different form and degree. How difficult does the believer find it to obtain such a clear and transparent conception of his own guiltiness, that the atoning work of his Redeemer becomes all luminous before his eyes, and he knows instantaneously that he needs it, and that it is all he needs! Usually, this crystal clearness of vision is reserved for certain critical moments in his religious history, when he must have it or die. Usually it is the hour of affliction, or sickness, or death, that affords this rare and unutterably tranquillizing view of the guilty self and the dying Lord. " We have the *blood* of Christ," said the dying Schleiermacher, as, in his last moments, he began to count up the grounds of his confidence on the brink of the invisible world. Here was a mind uncommonly contemplative and profound; that had made the spiritual world its home, as it were, for many long years of theological study and reflection; that, in its tone and temper, seemed to be prepared to pass over into the supernatural realm without any misgivings or apprehensions; that had mused long and speculated subtly upon the nature of moral evil; that had sounded the depths of reason and revelation with no short plummet-line, — here was a man who, now that death had actually come, and the responsible human will must now encounter Holy Justice face to face, found that nothing but the *blood*, the *atonement*, of Jesus Christ could calm the perturbations of his planet-like spirit. The errors and inadequate statements of his theological system, which cluster mostly about this very doctrine of expiation, are tacitly renounced in the implied confession of guiltiness and need of atonement, contained these few simple words: "We have the BLOOD of Christ."

It is related that bishop Butler, in his last days drawing nearer to that dread tribunal where the highest and the lowest must alike stand in judgment, trembled in spirit, and turned this way and that for tranquillity of conscience. One of his clergy, among other texts, quoted to him the words: " The *blood* of Jesus Christ cleanseth from all sin." A flush of peace and joy passed, like the bland west wind, through his fevered conscience, as he made answer: " I have read those words a thousand times, but I never felt their meaning as now." And who does not remember that the final hours of the remarkably earnest, but too legal, life of the great English Moralist were lighted up with a peace that he had never been able to attain in the days of his health, by the evangelism of a humble curate?

Such facts and phenomena as these, evince that it is difficult for man to know sin as guilt, and thoroughly to apprehend Christ as a Priest and a Sacrifice. But one of the best correctives of this tendency to underestimate both guilt and expiation, is found in the clear perception that the two are *necessarily* related to each other, and that consequently the death of the Redeemer has nothing arbitrary in it. When one is convinced that Christ "*must needs* have suffered," he is relieved from the doubts respecting the meaning and efficacy of the atonement, and surrenders his conscience directly to its pacifying influence and power. He that *doubteth* is damned, in this respect also. The least shaking of belief that this great gospel provision is absolutely necessary, if sinners are to be saved; the faintest querying whether it may not, in the nature of things, have been a superfluity; so far as it tends at all, tends to dull the edge of man's contrition, and destroy the keenness of his sense of the Divine pity.

It has often been remarked, that the Passion of the Redeemer performs two functions. It not merely removes the sense of guilt, but it also elicits it. The experience of the Moravian missionaries is frequently cited to prove that a contemplation of the sufferings and death of Christ sometimes accomplishes what the naked exhibition of the law fails to accomplish, in bringing men to a sense of their sinfulness. The stern commandment had been applied to the hardened conscience of the savage, and iron met iron. The pity of a dying, atoning High Priest was shown, and the rock gushed out water. And such, undoubtedly, is often the case in the history of conversions. But shall we not find in this instance, also, that the force and energy of the impression made, results from a perception, more or less clear, that this death of the Substitute was *inexorably necessary*, in order to the criminal's release? The operations of the human mind are wonderfully swift, and difficult to follow or trace. Though the Esquimaux passed through no long process of reasoning, he *felt in his conscience* the unavoidableness of that mysterious Passion of that mysterious Person, in case his own wicked soul was to be spared the just inflictions of the future. By a very rapid but perfectly legitimate conclusion, he inferred the magnitude of his guilt from the greatness and necessity of the expiation. For suppose the lurking query, to which we have alluded, had sprung up in his mind just at this moment, and instead of the felt necessity of an atoning sacrifice, the faint querying had arisen whether his sin were not venial without the satisfaction of justice, would he have *instantaneously* melted down in contrition? So long as men are possessed with the feeling that the New Testament method of salvation is an abitrary one, containing elements and provisions that might have been different, or that are superfluous, they will receive little or no moral impression from it. But when they see plainly, that in all its parts and particles it refers directly to what is ethical in both themselves and the Eternal Judge, and is necessitated by the best portion of their own constitution, and by the perfect nature of the Godhead, they will then draw a very quick and accurate inference with respect to the intrinsic nature of that transgression which has introduced such a dire and stark necessity. When a man realizes that the great and eternal God cannot pardon his individual sins except through a passion that wrings great drops of blood from every pore of incarnate Deity, he realizes what is involved in the transgression of moral law.

2. A second obvious inference from the doctrine, that the sacrifice of Christ is a satisfaction for both the Divine and the human nature, is, that such an atonement is thorough and complete. It leaves nothing unsatisfied, or dissatisfied, either in God's holy nature or in man's moral sense. The work is ample and reliable.

This is a feature of the utmost value and importance in a scheme of Redemption. For no method will be put to a more fiery trial, ultimately, than the gospel method of salvation. It undergoes some severe tests here in time. The dying-bed draped with the recollection of past sins and transgressions, the pangs of remorse shooting through the conscience, and the fears for the future undulating through the whole being, — all this solemn experience before the soul shoots the gulf between time and eternity, calls for a most "*sovereign* remedy." And we may be certain that the disclosures and revelations that are to be made in the other world, and particularly upon the day of judgment, will subject the atoning work of the Redeemer to tests and trials such as no other work, and especially no "dead work" of a moralist, can endure for an instant. The energy of justice, and the energy of conscience, and the power of memory, and the searchings of God the Holy Ghost, will at that bar reach their height and combination; and any provision that shall legitimately countervail that energy, and enable the human soul to stand tranquil under such revelations, and beneath such claims, will be infinite and omnipotent indeed. But the believer need never fear lest the work of the Eternal Word, who was made flesh, the co-equal Son of the Eternal Father, prove inadequate under even such crucial tests. He needs only fear lest his feeble, wavering faith grasp it too insecurely. If he does but set his feet upon it, he will find it the Rock of Ages. *All judicial claims are cancelled, because the oblation to justice is an infinite one.* " There is *no* condemnation to them which are in Christ Jesus."*

For we have seen that the very mercy of God, in the last analysis, consists in the entire satisfaction of God's justice by God himself, for the helpless criminal. What method of Redemption can be conceived of, more perfectly sure and trustworthy than this? " What com-

---

* Michael Angelo, that loftiest and most religious of artists, gives expression, in the following sonnet, to this natural shrinking of the soul in

passion," says Anselm, " can equal the words of God the Father addressed to the sinner condemned to eternal punishment, and having no means of redeeming himself: 'Take my only-begotten Son, and make him an offering for thyself;' or the words of the Son: 'Take me and ransom thy soul?' For this is what both say, when they invite and draw us to faith in the gospel. And can anything be more just than for God to remit all debt, when in this way he receives a satisfaction greater than all the debt, provided only it be offered with the right feeling?"* " The pardon of sin," says an old English divine, " is not merely an act of mercy, but also an act of justice in God." By this he means that mercy and justice are concurrent in the gospel method of Redemption,— mercy satisfies justice, and justice acknowledges the satisfaction. " What abundant cause of comfort," he adds, " may this be to all believers, that God's justice as well as his mercy shall acquit them! that that attribute of God, at the apprehension of which they are wont to tremble, should interpose on their

view of the fiery judicial trial that awaits it, and also to the cheerful reassurance induced by the recollection of Christ's Passion:

> "Despite thy promises, O Lord, 't would seem
> Too much to hope that even love like Thine
> Can overlook my countless wanderings:
> And yet Thy *blood* helps us to comprehend
> That if Thy pangs for us were measureless,
> No less beyond all measure is thy grace."
> *Harford's Life of Angelo*, II. 166.

How immensely deeper is the intuition of divine things, how immensely clearer is the insight into the nature and mutual relations of God and man, which is indicated by such a sonnet from the soul of him who poised the dome of St. Peter's and crowded the frescoes of the Sistine chapel with grandeur and beauty, than that of the modern brood of *dilettanti*, as expressed in much of the current literature, and the current art.

* *Cur Deus homo?* II. 20.

behalf, and plead for them! And yet through the all-sufficient expiation and atonement that Christ hath made for our sins, this mystery is effected, and justice itself brought over, from being a formidable adversary, to be our party, and to plead for us. Therefore the apostle tells us that God is faithful and *just* to forgive us our sins."*

Consonant with this is the well-known language of the elder Edwards: "It is," he says, "so ordered now, that the glory of the attribute of Divine justice requires the salvation of those that believe. The justice of God that [irrespective of the atonement] required man's damnation, and seemed inconsistent with his salvation, now [having respect to the atonement] as much requires the salvation of those that believe in Christ [and thereby appropriate the atonement], as ever before it required their damnation. Salvation is an absolute debt to the believer from God, so that he may in justice demand it on the ground of what his Surety has done." † Do these last words sound rash? But scruti-

---

* Bp. Ezekiel Hopkins's *Exposition of the Lord's Prayer.* Works, I. 124.

† Works, IV. 150. New York Ed. For the soteriology of this eminent writer, see his discourses on "Justification by Faith alone," "The wisdom of God displayed in the way of salvation," and "Satisfaction for sin." Among his positions are the following: Justification frees from all obligation to eternal punishment (IV. 78, 104, 150). Christ's suffering is equivalent to the eternal suffering of a finite creature (IV. 101, 551). Christ experienced the wrath of God (IV. 182, 195). God's wrath is appeased by the atonement (IV. 142). God cannot accept an atonement that falls short of the full claims of justice (IV. 94). The voluntary substitute is, in this capacity, under obligation to suffer the punishment due to the sinner (IV. 96, 137). Justice does not abate any of its claims in the plan of redemption (IV. 140, 552). Christ satisfied "revenging," or distributive, justice (IV. 150, 189).

Samuel Hopkins is equally explicit in maintaining the theory of a strict satisfaction, as is evident from the following: "One important and necessary part of the work of the Redeemer of man was to make atonement

nize them. "Salvation is an absolute debt to the believer *on the ground of what his Surety has done;*" not on the ground, therefore, of anything that the believer has done. It is merely saying, that the soul which feels its own desert of damnation, may plead the merit of Christ with entire confidence that it cancels *all* legal claims, and that there is nothing outstanding and un-

for their sins, by *suffering in his own person the penalty or curse of the law,* under which, by transgression, they had fallen . . . . The sufferings of Christ were, therefore, for sin, and consequently must be *the evil which sin deserves,* and that to which the sinner was exposed, and which he must have suffered had not Christ suffered it in his stead, or that which is equivalent.
. . . . The Mediator did not suffer precisely the same kind of pain, in all respects, which the sinner suffers when the curse is executed on him. He did not suffer that particular kind of pain which is the necessary attendant, or natural consequence, of being a sinner, and which none but the sinner can suffer. But this is only a circumstance of the punishment of sin, and not of the essence of it. *The whole penalty of the law may be suffered, and the evil suffered may be as much, and as great, without suffering that particular sort of pain.* Therefore, Christ, though without sin, might suffer the *whole penalty,* — that is, *as much and as great evil* as the law denounces against transgression. The evil which sinners may suffer, on whom the penalty of the law is inflicted, may, and doubtless will, differ in many circumstances, and not be precisely of the same kind in all respects, and yet each one of them suffer the penalty of the same law . . . . The evil of the sufferings of Christ, being, in the magnitude of it, commensurate with the dignity and worth of his person, *is equal to, is as great as, the evil which is threatened to the transgressors of the law, and as great as the sinner deserves;* yea, it is as great as the endless sufferings of mankind . . . . The curse of the law consists in the infinite evil, pain, and suffering which sin deserves. He who suffers this for sin, suffers the curse of the law, is accursed, or made a curse. *Jesus Christ suffered this curse, the infinite natural evil in which the penalty or the curse of the law consists;* and in suffering it for sinners, and in their stead, was made a curse. This might be consistent with his having the approbation of the Father, and his favor and love to the highest degree. The displeasure of God, which was the cause of his sufferings when he voluntarily took, and stood in, the place of sinners, was displeasure with sin and the sinner, and not with him who suffered, the state of the case being fully understood by the spectators . . . . It is evident from scripture, that the law of God does admit of a substitute, both in obeying the precepts, and suffering the penalty of it." — *Hopkins's Works,* I. pp. 321—341. Doctrinal Tract Society's Ed.

covered by that Divine atonement upon which it relies for justification. It is simply asserting that God incarnate, the redeeming Deity, can demand, upon principles of justice, the release of a soul that trusts solely in his atoning death ; because by that death he has *completely*, and not partially, satisfied eternal justice for it, and in its stead.* They are the bold words of a very cautious

---

* It is needless to remark, that Edwards does not concede that the mere atonement itself gives any and every man *a claim upon God for the benefits of the atonement,* — as is sometimes argued by the advocates of universal salvation. God is under no obligation to make an atonement for the sin of the world ; and, *after he has made one, he is at perfect liberty to apply it to whom he pleases, or not to apply it at all.* The atonement is *his*, and not man's, and he may do what he will with his own. Hence, according to Edwards, two distinct acts of sovereignty on the part of God are necessary in order to a soul's salvation. The providing of an atonement in the first place, is a sovereign act ; and then the application, or giving over, of the atonement, when provided, to any particular elected sinner, is a second act of sovereignty. The sufferings and death of Christ constitute the atonement ; and even if not a single soul should appropriate it by the act of faith, it would be the same expiatory oblation still, though unapplied. Hence, the second of these sovereign acts is as necessary as the first, in order to salvation. But when *both* of these acts of sovereignty *have taken place,* — when the atonement has been made, and has actually been given over to and accepted by an individual, — *then,* says Edwards, it is a matter of strict justice that the penal claims of the law be not exacted from the believer, because this would be to exact them twice ; once from Christ, and once from one to whom, by the supposition, Christ's satisfaction has actually been made over by a sovereign act of God. For God to do this, would be to pour contempt upon his own atonement. It would be a confession that his own provision is *insufficient* to satisfy the claims of law, and needs to be supplemented by an additional infliction upon the believer. It would be an acknowledgment that the atonement, when it comes to be actually tested in an individual instance, fails to satisfy the claims of justice, and therefore is an entire failure. The sum of money which was given to the poor debtor, with the expectation that it was large enough completely to liquidate his debt, is found to fall short, and leaves him still in the debtor's prison, from which he cannot come out "until he has paid the uttermost farthing."

That this is a correct representation of the views of Edwards is evident from the following answer which he gives to the question : What does God's sovereignty in the salvation of man imply ? — " God's sovereignty

and accurate thinker; but are they any bolder than that challenging jubilant shout of St. Paul: "Who is he that condemeth? It is CHRIST that died." As if, flinging his voice out into all worlds, and all universes, he asked: "What claims are those which the blood of the Eternal Son of God has not been able to satisfy? Is the atonement of the great God Himself not equal to the demands of his law? Is the Deity feebler upon the side of his expiation, than upon the side of his retribution?"

It is a false humility, and not unmingled with a legal spirit, that would prevent the believer from joining in these bold and confident statements respecting the amplitude and completeness of the work of his atoning Lord and God. He need be under no concern lest he underestimate the attribute of justice, if he make this hearty and salient evangelical feeling his own. He disparages no attribute of God, when he magnifies and makes his boast in the atonement of God. Christ was equal to all he undertook; and he undertook to satisfy the claims of the Divine law for the sin of the world, down to the *least jot and tittle*; to pay the immense debt

in the salvation of men implies that God can either bestow salvation on any of the children of men, or refuse it, without any prejudice to the glory of any of his attributes, *except where he has been pleased to declare that he will or will not bestow it.* It cannot be said absolutely, as the case *now* stands, that God can, without any prejudice to the honor of *any* of his attributes, bestow salvation on any of the children of men, or refuse it, because concerning some, God has been pleased to declare either that he will or that he will not bestow salvation on them; and thus *to bind himself* by his own promise. And concerning some he has been pleased to declare that he never will bestow salvation upon them; viz., those who have committed the sin against the Holy Ghost. Hence, as the case *now* stands, he is obliged; he cannot bestow salvation in one case, or refuse it in the other, without prejudice to the honor of his *truth*. But God exercised his sovereignty *in making these declarations.* God was not obliged to promise that he would save all who believe in Christ; nor was he obliged to declare that he who committed the sin against the Holy Ghost should never be forgiven. But *it pleased him so to declare.*" — *Edwards's Works*, IV. 530. N. Y. Ed.

to the *uttermost farthing.* "Think not," he says, "that I am come to destroy the law or the prophets. I am not come to destroy, but to *fulfil.* For verily I say unto you, Till heaven and earth pass, one jot or one tittle shall in no wise pass from the law till *all* be fulfilled." And the incarnate Deity did what he undertook. He had a view of the extent and spirituality of law, and of the demerit of sin, such as no finite mind is capable of entertaining, and he knew whereof he affirmed when, at the close of his life of sorrow and his death of passion and agony, he bowed his head and gave up the ghost, with the words, significant beyond all conception: "*It is finished,*—the oblation is complete." Jesus Christ, the God-Man, in the garden of Gethsemane and on the middle cross of Calvary, had a conception of the rigor of justice and the exaction of law, such as no human or angelic mind can ever have in equal degree; and the believer may be certain that when He invites him to rest his complete justification, and the entire satisfaction of all judicial claims, before that law, upon what He has wrought in reference to it, he is not invited to a procedure that will be a disparagement, or dishonor, either to law or to justice.

Man is not straitened in the atoning work of incarnate Deity. He is straitened in his own blind and unbelieving soul. He only needs to take a profound view of justice, a profound view of sin, and a profound view of God's atonement for it, to come out into a region of peace, liberty, and joy unspeakable. Feeble views upon any one of these subjects debilitate his Christianity. He should distinctly see how sacred is the nature of justice, and how indefeasible are its claims. He should distinctly feel the full impression and energy of this attribute. Then he should as distinctly see how complete and perfect is the liquidation of these holy claims, by the death of the incarnate Son of God,—that august Personage denominated by the prophet "the Wonderful, the Counsellor, the Mighty God, the Everlasting Father, the Prince of Peace."

That very interesting mystic of the Middle Ages, Henry Von Suso, enlarging in his poetic manner upon the compassion of God towards a sinful world, tells us that the "blood of Christ is full of love and red as a rose."* This roseate conception of the atonement is not the one that will meet the necessities of man's conscience, in the solemn hour of his mental anguish and his moral fear. There is love unutterable in that blood, but it was wrung from a heart to which all merely *sentimental* affection was as alien as it is to the vengeance of eternal fire. He only can appreciate and understand that love of principle, that love of self-immolation, who sympathizes thoroughly with that regard for the holiness and justice of God, united with compassion for lost souls, that led the Redeemer to undertake the full expiation of human guilt.

Whoever is granted this clear crystalline vision of the atonement, will die in peace, and pass through all the unknown transport and terror of the day of doom with serenity and joy. It ought to be the toil and study of the believer to render his conceptions of the work of Christ more vivid, simple, and vital. For whatever may be the extent of his religious knowledge in other directions; whatever may be the worth of his religious experience in other phases; there is no knowledge and no experience that will stand him in such stead, in those moments that try the soul, as the experience of the pure sense of guilt quenched by the pure blood of Christ.

* "Minnerichen, rosenfarbenen Blute."

SYMBOLS AND CONGREGATIONALISM.*

The constitution of the Congregational Library Association proclaims that it is the object of this society to establish a material centre for the denomination, about which it shall collect its scattered elements, and from which it shall radiate its forces. It is its design, in the language of its statutes, "to found and perpetuate a library of books, pamphlets, and manuscripts, and a collection of portraits," and to lay up in its archives "whatever else shall serve to illustrate Puritan history, and promote the general interests of Congregationalism." "It shall also be an object of the Association," says the constitution, "to secure the erection of a suitable building for its library, its meetings, and the general purposes of the body." Interpreting these articles and statutes in a broad and enterprising spirit, we find in them a desire to combine and unify the somewhat diffused characteristics of the Congregational denomination, by furnishing it a visible centre. This species of centre, and this sort of consolidation, though not of the highest order, though external in its instrumentalities, and external in many of its results, is nevertheless of great importance in the history of any organization. The influence of the national temple, the common visible

* A discourse before the Congregational Library Association, May 25, 1858.

home and resort of all the tribes, upon the Jewish church and state, is well known; and no external event, perhaps no event, contributed more to the downfall of the Old economy, and the Jewish cultus, and thereby to the progress and triumph of the new dispensation with its simpler and more spiritual worship, than did the siege of Jerusalem, and the destruction of the old ancestral temple. That building of the pagan temples which began in Greece, immediately after the Persian war was brought to a glorious close, did more than even that war itself to bring the various Grecian tribes into something akin to unity; and that so-called Sacred War which was signalized by the robbing of Delphi, and the scattering of its treasures, was at once the cause and the effect of the decline and destruction of Grecian patriotism, and Grecian unity. Mediæval Catholicism embodied its ideas, and centralized its forces, in the great Gothic cathedrals. That outburst of architecture in the thirteenth century, when Rheims and Rouen, Paris and Cologne, shot up their spires, and threw out their flying buttresses, with a suddenness and energy that looks like magic—that majestic series of material centres for the Papal church did much to strengthen it in its corruption, and to postpone the Reformation.*

The power and influence, then, of a centripetal point, even though it relate to externals, is not to be despised. It

* "The 13th century as a building epoch is perhaps the most brilliant in the whole history of architecture. Not even the great Pharaonic era in Egypt, the age of Pericles in Greece, nor the great period of the Roman Empire, will bear comparison with the 13th century in Europe, whether we look at the extent of the buildings executed, their wonderful variety and constructive elegance, the daring imagination that conceived them, or the power of poetry and of lofty religious feeling that is expressed in every feature and every part of them."—Fergusson's Handbook of Architecture, Part II., Book III., c. 9.

is indeed true that neither the library, nor the museum, neither the collection, nor the edifice in which the collection is garnered up, can be a substitute for the living spirit of learning in the mind of the individual scholar; and neither can the temple, nor the cathedral, nor any of the mechanism of an ecclesiastical denomination, be regarded of equal importance with the animating principle of piety in the hearts of church members. And yet neither science nor religion, neither the state nor the church, can wholly neglect these outward instruments of organization and union, without somewhat scattering their elements of power, and wasting their force.

Are we not then summoned by this "Library Association" to consider the need of more *centripetal force* in Congregationalism, in order to its greater efficiency as an ecclesiastical denomination? The Congregational edifice, the library, and the portrait gallery, imply that we require an ecclesiastical home, and are emblematic of the truth that the denomination needs to control its tendencies to vagueness, and diffusion, and to render its distinguishing characteristics more intense by concentration. But this cannot be done by merely erecting a building, or collecting a library and portraits. These are but the secondary, though, as we have remarked, the necessary instrumentalities. Our unity, and our consolidation, as one of the legitimate churches of Christ in the world, must ultimately proceed from a deeper and stronger force than anything visible and material. We have not been born of flesh and blood. We have been begotten of the will of God, with the *word of truth*, that we should be a kind of first fruits of his creatures. Our true growth, and our true strength, must lie in the line of our origin and birth. The ultimate organizing and centralizing influence, therefore, upon which we must place our main reliance as a
14*

religious denomination, is the *doctrine*, the *truth* of God This is one and homogeneous, and consequently unifies and harmonizes all that comes under its fair and full influence. But this supposes that eye sees to eye; and that there is a common doctrinal faith, and a common doctrinal creed, for the denomination.

Let us, then, consider *the necessity that exists in Congregationalism for a stronger symbolical feeling, and a bolder confidence in creed-statements, in order to its highest efficiency as a Christian denomination.*

Before proceeding to the discussion of this theme, we will cast a swift glance at the ancestral feeling and tendency on this subject. What was the attitude of the fathers and founders of Congregationalism towards the old historical theology that had preceded them, and particularly towards the Symbols that were then in existence? The answer to this question will require us to notice, very briefly, the theological position of the leading minds in the formative periods of Congregationalism, and the particular public action of the denomination itself.

It is a fact which will not be disputed, that the master spirits among the English Independents of the Cromwellian period were earnest and strong defenders, not merely of the doctrines of the Reformation, but of that particular shaping of them which is found in the creeds of the Calvinistic division of the Protestants. The English church previous to the days of Laud, it is well known, sympathized heartily with the theologians of Zurich and Geneva, and when that large and learned body of divines whose consciences compelled them to dissent from the increasing ecclesiasticism of the state establishment came out from it, they brought with them the very same *dogmatic* system which had been embodied in the 42 articles of Edward Sixth, had been compressed into the 39 articles of Elizabeth, and had been maintained by prelates like Whitgift, and Cranmer, and Usher, as the faith once delivered to the saints. As a natural consequence, the non-conforming theologians in England, however much they differed from one another, and from the old national church, upon secondary subjects, were characterized by an earnest and intelligent zeal for the old English, which was the old Calvinistic, faith and creed.

The Independents were not second to any in this feeling. Thomas Goodwin and John Owen, says Anthony Wood, "were the two Atlases and Patriarchs of Independency."* These two minds are the true representatives of the English Congregationalism of the 17th century, and they did more than any others to determine its type and character, both in doctrine and practice. Their theological position is as well known as that of Calvin himself. These minds were, also, of that exact and scientific order which requires for its own satisfaction the most unambiguous and self-consistent statement of religious truth. The treatises of the individual divine are, commonly, not so carefully worded as the articles of the council of divines; from the same cause that the best reasoned political disquisitions are not so precise in their statements as the technical phraseology of the political convention, or the political treaty. Yet even the practical treatises of Owen and Goodwin bear a much stronger resemblance than is common, or commonly practicable, in flowing discourse, to the concise and guarded enunciations of the council. The very structure of their sermons, and the very style of their discourses, evinces that these leading Independents were of their own free-will, and with their own clear eye, following on in that strait and narrow way of dogma

---

* Neale, II., 291. Harper's Ed.

which is the intellectual parallel to the strait and narrow way of life.

The Independents of England in the Cromwellian period had no quarrel with the Presbyterians in respect to matters of doctrine; even as the English Presbyterians had no quarrel with the low-church Episcopalians of this period, so far as relates to points of faith. Owen heartily adopted the Westminster Confession, and Twisse and the whole Westminster Assembly would have been content with the doctrinal part of the 39 articles. The Calvinists of England within the Establishment, and the Calvinists of England without the Establishment, were both alike opposed to Arminianism, and were equally earnest for those well discriminated creed-statements which mark off the faith of Geneva from that of Leyden.

The English Independents differed from the English Presbyterians solely upon the subject of ecclesiastical polity. And when, therefore, they appointed their committee at the Savoy in 1658 (exactly two hundred years ago) to draw up a confession of faith, that should organize the denomination, and hold it together, they instructed them to keep close to the Westminster upon doctrinal points, but to engraft the Congregational form of polity upon the old historical Calvinism that had come down to the Presbyterians themselves through Dort and Geneva.*

These well-known and familiar facts are sufficient to show that the founders and fathers of English Congregationalism were imbued with reverence for the ancient symbolism of the Protestant church, and felt that their small and feeble denomination, which was then struggling for existence amidst the convulsions of churches and states, must be held together, and made strong, by the

---

* Neale, II., 178. Harper's Ed.

strength of God's truth stated unequivocally and exhaustively in a creed-form.

The Congregational churches of New England were animated by the same feeling. Their leading minds, also, were of the same stamp, and theological affinities, with John Owen and John Howe. The pastor of the Plymouth pilgrims during their sojourn in Holland, the one who commended them to the protection of God when they embarked upon that hazardous voyage, and who told them that the Bible was not yet exhausted, and that " more light," he believed, was still to " break forth " from it, was John Robinson. But John Robinson believed in no light from the Bible that did not shine more and more upon the path of the Calvinist. John Robinson was a very vigilant observer of the most subtle and perplexing controversy in modern doctrinal history, that between Calvinism and Arminianism, and took a part in it. Bradford informs us that the pastor of the Pilgrims was " terrible to the Arminians," * and that too, it should be noticed,

* " In these times, also, were the great troubles raised by the Arminians; who, as they greatly molested the whole State, so this city in particular, in which was the chief university; so as there were daily and hot disputes in the schools thereabouts. And as the students and other learned, were divided in their opinions herein, so were the two professors or divinity readers themselves, the one daily teaching for it, and the other against it; which grew to that pass, that few of the disciples of the one would hear the other teach. But Mr. Robinson, although he taught thrice a week himself, and wrote sundry books, besides his manifold pains otherwise, yet he went constantly to hear their readings, and heard as well one as the other. By which means he was so well grounded in the controversy, and saw the force of all their arguments, and knew the shifts of the adversary; and being himself very able, none was fitter to buckle with them than himself, as appeared by sundry disputes; so as he began to be terrible to the Arminians; which made Episcopius, the Arminian professor, to put forth his best strength, and set out sundry theses, which by public dispute he would defend against all men. Now Polyander, the other professor, and the chief

at a period in the history of Arminianism when the little finger of the progenitor was not so thick as the loins of some of the posterity. The controlling spirits among the clergy of the first New England colonies were also men of the same theological character and tendencies with the Owens and the Robinsons. The membership of the first New England churches had been born into the kingdom, through the instrumentality of a style of preaching and indoctrination, searching, systematic, and orthodox, in the highest degree.

It was natural, therefore, that the Congregationalism of the New World should be marked by the same respect for the old historical faith which we have noticed in the English Independency. In 1648, ten years before the English Independents adopted their symbol at Savoy, the vigorous and vital churches scattered through the forests, and among the savages, of New England, sent their delegates to Cambridge, who drew up a confession of which the doctrinal part was adopted verbally from that of Westminster, while the polity of the symbol was made to conform to their own Congregational theory and usage. Thirty-two years after this, the churches of the province of Massachusetts met in synod, and drew up the only *original* symbol that has yet been constructed by an ecclesiastical body of Congregationalists. The Boston Confes-

preachers of the city, desired Mr. Robinson to dispute against him. But he was loth, being a stranger. Yet the other did importune him, and told him that such was the ability and nimbleness of wit of the adversary, that the truth would suffer if he did not help them ; so he condescended, and prepared himself against the time. And when the time came, the Lord did so help him to defend the truth and foil his adversary, as he put him to an apparent nonplus in this great and public audience. And the like he did two or three times upon such like occasions,"—Bradford's History of Plymouth C..ony, Congregational Board's edition, pp. 256, 257.

sion of 1680, still retained as its creed by one of the oldest churches in the city of Boston,* though modelled very much after those of Westminster and Savoy, purports to be the work of a Congregational Synod, and in this regard has more claim to the respect of the descendants of the Pilgrims than any other symbol. Twenty-eight years after the formation of the Boston Confession, the churches in the Connecticut colony sent their representatives to Saybrook to construct a symbol for their use. This synod adopted the Boston Confession of 1680, as an expression of doctrinal belief, and made a fuller statement of what they deemed to be the Congregational polity.

This brief survey is sufficient to show that those who laid the foundations of Congregationalism, in the Old world and in the New, were in hearty sympathy with that body of doctrine which received its precise and technical statement in the creeds of the Reformation, and more particularly in that carefully discriminated system which was the result of the debate between Calvinism and Arminianism. The carefulness, and the frequency (three times within sixty years) with which symbols were drawn up and sent forth by the first Congregational churches evinces that both the individual theologian, and the denomination as a whole, craved a distinct, and publicly adopted, rule of faith and practice, as that which should help them to study the Scriptures understandingly, and should bind them together ecclesiastically. Reverence for a common denominational creed belongs, then, historically, to the Congregational church, as it does to all those well-compacted churches whose career constitutes the history of vital Christianity upon earth. In seeking to deepen and strengthen this reverence, we are not going contrary to the primal instinct and native genius of Congregationalism; we are not

* The Old South.

engrafting any wild shoots into the church of our forefathers; we are simply inhaling and exhaling their pure, their exact, their thorough-going spirit.

1. Passing now to the discussion of the theme itself, we remark, in the first place, as a reason for a stronger symbolical feeling in Congregationalism, that an intensely free system, like our own, is the one that derives all the advantages, and escapes all the evils, that result from the organific power of a symbol.

Were the church which we honor and love already rigid and solid by reason of an inherent tendency of its own to centralization, there might be reason to fear any and every consolidating influence. But Congregationalism is made up of dynamic forces and flowing lines, and its intrinsic tendency is to liberty and diffusion. There is no church that has so little of form, and figure, and organization, as our own. Like the church gathered in the upper room, its constitution is almost invisible. We are vastly nearer to pure spirit than to pure matter. Our body is nearly as immaterial as some souls. There is little danger, therefore, that Congregationalism will receive detriment from a centripetal force, particularly if that force does not issue from polity, or judicatories, but from doctrine. And there is no danger that it will proceed from either government or ecclesiastical mechanism. The political structure of our denomination is as well defined and settled as that of the Papacy itself, and stands even less chance of alteration. No centralizing force can be brought to bear from this quarter. The very attempt to establish judicatures within Congregationalism, and to unify and consolidate the denomination by means of polity, would be suicidal; and, therefore, though there may be secessions and departures from it, there can be no internal change of the denomination as a whole, unless we suppose an entire transmutation of it into something that is not Congregationalism.

The only power, then, that can unify the denomination, and make its various atoms and elements feel that there is a deeper life and bond of union than that of polity, is the power of *doctrine;* the power of a *common faith;* the power of a *self-chosen denominational creed.* And this is both a salutary and safe power, in reference to a system so highly republican as our own. For in this exuberance of democratic life, and this expansive freedom, lies our danger. The centrifugal force, if unbalanced, will shoot the star madly from its sphere. Considering that our natural tendencies are those of growth, progress, and liberty, and that all natural tendencies perpetuate themselves, our watchfulness ought to have reference to such traits as unity, solidarity and harmony. That which is spontaneous need give us no anxiety; but that which is to be acquired, which is the result of effort and of self-education, should be the chief object in the eye.

We may derive an illustration from the province of political philosophy. The question whether conservatism or progress shall be the preponderating element in the state, will be answered by the wise man in view of the general condition of things in the commonwealth. He whose lot is cast among the hereditary prerogatives and orders of the English state, if he follows the wise course, will side with the Liberals; while the very same man, if called to live and act in the midst of the fierce democracies and conflicts of a new and rankly growing nation like our own, will side with Conservatism. For there is little danger, in the early and formative eras of a nation's history, particularly if there be an immense fund of vital force, and vast continental spaces to spread over and work in, of too much regulation and education. The training is more liable to err upon the side of laxness than of strictness, when the thews and muscles of a giant are forming, and the gristle is hardening into the bone of a Hercules. Besides this, in a republican commonwealth, if the tendency to centralization does become too strong, and power really begins to steal from the many to the few, the remedy is close at hand, and in the hands of the citizens. In a monarchy, if the just equilibrium has been disturbed, it cannot be restored without a revolution; but the adjustment in a republic takes place by an inevitable law and a tranquil movement, like that which equalizes the pressure of the atmosphere. In all free systems, therefore, where the instinct and the spontaneity runs to liberty and diffusion, the hazard is not in the direction of conservative methods and influences.

All this holds true in its full force of the democratic church, as well as of the democratic state. As there is no lack of inward energy in Congregationalism, and as there is no external restraint from its political structure and arrangement; as there are no judicatures, and nothing, consequently, but good advice by which to hold the denomination together; there is little danger of an excess in the moral and spiritual forces that must do this work, if it be done at all. As that individual who stands up isolated, and independent of all outward restraints, ought for this very reason to feel the strongest possible inward limitation, so should that ecclesiastical body which has least of mechanism and of polity, subject itself to the strongest possible doctrinal and spiritual constraint. Let then the symbol be melted into the soul of the free and vigorous churches. Let it permeate them as quicksilver does the pores of gold. Let the clearly defined, and the accurate dogma become the sinew and fibre of the otherwise loose and slack organization.

2. Secondly, Congregationalism needs a stronger confidence in creed-statements because, as a denomination, it is unusually exposed to the sceptical influences of literary culture and free-thinking.

It so happens that the simplest form of church polity is the dominant one, the "standing order," in the oldest and most highly educated portion of the United States. The Congregational churches of New England are planted in the midst of the most artificial civilization upon the Western continent, and their membership is more exposed to the good and bad influences of secular refinement and literary cultivation, than is that of any other denomination in the land. The first-settled, and most densely-settled, part of any country always contains more of *irreconcilable* varieties of social, literary, and religious opinion than the newer regions. There may not be more apparent and superficial variety, but there will be vastly more of the latent and profounder differences of sentiment. There are, it is true, a much greater number of sects in our Western states than in the Eastern, but then these sects themselves are founded in religion of some sort, and not in scepticism. The pioneer, though illiterate and rude, it may be, is characterized by religious sensibility, and he is continually thrown into circumstances and emergencies that cause him to feel his dependence upon his Maker. As a consequence, he is, like the ancient Athenians to whom Paul spoke, very much inclined to religion and worship. The older parts of our land, on the other hand, may exhibit fewer external marks of difference; fewer sects may come into existence, and to the eye of the superficial observer, there may seem to be a very general sameness in the external phenomena of the region, and yet there be forming, and formed, beneath, in the hearts and minds of a class of community, a disbelief in all that is properly called religion that throws them "whole equinoxes apart" from those who are living, thinking, praying, and dying by their side. This radical divergence of the parties from each other is seen whenever any great religious movement takes place. The motley and mottled population of the new region, being only superficially separated, flows together when the common Christian faith and truth is set home with unwonted power and by unwonted influences, while the seemingly homogeneous population of the educated and refined portions of the country only have their latent and irreconcilable antagonisms elicited by such influences. Hence it is that the extremes of faith and unbelief will always meet, in their severest conflict, in the older and more highly cultivated portions of a country. And that church which is called to defend and propagate the faith amongst such a population, is consequently exposed to unusual temptations, and needs uncommon aids and appliances.

Such, if we are not mistaken, is the position and the function of Congregationalism. The most careless observer must acknowledge that there is more of *radical* conflict of opinion in New England than in any other portion of the United States. That scepticism which invariably springs up out of belles lettres when belles lettres is divorced from deep thinking, is more rife and forth-putting here than anywhere else. These older states contain more of that religious indifferentism which always arises when literature is separated from philosophy and theology, and which exhibits its opposition to New-Testament Christianity, sometimes by the elegant languor of its over-refinement, and sometimes, when exasperated into some emotion, by a bitterness that borders upon malignity. The Congregational churches are set for the defence and spread of the humbling doctrines of guilt and atonement, among a population which is feeling in an increasing degree the stupefying influences of wealth, and the inflating influences of earthly culture. The structure of society around them, like that of England or France, is growing artificial, and, in so far, irreligious, by the very lapse of time, and the influx of a more elaborate civilization. Loose thinking, and radical differences of opinion upon fundamental subjects, are the natural attendants upon such a social state and condition, and it becomes much more difficult for Christianity under such circumstances to overcome the antagonisms and mould society internally and from the centre. The newer states, and the less sophisticated populations, are much more plastic, and, in all their internal characteristics, much more homogeneous, and hence the church that is planted in them only needs to enunciate certain leading truths with boldness and fluent eloquence, to create currents that will roll like the Mississippi itself through the whole length of the land. But it is different in the older and over-civilized portions of the country. The statements of the pulpit, here, must not only be bold, but exact, and drawn from the deep places. The preacher must be an anatomist, and not merely a painter. He cannot break up moral indifference, or vanquish religious scepticism, in the wellbred and well-read hearer before him, by a merely pictorial method. He must prove himself to be a psychologist, and by an analysis of character, by a subtle penetration into the springs of motive and feeling, elicit some religious consciousness in his careless and unbelieving auditor, and probe it until he writhes. Christianity, among old institutions, and matured methods of mental discipline, must verify itself as the commanding truth, by the energy of its abstraction, the clearness of its discrimination, the penetrating force of its elements, the comprehensiveness of its grasp, and the patient thoroughness of its details.

But all this necessitates the *symbol*. This conflict of opinion in cultivated Christendom can be stilled only by that church which looks down upon it from the higher position furnished by historical Christianity. That denomination which thinks to dispense with the results of past theologizing, and which supposes that, of and by itself, it can solve all the problems that press upon the natural mind, and refute all the arguments advanced by the carnal reason, will find that it has over-estimated its strength. It will be forced to fall back into the solid columns that are behind it, and to fight the battle in company with the whole church militant. For the creeds have themselves been born of intellectual conflict; of a deeper conflict than is ever witnessed by any single church, or any single generation, because they are the slow growth of many churches and many generations. The historical symbol contains the key to those very problems which are troubling every new generation of unbelievers, because they are vainly thinking that the individual is wiser than the Christian church, and wiser than the human race. That church, consequently, which, calmly and with intelligent foresight, has adopted it, and wrought it into its understanding and its affections, will be able to still the conflict that is going on, either by lifting the doubting or opposing mind up to its own serene height of vision, or by an argumentation that leaves the truth triumphant and firm, whatever becomes of the opponent.

3. In the third place, a stronger symbolical feeling is required in Congregationalism, because of the laxness with which the Bible itself is now interpreted by many minds in the Protestant world.

In the preceding division of the discourse we have

spoken of the dangers that assail us from that scepticism which rejects the Bible altogether; we have now to speak of those latitudinarian influences which issue, not from a rejection of Revelation, but from an inadequate and defective understanding of it. When the Scriptures have become venerable and sacred in an old Christian commonwealth, and yet there is a declining interest in their cardinal doctrines, nothing is more natural than an exegesis that empties them of these doctrines. "The Bible is the religion of Protestants" is a dictum accepted at the present day by Protestant parties that stand poles apart in their interpretation of the Bible, and their theological belief. This dictum meant something when the church was just escaping from the crushing authority of tradition and of the Papacy. It taught that the human mind must seek for an *infallible* rule of faith, and source of truth, in the word of God, and not in the church. But the Reformers held, and with very great earnestness too, that the Bible teaches but one set of doctrines, and contains but one homogeneous system. They were themselves strict constructionists and exegetes, and every line and letter of their creeds evinces that *they* could discover within its pages only that same doctrinal system which the Patristic church,* as distinguished from the Papal, had found in them. The Reformers had no notion that the Bible is a nose of wax. It could not be made to teach two or more systems radically contradictory to each other. When, therefore, they called the church back to Divine Revelation, as the only *unerring* source of truth, they did not

* And the *Western*, rather than the Eastern, Patristic church, it should always be observed. Luther and Calvin fortified themselves, in their contest with the Papal theologian, who asserted that the Protestants were leaving the faith of the "Fathers," by citing the stricter views held by the Latin, rather than the milder tenets adopted by the Greek, divines.

suppose that they were sending it to a Delphic oracle, uttering ambiguous voices, like those of Paganism. And neither did the first Protestants themselves find two antagonistic lines of doctrine in these Scriptures. From Genesis to the Apocalypse, the modern Protestant church, as had the ancient Patristic before them, discovered but one generic and homogeneous teaching respecting the being and attributes of God, the actual character and destiny of man, and the method of his redemption by a Mediator. And they embodied the results of their profound and systematic study of the Bible, in that remarkable series of symbols, which more than anything else of a human sort consolidated Protestantism, and gave it a firm fibre and organization, whereby it stood strong amidst all the distractions of the time. Had there been radical differences among the Reformers in their understanding of the Scriptures; had Luther and Calvin been unable to see eye to eye upon the leading truths relating to God, Man, and the God-Man, and had they constructed creeds for the German, Swiss, and Holland churches, that were antagonistic to each other upon these subjects; had there not been in this remarkable age the most profound and exhaustive study of the word of God, and as a consequence, a most *harmonious* understanding of its contents, Protestantism would have been broken down, and crushed into the earth, by the massive, time-honored, though merely mechanical unity of the Papacy.

But in process of time, the term *Protestant* acquires the same vague and loose meaning which the term Christian has received. When the disciples of Christ were first called by this name at Antioch, it denoted only those who had come to a personal sense of sin, and a living faith in the Redeemer. It now, besides this, designates all of the human family who are not Pagans or Mohammedans. In like manner the term Protestant, in the beginning, had exclusive reference to religious and doctrinal characteristics, while now, it has certainly an equal reference to intellectual traits. Protestantism, at first, meant justification by faith, in distinction from justification by works. It now means, over and besides this, freethinking and private judgment, in distinction from hereditary trust and unreasoning assent.* As a consequence, the intellectual characteristics of Protestantism are apt to overcome and suppress its evangelical and theological ones, in those periods when civilization and literary culture become separated from doctrinal Christianity. As matter of fact, the Protestantism of the present day includes within itself an amount of rationalistic and antievangelical elements, at which the Reformers, the original Protestants, would have stood aghast.

But this condition of things directly affects the interpretation of the Scriptures. All Protestants, of whatever grade, must accept the dictum that distinguishes Protestantism from Popery; otherwise they fall into the ranks of the Pope. Chillingworth's saying: "The Bible is the religion of Protestants," becomes the watchword for Socinus, equally with Calvin, and for all the intermediates between these two representative men. In order, therefore, to an unambiguous and well-accented denominational character, every Protestant denomination requires a symbol that shall express, and proclaim to the world, what *it* finds in the word of God. In the present condition of Protestantism, and amidst the variety of interpre-

* This is the preponderating conception of Protestantism, in Mr. Hallam's representation of the Reformers and of the Reformation. A deeper acquaintance with the *theological* problems and aspects of those men and times would have preserved the history of the Literature of Europe from the only grave bias that now injures it.

tations that are put upon the Scriptures, it is not sufficient for an individual, or a church, to say: "My religion is in the Bible." Well do we remember the humor with which a venerable theological teacher was wont to allude to the zeal of a well-meaning man, who proposed to unite into one body all the various denominations that checker and speckle our land, by issuing an edition of the Scriptures with a sufficiency of blank leaves, and inviting all persons to fall to, and subscribe the Bible! It is not enough, in the present condition of Christendom, for an individual to point at the word of God, as it lies upon the table, saying: "My doctrinal belief is between those covers." As we cannot determine, in these days of naturalism and pantheism, what lessons the scientific man learns from the book of Nature, until he has stated them in the exact nomenclature and precise phraseology of science, so neither can we decide what teachings the Protestant now finds in the book of Revelation until he has written out his creed.

"The subscription to Scripture," said Edmund Burke, "is the most astonishing idea I ever heard, and will amount to just nothing at all. Gentlemen so acute have not, that I have heard, ever thought of answering a plain obvious question: What is that Scripture, to which they are content to subscribe? They do not think that a book becomes of divine authority because it is bound in blue morocco and is printed by John Basket and his assigns. The Bible is a vast collection of different treatises: a man who holds the divine authority of one may consider the other as merely human. What is his canon? The Jewish—St. Jerome's—that of the Thirty-Nine Articles—Luther's? Therefore to ascertain Scripture you must have one article more; you must define what that Scripture is which you mean to teach. There are, I believe, very few who, when Scripture is so ascertained, do not see the absolute necesity of knowing what *general doctrine* a man draws from it, before he is sent down, authorized by the State, to teach it as pure doctrine, and receive a tenth of the produce of our lands. The Scripture is no one summary of doctrines regularly digested, in which a man could not mistake his way. It is a most venerable, but most multifarious collection of the records of the divine economy; a collection of an infinite variety of cosmogony, theology, history, prophecy, psalmody, morality, epilogue, allegory, legislation, ethics, carried through different books, by different authors, at different ages, for different ends and purposes. It is necessary to sort out what is intended for example, what only as narrative, what to be understood literally, what figuratively, where one precept is to be controlled and modified by another, what is used directly and what only as an argument *ad hominem*, what is temporary and what of perpetual obligation, what is appropriated to one state and to one set of men, and what the general duty of all Christians. If we do not get some security for this, we not only permit, but we actually pay for, all the dangerous fanaticism which can be produced to corrupt our people, and to derange the public worship of the country. We owe the best we can (not infallibility, but prudence) to the subject: first sound doctrine, then ability to use it." *

In order, therefore, that the Congregational churches

---

* Speech on the Acts of Uniformity.—It may be said, that the Congregational churches *do* write out their creed, each one for itself, and therefore do not need a denominational symbol. But upon this method, they are less assisted by a *common* and *self-authorized* interpretation of the Scriptures, than most other denominations; and less than their ancestors were a century and a half ago, if we are to judge from the denominational action at Cambridge, Boston, and Saybrook. Have we not applied our theory respecting church-discipline, to church-doctrine, somewhat to our own disadvantage, from overlooking the difference between the two things? It is our belief, as it was that of our forefathers, that it is expedient that government and discipline should be

may escape the evils incident to the great Protestant right of private judgment, and the freedom of speculation which always goes along with it, and may derive only the advantages flowing from it, they need, as a denomination, to state their own judgment, in the most exact and distinct manner, with respect to the meaning and doctrinal contents of the Bible. For in this way alone can they prevent the private judgment of other Protestant parties and denominations from being imposed upon them for their own. As this is a point of some importance, we will dwell upon it for a moment. There is little danger that a denomination like our own should be much affected, in

confined as strictly as possible to the local church, and that as little as possible even of advice should be called in through councils, associations, or the denomination as a whole. And it also seems to be our belief, as it was not that of our forefathers (judging from their denominational action), that it is equally expedient that the doctrinal creed should be drawn up by every local church for itself, and that a common concert and coöperation of the churches of the denomination, in this respect, is as undesirable as with respect to cases of church discipline. But are we not mistaken in this, from not observing the great difference there is between doctrine and discipline? While it is well that all those secondary affairs which pertain to church government should be guided as much as possible by each individual church for itself, and there should be all the variety of adjustment incident to the great number and variety of such affairs, is it as well that the primary matter of doctrinal statement, which from the nature of the case is a fixed quantity, should be exposed to all the liability to variation and divergence from the exact truth that necessarily attaches to individual and local action repeated every time that a church is formed? This work, unlike the other, does not require to be performed anew every day, and continually. Truth is unchangeable. The creed for the denomination ought, therefore, to be the work of the denomination, and be constructed once for all. But church discipline is required anew and afresh every day, because it grows out of the ever-changing circumstances of the day. It may, therefore, be administered by the day—that is, whenever the occasion arises, and by the local body, because the local body is concerned in the speciality of the case.

the outset, by those forms of Protestantism which reject the *essential* doctrines of Christianity. The difference between Rationalism and Supernaturalism is too great for influences to pass *directly* from one to the other. The chasm between these parties is so wide that they cannot hear each other's voices across it. The latitudinarian influences (latitudinarian as we must regard them from *our* denominational position) will first come in upon us from those *evangelical* divisions in Protestantism who hold the doctrines of grace, but who, according to our denominational judgment, do not hold them with sufficient *self-consistence* and *comprehensiveness*, to render their *creed*, and their *theologizing*, as accurate as our own. The nice point, and therefore the point of most danger, for Congregationalism, and for all other denominations that occupy the same doctrinal position with it, is the right adjustment of its relations, not to downright heresy, but to a looser and less defined form of orthodoxy than Congregationalism thinks itself can stand upon. We may illustrate our meaning by reference to the great controversy which has gone on from the very first ages to the present time, between the two grand divisions of evangelical Christendom. We refer to that standing difference of opinion among believers in the *general* doctrines of grace, which, in the Patristic church, showed itself in the Augustinian and Semi-Pelagian divisions, and, in the Protestant church, in the Calvinistic and Arminian controversies. In these two great divisions of ancient and modern evangelical Christendom, we find a difference of sentiment, not with regard to the *general* facts and truths of New Testament Christianity, but with respect to the more *specific* and *exact* definitions of them.* And it is with reference to

* " That man is no longer in his pure and primitive moral condition, and that the mere cultivation of his present natural powers and sus

this *specific* enunciation of the general doctrines of grace that the principal controversy has gone on, and is still going on, within the evangelical world. For it is a great mistake to suppose that the Patristic church was very much convulsed by the controversy with mere and sheer Pelagianism; or that the Protestant church has been very much excited or tasked by mere and sheer Socinianism. Both of these schemes are so totally different from the plain teachings of the entire and unmutilated Scripture that there was no opportunity for a profound argument, and a permanent debate; and hence both of these schemes alike dropped back into their own private and local circles, while the great mass of the Patristic, as of the Protestant church, retained, and defended the *evangelical* theology. But upon *this* basis of *general* evangelism, there was an opportunity for an argument, and an honest difference of sentiment, among true believers in Christ. The ancient Semi-Pelagian, like the modern Arminian, while confessing his sin, and trusting in the blood of Christ, could sincerely urge what he believed to be a strong argument against the doctrines of predestination and irresisti-

ceptibilities cannot possibly suffice for the attainment of the true end of his creation; that, on the contrary, his original divinely-created nature has become corrupted and ruined by the dominion within him of the principle of self-will, and that in order to live conformably with his own original constitution, and to practice holiness from a holy disposition, he needs an inward change through a divine power—all this, in a *general* form of statement, had been the doctrine of the church from the first. It was only when still more *strict* definitions and statements were attempted—and particularly when such questions as these arose: Is there in the fallen soul any power of self-restoration? if so, to what degree? and what is its relation to the renewing power of the Holy Spirit?—that the church of the first four centuries found itself not fully agreed. There was constantly a difference, in this respect, between the Oriental and Occidental churches, and to some extent also within the Occidental church itself."—Guericke's Church History, § 91.

ble grace,* and that particular statement of the doctrine of original sin out of which the doctrines of predestination and irresistible grace issue as necessary corollaries. And his opponent showed his respect for that belief, by entering into the debate, and defending what he believed to be the more exact, and self-consistent, and all-comprehending statement of that same evangelical system. Not with reference, then, to the tenets of Pelagius and Socinus, but to those of Chrysostom and Arminius, as distinguished from those of Augustine and Calvin, do the Congregational churches need a strong symbolical feeling that will identify them yet more thoroughly with the stricter of those two great systems of theology, whose fraternal (and may it ever be fraternal) conflict and debate constitutes the sum and substance of evangelical doctrinal history.

For Congregationalism, it is agreed upon all sides, does not adopt the Arminian system as its doctrinal basis. The early history of the denomination has shown that the fathers and founders were strictly Calvinistic, in reference to the points at issue between Geneva and Leyden. Says the respected secretary of this Library Association, at the close of a most instructive historical sketch of the Congregational churches in Massachusetts : " Calvinism as a system of religious faith, and Puritanism as a code of morals (the two toughest things that ever entered into the composition of human character), were the original soul and body of these Congregational churches." And this Calvinism, he adds, was " that unadulterated Calvinism which had been filtered of every Arminian particle by the Synod of Dort,

---

* "Irresistible," it is needless to remark, not in the sense of never being resisted by the enmity of the carnal mind (Rom. 8: 7), but in the sense of being able to overcome, and actually overcoming, the utmost energy and intensity of that resistance.

whose ablest defender was John Robinson." * And no one can follow the tremendous cogency of that logic by which the great head of New England theology crushes to its minutest fibre the Arminian theory of indetermination, and the Arminian statement of the doctrine of Original Sin, without perceiving that there was a most profound harmony and agreement between the mind at Northampton, and the minds at Dort and Westminster. The successors of Edwards, New England divines of all varieties, alike repel the charge of Arminianizing proclivities ; and, though there may be a difference of opinion respecting the success with which the several schools that have arisen among us have untied the knots, and unravelled the intricacies of the Calvinistic system, there can be no doubt that all of our leading thinkers have intended, and done their utmost, to be true to the historical faith of their denomination.

The influence of the symbol is required to strengthen and perpetuate in Congregationalism this same primitive energy and decision in favor of the stricter of the two systems of evangelical theology. For the creed-statement evinces that there is no logical middle position between Calvinism and Arminianism, and that the choice of an individual or a denomination, consequently, lies between the one or the other. Semi-Pelagianism was a real midpoint between the tenets of Augustine and those of Pelagius ; but there is no true intermediate between the system of Arminius and that of Calvin. In the history of doctrine there are sometimes semiquavers, but demi-semiquavers never. In marking off the true scientific difference in this way, in making up the exact issue, between

---

* Congregationalist, Feb. 12, 1858. These valuable sketches have recently been collected, and published with additions, by the Congregational Board of Publication.

the two great theological systems of Christendom that are kindred but not equivalents, the historical creed is an educating force of the highest value to a denomination. It imparts frankness and clearness to all minds within it, and frankness and clearness are twin sisters to generosity and catholicity.

4. Fourthly, a stronger symbolical feeling, operating in Congregationalism, would tend to harmonize its own theologians among themselves.

It is the tendency of our highly republican system to call out vigorous and independent thinking. As a consequence, our denomination more than others, has from the beginning been stimulated, and sometimes startled, by the uprising of those salient minds who become the nuclei of parties, and the heads of schools. Minor and somewhat local systems, each in its own time and place, have thus radiated their influence through the denomination, have come more or less into collision with each other, and have thereby imparted to Congregationalism that varied and somewhat parti-colored aspect which it wears when compared with ecclesiastical bodies in which there is less boldness of speculation. This is the genius of Congregationalism, and we would not transform it if we could. This desire to evince the reasonableness of Christianity, this inquisitive and enterprising temper, this scholasticism of the nineteenth century, is the vitality by which theological science in every age has been built up. But vital force must always have materials to work upon, and ideas to work by. And these we would find, *for the theologian*, in the denominational symbol. For it is not enough to refer *him* to the Bible without note or comment. Were he a convicted sinner only, and were it his object to seek his own personal salvation, this direction would be sufficient. But he is a theologian, and as such it is his purpose to construct a great comprehensive system that shall do justice to the entire word of God—that shall not omit a single truth, and shall place every doctrine in its right relations and proportions—and therefore he, in the capacity, and exercising the function of a *theologian*, must be assisted in this collection and combination of the contents of Revelation by the labor of all his predecessors. To shut up a single individual with the mere text of the Scriptures, and demand that, by his own unassisted studies and meditations upon it, he should during his own life-time build up a statement of the doctrine of the Trinity like that of Nice, of the doctrine of the Person of Christ like that of Chalcedon, of the doctrine of the Atonement like that of the Augsburg and Helvetic Confessions, of the doctrines of Sin and Predestination like that of Dort and Westminster, would be to require an impossibility. It would be like demanding that a theologian of the year 150 should construct, in his single day and generation, the entire systematic theology of the year 1850; that a Justin Martyr, *e. g.*, should anticipate and perform the entire thinking of a thousand minds and of seventeen hundred years! And yet the substance and staple of all this vast and comprehensive system of divinity was in that Bible which Justin Martyr possessed without note or comment.

The *theorizing* spirit of the individual divine needs, therefore, to be both aided and guided by symbols. In proportion as individual thinkers can bear in mind that the church which they honor and love has already earned a definite theological character, and has given expression to its theological preferences in its own self-chosen creed, they will come under a unifying influence. Their differences and idiosyncrasies, instead of being exaggerated by themselves or their adherents, will be modified, and harmonized, by the central system under which all stand, and to which the whole body has given assent. There will be no loss of mental vigor upon this method, nor of true mental originality, any more than there is when the mathematician's genius is guided and stimulated by the axioms and theorems of a science that was wrought out before he was born. He does not copy, but he reproduces, the mathematical processes of the past, within his own intellect, and in and by this reproduction is conducted to fresh and original products that are also in the true scientific line. In what other way will the active and ingenious minds of a denomination be likely to see eye to eye, and the sum-total of their speculations constitute a homogeneous theology, except as they revere the symbolism of their ancestors? It is when differing, and perhaps diverging, minds are called upon to defend the peculiarities of a common denominational faith, that their differences are dissolved. So long as it is an open question what the common faith is, and the thinkers of a denomination are at leisure to cultivate their peculiarities, so long there must be collision and debate. But the very instant it appears that there is a recognized denominational creed, and it becomes necessary to maintain this creed as vital to the very existence and growth of the denomination, all sincere members of it rally to the defence; and the tendency of defences, as the whole history of Apologies proves, is to harmonize and unite.*

5. Fifthly, and finally, Congregationalism needs a

---

* When the doctrine of vicarious satisfaction was attacked by Duns Scotus, Thomas Aquinas rushed to its defence, and in so doing substantially retracted positions which he himself had previously taken; because he *now* saw, as he did not before, that it was impossible to defend the faith of the church if he retained them. And the whole history of Calvinism proves that it has been enunciated with most unanimity, and defended with greatest power, when the Calvinistic divines were hardest pressed by their Arminian opponents.

stronger symbolical feeling, in order to success in its present endeavor to extend its denominational limits.

The two forms of evangelical Christianity which are to spread over the United States are the Calvinistic and the Arminian. The history of the church upon this Western continent will be substantially the same with its history in the Eastern. One portion of American Christendom will demand the more exact and self-consistent statement of Biblical doctrine, while the other portion will be content with that less precise and comprehensive enunciation of it which emphasizes, indeed, with evangelical energy, the doctrine of forgiveness through the blood of Christ, but rejects the predestination and irresistible grace that *secures* the vital acceptance of the Gospel provision. Throughout the land, there will be those, on the one hand, who, in the phrase of Edward Irving, " will rest content with the infant state of Christ, and see no more in the rich treasures of God's word than a free gift to all men, shrinking back with a feeling of dismay from such parts of the sacred volume as favor a system of doctrine suited to the manly state of Christian life ; " and those on the other, who " will not be content evermore to dwell in the outer court of the holy temple, but who resolve for their soul's better peace and higher joy to enter into the holy and most holy place, which is no longer veiled and forbidden, and find a full declaration of the deepest secrets of their faith, expression for their inmost knowledge of the truth, and forms for their most profound feeling, upon the peculiar, and appropriate, and never-failing love of a covenant God towards his own peculiar people." * The American church, like the old Patristic, like the modern European, will crave, according to the grade of its Christian culture,

---

* Irving's Preface to Horne on the Psalms.

either the milk that is for babes, or the meat that is for strong men.

Congregationalism now proposes to go from East to West, from North to South, upon its mission of love. Outside of its old ancestral home, it is not yet strong. It enters into a friendly rivalry with other branches of Christ's church, upon fields which they have preoccupied, and upon which it has yet to get a firm foothold. Shall it give up or modify, its old historical character, and adopt the laxer of the two great systems of evangelical doctrine, and seek to build up churches upon the same doctrinal basis with the pioneering, the fervid, the beloved * Methodist? If it does, it will fail; first, because it will not be true to its own genius and antecedents, and second, because the wonderfully effective and persistent " method " of Methodism will absorb all its acquisitions, upon *this* basis, into itself.

It only remains, therefore, for Congregationalism to carry into the new regions which it proposes to enter, the very same doctrine, and the very same creed, which it brought over from England and Holland. The denominations with which it has most affinity, and with which it will come into nearest contact, are themselves built upon the Calvinistic foundation. The several Presbyterian bodies have become strong and consolidated in those regions by their persevering attachment to their historical symbols. If they are true to Christ and the New Testament, they will welcome, and not repel, all who stand upon the same doctrinal platform with themselves. The merely secondary matter of polity will never, in the long run, alienate denominations who are one in doctrine, and

---

* We use this word advisedly. We feel a deep and warm affection towards that large denomination which goes everywhere preaching the doctrine of man's *guilt*, and his forgiveness through *atoning blood*.

in the experimental consciousness that grows out of doctrine. Standing firm upon the creed of Owen and Robinson, and equally firm upon the polity of Owen and Robinson, who can doubt that an advancing career is in reserve for the Congregational churches? Thorough orthodoxy (which means thorough accuracy) in the technical statement, in friendly alliance with the utmost freedom and simplicity in the political structure—the longest and firmest of roots bursting out into the brightest and most delicate of flowers—this will be a phase of Christianity that must attract and influence. It lies within the province of Congregationalism to originate and exemplify a style of Christianity that will be somewhat unique in the history of the church. Exactitude of doctrine has sometimes been associated, in ecclesiastical history, with rigid and stately forms of polity. The muscle has been enveloped in tissues as tough and fibrous as itself. It is now competent for the most republican of the polities to clothe the bone and sinew in the warm and flexile flesh; to exhibit the most profound and scientific type of truth in the most simple form of church government, and the most ethereal style of church life. In so doing, Congregationalism will find a welcome from all the true friends of Christ, the world over. And particularly will it be welcomed by that large portion of evangelical Christendom to whom the theology of Augustine and Calvin is precious as the apple of the eye. There can be no collision and no hostile rivalry between denominations that see eye to eye in respect to an exact and a living orthodoxy. How was it in the days when the Reformers on the Continent fraternized with the Reformers in the British Islands? There was much more difference between the Presbyterianism of Geneva and the Episcopacy of London, than there is between the Presbyterianism of the Middle and

Southern States, and the Congregationalism of New England. Yet how respectful was the feeling of Richard Hooker, the great defender of prelacy, towards John Calvin. Read the Zurich Letters, and see how deep was the interest which the English prelates took in the prosperity of the Swiss pastors. And yet there was no sacrifice of principle, or of conviction, upon either side, even in regard to polity. Bishops Grindal and Jewell will not be called lax Episcopalians. John Calvin and Henry Bullinger will not be regarded as indifferent Presbyterians. Each stood firm upon his own ecclesiastical position, and each labored, in every legitimate manner, for the upbuilding of the particular branch of Christ's church with which birth, and education, and personal conviction had connected him. But both knew that there is a higher, a more august thing than the external regimen of the visible church. Both felt the mutual respect, and mutual fellowship, which springs out of a common reception of a common type of doctrine.

And so will it be upon the wider arena of denominational life and action. By identifying itself, always and everywhere, with that theological system whose most fitting material symbol is Plymouth rock, while yet it maintains, always and everywhere, that simple and spiritualizing form of polity which is in such perfect keeping with the doctrine which it enshrines; by uniting the firmness and solidity of the œcumenical symbol with the freedom and flexibility of the local church, Congregationalism will receive the "God speed" of the Church universal. Go where it may, upon this continent or upon other continents, it will hear from the lips of the worn and weary penitent, the warm words of the hymn:

> "Brethren! where your altar burns,
> Oh! receive me into rest."

We have thus, Brethren and Fathers, considered some of the reasons for the cultivation, among ourselves, of a stronger symbolical feeling, and a bolder confidence in creed-statements. In so doing, we are well aware that we tread upon difficult ground. In the minds of some, the symbol has come to be associated with rigid, and more or less monarchical forms of church polity. The adoption of an exact denominational creed seems to carry with it the renunciation of Congregational freedom, and to pave the way for judicatures, and a central government in the church.

But there is no necessary connection between strict doctrine and high-church polity. Each subject stands, or falls, upon its own merits. No one will deny that John Owen was as thorough a Calvinist as ever drew breath; and that he was as thorough a Congregationalist is equally certain. What hinders any denomination from being inspired with the very spirit of Dort and Westminster, so far as doctrine is concerned, while yet it cleaves to the most democratic republicanism in polity?

For this matter of doctrine is an inward conviction, a voluntary adoption, if it is anything at all. The denominational symbol is not to be forced upon a denomination. It cannot be. It must be the free act, the self-chosen creed, of the churches. Hence we have spoken of a symbolical *feeling*, a denominational *confidence* and *respect* towards creeds, rather than of any particular measure, or method, by which a symbol might be cunningly insinuated into a church, or sprung upon it as a surprise. That which is inward and spiritual must first exist, in order to that which is outward and formal. While, therefore, we would not, if we could, impose and inflict a creed upon any unwilling church, we confess that we would, if we could, inspire every church upon the globe with an intelligent and cordial affection for that "form of sound words," around which the sublimest recollections of the church militant have clustered, and out of which its purest and best religious experience has sprung.

To deepen a feeling which already exists in Congregationalism; to strengthen a confidence which has never died out, has been the purpose of these remarks. Whether this feeling and confidence should once more give itself expression in the formal action of the denomination is a question that will be answered variously. But will not all agree that the action of the denomination at Cambridge, and Boston, and Saybrook, has never been *repudiated ;* that if Congregationalism has any corporate existence, and any organic life, by which it maintains its identity from generation to generation, it is *still committed to the symbols* that were then and there made public. Shall we not do well, then, to cherish the recollection of what was done when the foundations of the Puritan church were laid in this Western world? Associated and assembled, as we are, to collect and preserve the memorials of our denominational history, ought we not, more than ever, to think of, and prize, that *system of truth* which has made us historic, which has given us our position among the churches of Christ in the world, which is the secret of our active and tenacious vitality, and without which we should long ago have crumbled and disappeared like the seven churches of Asia?

CLERICAL EDUCATION.*

"How shall they preach, except they be sent?" is the concluding question, in a series of interrogatories designed to show that Christianity, as a universal religion, should obtain a universal proclamation. The *substance* of this religion, St. Paul affirms to be, simple faith in the work of Christ. "If thou shalt confess with thy mouth the Lord Jesus, and shalt believe in thine heart that God hath raised him from the dead"—if thou shalt simply and cordially appropriate what is involved in that death— "thou shalt be saved." The *range* of this religion, he teaches, is the whole world of mankind. "There is no difference between the Jew and the Greek; for the same Lord over all is rich unto all that call upon him. For whosoever shall call upon the name of the Lord shall be saved." These two facts being established, it follows immediately that this religion, so simple in its nature, and so catholic in its aim, should be preached to every human being. Were Christianity complicated and difficult to be understood and complied with, or were it designed for only a particular people or class of mankind, the contrary inference would be drawn. The proclamation of an abstruse or esoteric truth should be cautious and circumspect.

* A discourse before the American Education Society, May 28, 1855.

There should be initiation, and secret instruction, in case the religion is complex and sectarian. But when, as in the instance of the Christian religion, the essential truth of a system is simple as childhood, and to be received by a child's act, and when it is designed for all ages, sexes, conditions, classes, and nationalities of mankind, its promulgation ought to be as loud as thunder and free as the winds. The sound of it should go out through all the earth, and its utterance to the end of the world.

But the question implies that the Christian religion is not self-proclaiming. As a revelation of truth, it had been furnished solely by God. As a plan and work of redemption, there had been no co-operation of man. The Deity imparted a body of knowledge, made an atonement for sin, and poured out supernatural influences, by himself alone; and in reference to all this substance and foundation, man was neither taken into counsel nor permitted to assist. As truth and as fact, Christianity originated from another sphere than the human, and is the pure product and gift and work of God alone.

Yet, though having such a transcendent origin, and being so perfect in its nature, its Author made no supernatural provision for its spread among the nations and down the ages. Under the arrangements of Providence, this supernatural religion is as dependent upon the agency of man, for its extension, as if it were a merely human production. The heavenly treasure is committed to earthen vessels; and Christianity, though a heaven-derived and perfect system, is compelled by its great Author to rely for its diffusion among mankind upon the very same contingencies by which literatures, sciences, arts, and all earth-born knowledges, are disseminated and perpetuated. God might have sent twelve legions of angels to proclaim the truth, with their eyes of light and tongues of flame. He might nave continued to train up preachers to the end of time, by his own direct inspiration and personal instructions, as he did in the beginning. He might have intrusted the heavenly treasure to a celestial vessel and agent. But he did not. He left this wonderful system of truth, which he had been slowly revealing for four thousand years, by prophecy, by type, by miracle, by institute and dispensation, and which he finally crowned and perfected by the incarnation of his Son: he left this wonderful religion, thus originated and constructed, to be diffused among the race for whose benefit it had come into existence by their feeble and unreliable agency. It *looks* as if the Architect were deserting his work; as if this stupendous plan, originating in the counsels of eternity, and moving forward through some centuries of time with energy and success, were suddenly dismissed to a lame and impotent conclusion. As the Gospels and Epistles themselves, in the early ages of the church, were left floating about on a few manuscripts, like the future legislator in the ark of rushes on the Nile, so that, as we look back, we wonder that the archives of our faith were preserved at all in those ages of fire and blood and vapor of smoke, so has the Christian religion been committed to an agency, in itself considered, utterly feeble and totally unreliable, and as we look back over the history of Christianity, we wonder that the world has known and felt so much of its influence as it has. The doctrines of a special divine influence, and a special superintending Providence, alone, dispel our wonder in each of these instances. The human agent worked, and worked well, notwithstanding his intrinsic unfitness and unreliableness, because God worked in him to will and to do. The events and contingencies of this earthly state, the adverse events and unexpected contingencies of human history, conspired to the extension of the Christian religion, instead of its overthrow, because a divine Arm was outstretched to uphold and guide the vessel through the billows.

These reflections, suggested by the interrogatory of St. Paul, lead to the consideration of *some reasons why the Church should address itself to the particular work of Clerical Training and Education.*

1. The first reason is found in the fact, that unless the churches devote their energies and means to this special object, their clergy will not be a sufficiently *numerous* profession.

It is never safe, nor prudent, to rely upon the operation of extraordinary causes, in laying a plan for permanent operations. Inducements and impulses need to be employed, to elicit the latent disposition and power, otherwise this latency will continue to slumber. Hence the church within its own sphere, like the world within its, must make use of average materials, and ordinary appliances, in carrying forward the enterprise that has been committed to it. The common piety of a regenerated man, and not the uncommon holiness of a seraph, is the material which the church should take and mould into the earthen vessels that are to hold the treasure. The churches cannot, wisely or successfully, insist upon a degree of piety, in the Christian young men of this age or of any age, so intense and angelic as to carry them over all obstacles, and without any stimulus or encouragement, into the Christian ministry. Means and facilities for clerical education will never be rendered unnecessary, by a zeal like that of some few missionaries, in some few periods of church history, who penetrated heathenism alone and unassisted, and who laid down and died in the beginning of their career; the zeal of God's house having literally eaten them up. Extremes are dangerous, and those are not the best periods in the history of the church, when remarkable apathy in the mass of Christians was both supplemented and shamed by the intense self-martyrdom of a few individuals. For the church to coldly look on, while the youthful warrior fights his way through a conflict which a little self-denial on the part of his fellow-Christians might have spared him, is unwise and unchristian. All that we should expect or demand, in candidates for the ministry, is a grade and type of Christian character that originates in the bosom of the church itself, possesses the average excellencies and deficiencies, and needs the stimulus and purification of ordinary means and appliances.

Some thirty or forty years ago, that remarkable and interesting man, Edward Irving, was called to preach a sermon before the London Missionary Society. Seizing rankly upon the example of our Lord, who sent out the seventy without purse or scrip, and forgetting the altered circumstances of both the church and the world, and particularly the absence of those miraculous gifts with which those first missionaries were endowed, he deduced the doctrine, that the whole modern missionary movement ought to be left to the spontaneous, unorganized, unaided energy and vehemence of the individual Christian mind. On his scheme, the church had a right to demand that the missionary, in devotedness and zeal for God, tower high above the level of clerical character; that the piety of the herald of the cross should be of such an extraordinary type, that it would bear the missionary, as on the wings of the wind, over land and sea, through all species of populations, and inspire him with a pentecostal energy by which he should electrify and overcome the masses of heathenism. He announced this theory with a wonderful boldness and energy, and threw over it, and all about it, the sheen and the splendor of a most affluent imagination, and a most gorgeous rhetoric, and set the whole all aglow with the fire of an undoubted zeal for God and human salvation.

But no wise man, from that day to this, has supposed that Christian missions can be successfully carried forward on such a scheme. The church cannot rely upon the unusual in feeling, and the extraordinary in character, because, if for no other reason, it is not to be found in sufficient abundance for working purposes. It must rely upon an average piety, and fill out what is lacking, by wise and judicious means and appliances.

It is, consequently, not to be expected, that the attention of Christian young men, in sufficient numbers, will be turned to the work of the ministry, unless facilities are afforded by the church for access to this work. A few men, of remarkable holiness and zeal, might perhaps have crowded and forced their way into ministerial life, by individual and unaided effort; but the greater portion of the present generation of clergymen, who are now actually preaching the word, would not be so doing, if the church had not, by its organizations and charitable foundations, and literary and theological institutions, thrown up a highway into the Christian ministry, and wooed them on into it. And this fact is not specially derogatory to the clerical profession. It implies, indeed, that the clerical mind is not yet filled with a cherub's knowledge of eternal things, and a seraph's love for them. But neither is the church at large. Both clergy and laity have a common type of piety, which, in each case alike, requires aids, and encouragements, and stimulants, and in neither case, alike, can be rightfully called upon to exercise a superhuman virtue, that the other may exercise none at all.

The Christian young man, therefore, at certain turning-points in his educational career, needs an impulse to carry him over into the ministry. His mind is balancing; and if, in this mental state, he sees the church indifferent and apathetic, in reference to that self-denying profession whose claims he is weighing, he will, in too many instances, conclude that a layman's position is not incompatible with his soul's salvation.

If, as he is hesitating in respect to the course he should pursue, he casts his eye forward, and sees that even the years of proposed professional study will be overhung, not merely with poverty but increasing embarrassments, and then usher him into the most anxious and laborious and ill-paid of occupations; if he sees that this obstacle, in the outset, is owing to the neglect, or indifference, of that very Christian church to whose service he proposes to devote himself, what is more natural than that, in a majority of cases, the professedly and really pious young man slides down to a lower level of character and feeling, and enters upon some other course of life and labor? But if, on the other hand, as he looks off in this hour of hesitation, he sees that the wise and good, of the past and the present, have smoothed the pathway to the laborious but noble field of clerical effort, and, by their institutions and scholarships, and benevolent societies, and faculties of instruction, and libraries of books, have made all things ready to his hand, and have placed a professional training within his reach; if, we say, all this preparation and emphatic invitation, on the part of the churches, strike the mind of the hesitating young man at this crisis in his history, how very few truly religious young men would or could find excuses for declining the clerical profession.

In so far, therefore, as the church addresses itself to the work of raising up a ministry, by furnishing *ample* means and apparatus for a professional education, does it take the surest method of securing a numerous clergy; a profession sufficiently well stocked to meet the ever-increasing demand, in this country and age, for religious teachers. And, just in proportion as it leaves the pathway to ministerial life full of obstructions, by neglecting to provide the necessary facilities for clerical education, will it lose the service of a great number, who, under these slight outward influences and impulses from benevolent assistance, would have entered the ministry, and have proved good and faithful laborers in the vineyard of the Lord.

It may be, and has been, urged as an objection to this multiplication of facilities for entrance into the ministry, that the clerical profession will become secularized by the admission of large numbers who are unwilling to exercise that fair and acknowledged degree of self-denial which is required in a true minister of Jesus Christ. There is, however, little danger under the voluntary system of clerical support, that this will be the case. Were there in this country a rich and powerful ecclesiastical establishment, to provide amply for the wants of the incumbents of the sacred office when they enter it, there might, perhaps, be some need of rendering the access to the profession as difficult as possible. But when, as is the case in this country, the clergyman, immediately on leaving his professional course, enters upon a career for life of the most trying and self-sacrificing character, surely the objection above-mentioned loses all its force. The few brief years of preparatory study ought, therefore, to be rendered as pleasant and free from anxiety as possible, in order that the mind may enter, with boldness, and buoyancy, and courage, upon that ministerial life which becomes more and more solemn, and more and more weighty, to the end of it. The church need be under no concern lest, by a full educational treasury, and the multiplication of endowments and scholarships, by the accumulation of books and all the means of clerical training, it shall be instrumental of introducing too many men into the Christian ministry. There is *a work for life* to follow the professional course that will be a sufficient check upon any apprehended glut of clergymen. The few years of education are soon passed, and the long, long years of service begin. Perhaps there is no transition more marked than that from the college and professional school into the parish. The youthful mind has been spending a decennium in the still air of delightful studies, under the guidance of accomplished teachers, and in association with kindred youthful minds. It has been free from care. It has felt only those private responsibilities, which relate to the keeping of one's own heart, and the education of one's own mind. But now it passes into public life. The youthful disciple becomes a religious teacher, is laden with the cares and responsibilities of a great profession, and finds that the days of spirited and hopeful self-education are passed, and the days of persevering, arduous toil for others have come. Looking at this transition from a merely human point of view, there is none more fitted to deter. Were there no higher considerations of usefulness to man and of glory to God, how many a youthful mind would start back at the change, and even on the very threshold of the profession, return to the more inviting fields of literature and authorship, or the more dazzling and exciting arenas of the bar and the senate-house. All that Wordsworth tells us of the passage from the early and romantic age of human life, to the sober gray realism of its later periods, applies, with very deep truth and force, to the transition from the days of professional training, to the days of professional toil. So far as this world is concerned, the journey is ever "farther from the East," and the light fades more and more into that of "common day."

In the great and toilsome *work*, then, which is to follow the professional course, and which must be performed with no assistance from institutions and establishments, but solely in self-denial, and faith, and prayer; in the weight and solemnity of the ministerial profession itself, we find the check needed to prevent the indolent, the ambitious, and the irreligious, from availing themselves of the introductory facilities of the professional course.

Let, then, the church, by making the avenue to ministerial labor as broad and pleasant as possible, while it leaves the labor itself as toilsome and as self-denying as God in his providence has seen fit to constitute it, elicit the greatest possible amount of clerical talent, get it committed to the clerical profession, and thus train up the greatest possible number of clergymen.

2. The second reason why the church should address itself to the special work of ministerial education, is found in the fact, that without such patronage and assistance the ministry will not be a sufficiently *learned* profession. We shall here employ the term "learning" in its widest signification, and under this head shall discuss several topics, some of which pertain to the literary, and some of them to the theological education of the clergyman.

Taking up, in the first place, the conditions of learning, we shall see the need of a special attention and assistance on the part of the churches. Learning depends upon these three conditions: first, upon freedom from mental distraction and task-work, during the period of study;

secondly, upon thorough teachers and the discipline of a curriculum; and, thirdly, upon access to large libraries.

During the period of study, the mind requires to be calm and unembarrassed, in order that it may give its powers a single direction and concentrate them upon a single point. The whirl of business, and the excitement of gay life are unfavorable to scholarship, even in case there be no exacting demands made upon the student's mind and time. Hence, the cloister life of the middle ages was far less injurious to the scholarship of that period, than it was to its piety. In all ages, tranquillity and serenity have been found favorable to culture, even though other interests may have suffered from a life of undue seclusion.

But when, in addition to the lack of scholastic retirement during the years of professional training, there is added the laborious occupation of the mind in other pursuits than those of study and self-discipline, great injury must result to the ultimate professional power and stamina of the individual. He, who is compelled to earn his daily bread while laying the foundations upon which the future structure of ministerial labor is to be reared, will find, to his regret, when he comes to perform that life-long service, and feel that unintermittent draught upon his ideas, that he was obliged to be hasty and superficial at a point, where, of all, there is need of slowness and thoroughness. The human mind cannot well do two things at once, and, therefore, from the beginning to the end of the course of clerical education, there ought to be secured to the rising ministry, the greatest possible freedom from the excitement of gay and secular life, and the exactions of poverty. Only in academical quiet and unembarrassed finances, can the foundations of a broad, deep, and powerful clerical scholarship be laid.

Again, the influence of a faculty and a curriculum is needed, in order to the existence of a learned ministry. Doubtless much thorough discipline in a single direction, and with respect to a single topic, may be obtained from a single strong and original mind. The minds that were trained in the last century, in the study-chambers of the distinguished divines of New England, were very able in regard to their specialty, or that of their teacher. They had their forte, and they had their foible. For it is impossible that a single mind should be able to impart the entire encyclopædic knowledge and discipline of a faculty of learned men, each of whom devotes himself to a particular department, while he co-works with his associates. It is impossible that the professional culture which flows out from a single fountain, however ebullient, should exhibit the powerful and broad current that results from the union of head-waters. It was for this reason that the churches were compelled, so soon as the colleges of the land ceased to impart that clerical training, for the sake of which they were first founded, to establish the ecclesiastical professional school, and subject the rising ministry to the influence of a faculty and a curriculum.

And, lastly, a learned profession can live only in the atmosphere of libraries. The influence of large collections of books, upon both faculties and students, is a subject deserving the increasing attention of all who are interested in the formation of a yet more thorough culture in our lively age and country. The consciousness of ignorance, which is generated by an exhibition upon the shelves of a library of what the human mind has accomplished in the past, is one of the sharpest spurs to personal investigation; is one of the keenest corrosives of intellectual conceit and vain-glorying. And the professional mind, equally with the popular, needs to come under this influence: for it is as true in the intellectual sphere, as it is in the moral, that he that humbleth himself shall be exalted.

These conditions of thorough scholarship can be secured to the candidate for the ministry only by the church at large. The individual cannot originate and maintain them for himself, any more than he can originate courts of law, and juries, and benches of judges. The institutions and endowments requisite in order to the very existence of a clerical discipline are the proper care of the churches; and just in proportion as any particular branch of the church fosters or neglects them, will be the strength, or the weakness, of its clerical body.

But the strength of this argument, from the fact that the ministry will not be a learned body unless it is supplied with the conditions of scholarship, is greatly enhanced, as soon as we consider one or two peculiarities in the present state of the world, which create an unusual necessity for thorough learning and discipline in the clerical profession. It is to this part of the plea that we would invite particular attention.

In the first place, then, a very high mental discipline is required, at the present time, in order that preaching may be simple, plain, and powerful. It was a remark of Archbishop Usher to the clergy of his diocese, "It takes all our learning to be simple." To preach plain and simple, says Luther, is a great art. These statements are true ones, though paradoxical, and contrary to a common notion respecting the influence of learning. It will however be found, that in proportion as the human mind becomes a profound master of the truth, it becomes able to unfold and express it in such a manner, that the wayfaring man need not err, and also in such a way that the cultivated mind feels the very same influence from the actual verity. We see this illustrated in secular literature. The greatest minds, in any department, address the two extremes of human culture, as well as all the intermediates. Shakspeare is the poet of the masses, and also of the "laureate fraternity" of poets. That homely sense, which speaks like a swain to the swain, and that ethereal discourse, which is the admiration and the despair of the cultivated reason and imagination, both alike, flow from a thorough apprehension and a perfect knowledge of man and of nature. Lord Bacon's understanding addresses both the peasant and the philosopher, because it grasped what it seized, and saw entirely through what it looked at. And, to come down to our own time and country, and into a department that more than any other is both practical and popular, how powerfully does the eloquence of Webster affect all grades of intelligence, because it sprang, so uniformly, out of an entire mastery of the subject. In each of these instances there was learning, in the sense of clear and thorough knowledge. From whatever source it be derived; whether from intercourse with man and self, or whether it is drawn more immediately from books; if there be a clear understanding, a perfect mastery, there will be plainness; and if there be plainness, there will be power.

In no sphere is there greater need of this learned plainness than in religion, and especially in no age more than our own. The public mind is now distracted by a variety of information. It has read and heard too much. It is discursive, and disinclined to ponder upon fundamental truths. Consequently, simplicity, depth, and clearness, are qualities specially required in the public religious address of the day, in order that men may be called back from this wandering over a large surface, and induced to take a descending, instead of an expatiating, method. Never did man more need to be brought back to his individuality, which is a very simple thing, and to his few relations to God, which are yet more simple, than now. Even good men find, upon their death-beds, that they have been too discursive, even in their religious study and experience. Said a dying theologian, "My theology is now reduced to these two points, that I am a guilty sinner, and that the blood of Christ expiates human guilt." But if the religious and theological mind finds that it is unduly inclined to career over large spaces, and examine curiously into collateral topics, to the neglect of the vitalities and simplicities of faith, and of life, what shall be said of that secular mind, which, in this age of new discoveries, and vast accumulations of facts, roams over all this oceanic expanse, but finds no time for soundings?

In this connection, is it not natural to query, whether even the mind of the church has not been too much distracted by that large and important class of subjects which fall within the sphere of Ethics, as distinguished from that of Christianity? Whether the whole great subject of Reform has not been made to yield up such a mass of topics, and such an influx of ideas and sentiments, as to deluge the mind, and leave no room for the distinctively religious topics of sin and guilt, of atonement and regeneration, of faith and repentance, of hope and of love? Has not this variety of topics and of information, drawn from the ethical rather than the evangelical domain, brought the public mind into such a confused condition, that it needs, more than ever, to be brought back to the few and simple truths of the gospel and godliness?

But how is this to be done? Not by mere fault-finding,
16*

and moaning over this unfavorable state of the case, but by a cheerful, manlike, and powerful method. The Christian religion does not *whine* over human nature. Its meekness and sorrow are not pusillanimity, and, in the phrase of Thomas Paine, "the spirit of a spaniel." The Lamb of God is also the Lion of the tribe of Judah; and while Christianity, with a yearning love for human welfare, utters its tender: "Come unto me, all ye that are weary and heavy laden," it also utters its high and authoritative: "He that believeth and is baptized shall be saved, and he that believeth not shall be damned." A calm, uncomplaining, and commanding tone, should therefore ever be preserved by the Christian ministry, in the midst of all the waywardness and self-ignorance of the generations of men.

Not, then, by lamentations over the present, and forebodings in reference to the future, but by such a clear, bold, and penetrating statement of the truth that slays, and the truth that makes alive, is the altered mood and tendency to be brought about in the public mind. When the "commandment" shall "come," with clearness, and plainness, and power, all these secondary truths, now unduly occupying the attention, will, of themselves, fall back into their proper places, in the thought and feeling of both the church and congregation.

But this implies no slender discipline of head and heart in the clergyman. It requires a most learned, and a most spiritual mind; a clergy full of evangelical ideas, and full of vital energies; the eye of the hawk, and the fire therein; the eye of the dove, and the love therein. For the auditor will not leave that animated arena which is now engaging and exacting his powers, unless there be a substitute; unless another realm, of vaster solemnity and grandeur, is opened upon him. The streets of Vanity Fair will never be deserted until eternity, in all its terrors and splendors, be actually made to dawn upon them. The hearer will not leave his spirited careerings over universal space, and sink a narrow dark shaft into the depths of his own heart, unless his religious teacher actually goes before him, bringing him to consciousness, and interpreting to him his own perishing religious necessities.

The preacher, consequently, must have a *masterly* knowledge of gospel doctrines. He must know them with thoroughness, so that he can make them come into actual contact with the human mind. Then there will be an effect. Bring the human mind, and especially the sinful human mind, into vivid connection with the bare, real, single, simple, verity, and the result is like that of the mingling and war of the elements in the old cosmogonies. But the power of thus handling the few and simple truths of Christianity rests, so far as it rests upon a human foundation, upon discipline, deep, clear, and persevering. The truths of Christianity are few in number, but vast in their capacities and implications. Hence a profound, rather than a discursive talent, is required in him who is to proclaim them. He who cannot say the same thing in a variety of modes is not qualified for the work of the ministry. He who cannot find the new in the old is not fit to preach the gospel. If we examine the preaching of the great and evangelical divines of the church, in all ages, we find but one general strain and tone. Everything is tinged with sin and redemption. The fall and the recovery of the human soul, paradise lost and paradise regained, are the substance of their sermonizing. Like some of the great painters, they are monochromatic; they employ only one principal color. And yet there is variety in this unity. For the Christian mind never tires of these repeated lessons from *them*, any more than it does of the often-reiterated teachings of Scripture itself. The one subject is ever new and fresh. Be it sin, or be it redemption, it is treated thoroughly, and brought into direct contact with the heart and experience, and wherever this is done there is freshness. The peculiar interest of the public mind in the subject of religion, during an effusion of the Holy Spirit, does not spring from the novelty, or the number, of the truths presented to it. They are the same old and simple doctrines, and exhibited with even less of collateral matter than common. For it is wonderful to observe how both hearer and preacher, at such times, are dissatisfied with everything that is not distinctively and intensely evangelical. Heretofore, perhaps, both parties had preferred to expatiate over that border-land which skirts the legitimate field of sermonizing, in order to find topics of intellectual entertainment. But now a meaning and power are discovered, in the few and old truths of Scripture, which the whole varied, vivid universe of science, literature, and art cannot furnish.

Now we freely concede, that the work of the Spirit is needed, in both preacher and hearer, in order that this interest in distinctively evangelical subjects may reach its highest form, and were the work of the Spirit our theme, we would insist upon this great truth. But at this time we are treating of human discipline, and speaking of those intellectual methods that are best adapted to favor the operation of the truth and the Spirit of God. And, speaking in this connection, we are bold in affirming that a learned and thorough theological discipline contributes to this simplicity in the subjects, and to this directness in the exhibition of them. Learning does make us plain and powerful teachers. A shallow education, and a lively, but illogical mind, cannot find the elements of power in the doctrines of Jesus and the resurrection. Such are compelled, by their undue discursiveness, and their lack of thoughtfulness, to seek pulpit effect in a multitude of topics, and in novelty of themes.

Again, in the second place, the existing, and the coming conflict with educated skepticism, calls for a ministry that has been made learned, by the discipline of institutions and curriculums. Modern infidelity assumes a greater variety of forms than the ancient, although its essential character remains the same. We should expect this would be the case in an age which, as we have already observed, is inclined to variety rather than to unity, in all its manifestations. The infidelity which the ministry has to combat is, as usual, protean ; and when refuted in one shape, instantaneously reappears in another. One of its most specious forms, and the only one we have time to notice, springs out of the connection of natural religion with revealed. It involves the relation of Ethics to Christianity. In our country, in particular, this form of infidelity associates itself, parasitically, with the reformation of society, and thereby becomes doubly dangerous to the Christian church, which ever takes a deep interest in the removal of social evils. That the reconstruction of society is made to supersede the regeneration of the individual is not the whole, or the worst. Reform is not merely divorced from evangelical Christianity, but is at enmity with it. A class of minds are loudly proclaiming the truths of ethics and natural religion, from beneath the sounding-board of Reform, for whom the doctrine of the cross is a most hateful offence, and whose temper towards those peculiar truths which are the life and life-blood of the Christian Religion, is marked by a malignity, and a virulence, which finds its parallel only in the first, and original " generation of vipers."

Nothing but learning in the clergy can overmaster this

error. Nothing but broad scholarship, profound insight, and power of distinct statement can exhibit the true functions of both Ethics and the Gospel, and carry the public mind against this half-understanding of the enemy of Christianity, and his covert attack. For the opponent of the ministry, and the gospel, now plants himself upon Ethics, and not upon mere, sheer, sensual infidelity. He professes a moral end and aim, and his own character, in most instances, is moral and proud. He professes to call men back, from a mysterious and complicated religion, to the few first principles of justice, and virtue, and benevolence. He derives no little authority and influence, before the judgment and conscience of men, because he advocates the claims of the great and noble department of moral philosophy. Hence the clergyman, in this age more than in any other, must be able to draw the line between morality and religion, and especially to make men see what all history teaches, that there is no *self-realizing power* in moralism; that all this Ethics must follow in the rear of evangelical Christianity, in order to be operative among mankind. Men need *life*, renovating and sanctifying *life* from God; and not merely light from nature and reason, or even from revelation; for the Bible itself is powerless without the Holy Ghost. The truths of ethics and natural religion can become the ruling principles of individual and social life, only in case the individual and society come under the power of revealed religion. Ethical justice, and ethical truth, and ethical benevolence, cannot prevail on the earth, except as evangelical faith, and hope, and love, renovate human nature in its fountains. Only through the *vitality* and *regeneration* of Christianity can the cold, clear reason of ethics be transmuted into feeling, and be realized among mankind. Only the renewed soul can actually obey the hard and high law. Theorists are setting the Christian religion upon the same level with that of Confucius, because the Chinese sage taught the "golden rule." Suppose it to be true (which, however, we deny) that Confucius did teach the golden rule as clearly and as fully as Christ taught it in the Sermon on the Mount, would this make Confucius equal to Jesus Christ? It would, provided that Christ did no more than merely *teach* the rule. But he does far more than this. He imparts a disposition to obey the rule. This Confucius never did while upon earth, and has never done since he left it. It is easy enough to point to the north star—any child can do this. But to carry a human being to the north star is beyond the power of man. When Christ said to the paralytic: "Arise, take up thy bed and walk," he empowered him to the act. He imparted a vital force that enabled the patient to do what he was commanded to do. But when these natural religions of the globe, for which an equality with Christianity is claimed, say to the moral paralytic: "Do right," "Be perfect," they bestow no spiritual power along with the command, and hence accomplish nothing.

It is surprising to see how this great difference between Christianity and the natural religions of the globe is overlooked in the contest now going on between naturalism and supernaturalism. The utmost that Confucius, Sakyamuni, and Socrates can do is to give good advice. They cannot incline and enable men to obey it. Socrates confesses this with sadness. It is the burden and grief of his soul that men will not hear, and that he has no power to move their hearts. But Jesus Christ possesses this marvellous power. He can not only say to men: "Whatsoever ye would that men should do to you, do ye even so to them," but he can actually dispose them to do it. Men for centuries, of all grades of civilization and culture, have come under the power of the gospel, and have found in themselves a new heart. This is not theory, but fact. That Christianity possesses the wonderful power of originating character, and spiritually transforming men, is as certain as that magnetism affects iron. It is demonstrable by actual experiment and observation. St. Paul, speaking of the superiority of the gospel over the moral law, remarks that, "if there had been a law given which could have given *life*, verily, righteousness should have been by the law." Now this imparting of moral life is precisely what no religion but the Christian is competent to. If the human heart could have been inclined and persuaded to practise the golden rule by the mere teaching of the rule, by Confucius or any other mere teacher, there would be some color of reason for the assertion that Confucius and Christ are equals. But the human heart remains the same selfish and self-seeking thing from generation to generation, until the Christian herald proclaims the religion of that redeeming God who says: "A new heart will I give you, and a new spirit will I put within you; and I will take away the stony heart out of your flesh, and I will give you an heart of flesh."

The infidelity of moralism, then, so covert and so specious, calls loudly for an evangelical ministry that knows exactly the difference between the law and the gospel; that can meet the opposer upon his own ground, and instead of vilifying ethics, and natural reason, and religion, can apply their truths and principles so hotly and terribly to the human soul *at variance with them*, that they shall be a schoolmaster to lead it to Christianity. "Tell me, ye that desire to be under the law, do ye not hear the law? The law is not of faith," it stands in no relation to mercy, "but the man that *doeth* them shall live by them." And the contrary follows inevitably: "The man that doeth them *not*, shall die by them." It is because mankind have not obeyed the principles of natural religion, and are under a curse and a bondage therefor, that the peculiar doctrines of revealed religion are needed; and he who in this age, or any other, preaches the truths of natural reason and conscience, and there stops, preaches the eternal and inevitable damnation of the human soul. He may not know what he is doing. He may announce the ideas of ethics and natural religion, as evidence that human nature is upright, and needs no redemption, forgetting that a Plato, a Plutarch, and a Cicero, found in the fact that they are in man's *reason* but not obeyed and realized in man's *will*, the most convincing evidence that humanity is at schism with itself, and therefore depraved and fallen, while they knew no mode of deliverance. He may expand these old and obvious doctrines of ethical morality, as something new and original with himself, forgetting that a single dialogue like the *Phædo*, or a single tract like the *De Natura Deorum*, contains more of the pure and dense reason of the finite mind than he has been able to flatten out into many volumes of essays and so-called sermons. He may suppose in all this, that he is dispensing with the necessity of revelation, and taking the most effectual method to destroy its influence among mankind. But the well-disciplined Christian preacher can take all this asseveration respecting the immutability of ethical distinctions, and all this emphatic assertion of the sacredness and worth of justice and truth and benevolence and all the forms of virtue, and from it deduce man's perishing need of God's mercy and redemption. For where is the conformity to all these statutes and commandments? Who realizes these truths of natural conscience in his daily life? Who will not be found guilty before the bar of natural religion, that is, the bar of his own conscience? Who will not need that atonement for failure to live up even to the light of nature which is the key to that sacrificial system which makes a part of all the more thoughtful and respectable religions of paganism?

The connection between natural and revealed religion is the point where the most dangerous infidelity of the time takes its stand; and the ministry needs, more than ever, a profound and clear understanding of the distinctive character and relations of each, in order to meet the adroit attacks of enemies, to relieve the sincere doubts of inquiring minds, and more than all, to make the law, in all its forms, tributary to the gospel of Christ. But this power rests upon learning; upon a profound acquaintance with what that learned Puritan, Theophilus Gale, denominates, "the wisdom of the Gentiles," and a yet more profound acquaintance with the wisdom of the Scriptures. Here is the whole broad field of human reason and divine revelation to be traversed, and nothing but that thorough understanding of their true meaning and mutual relations, which characterized both the conforming and the non-conforming divines of England in the seventeenth century, will prepare the ministry of the present, and the coming age, to meet the skepticism present and to come. The English deism of that century and that age was learned, was able, was subtle. It contained all shades, from the lofty and virtuous deism of Lord Herbert of Cherbury, to the low and sensual deism of Mandeville. But it was thoroughly met by the Christian ministry of that century, because the truths of natural religion itself were more philosophically and correctly apprehended by the defenders of revelation, than they were by its opponents. The Deist found that the Christian preacher was at home in the Pagan as well as in the Christian theology; and, before the controversy was over, learned that by far the justest estimate of what the uninspired human mind is capable of doing, and of what it is incapable, is formed by the mind that occupies the higher point of view afforded by a supernatural revelation. The Deist discovered that John Howe had read Plato, and that Bishop Stillingfleet was learned in all the wisdom of the Egyptians, and that both alike, while the farthest possible from disparaging the just dues of reason and conscience, were able, convincingly, to show the powerlessness of both, in reference to the two great needs of human nature, the forgiveness of sins and the sanctification of the soul; in reference, not to a mere illumination that like moonlight in nature warms nothing and stirs nothing, but to a deep central renovation and restoration to holiness and paradise, of a race that, for six thousand years, has had full opportunity to try the recuperative virtues supposed to inhere in the uninspired human mind and the unrenewed human will.

We have, then, these two general reasons why the Church should address itself to the work of training a ministry: first, that the ministry may be sufficiently numerous to supply the increasing demands for public religious teachers; and, secondly, that the ministry may be sufficiently disciplined, to exhibit the few and simple doctrines of Christianity in a plain, fresh, and powerful manner to the general understanding, and sufficiently learned to thwart the present attempt of infidelity to substitute natural for revealed religion.

There are other fundamental reasons for this procedure that might be urged, but we prefer to seize upon two strong points, and rest the plea upon them alone. The two considerations of number and of power in the ministry are sufficient to evince the duty of the church in respect to clerical education. We are the more ready to rest the case upon these two points, because they are both unusually practical, at this juncture. The opening of new nations to Christianity is destined to make a great demand for preachers of the Word during the next century. The indications now are that the unchristianized world is simultaneously waking up to a sense of its spiritual wants, and being thrown open to Christian enterprise. The heathen are ready and waiting to hear the living Word from the living tongue and eye. While, therefore, missionary schools and seminaries cannot safely be neglected, and will not be, it is becoming more evident every day that the number of preachers must be very greatly increased, so that, as in the apostolic age, Christianity may run like sacred fire over large spaces in short time. It is by preaching tours and missionary journeys, like those of the apostolic age, taking their start from the missionary station, that the world is to be evangelized. Companies and bands of heralds, penetrating in every direction, and carrying the truth to every hamlet and heart, will speedily be needed, if the church would see the millions who are now coming under the influences of civilization, also coming under the influences of Christianity.

And, certainly, the other consideration which we have urged, viz., the fresh, vigorous power of the clergy, appeals with equal force to our minds, when we consider the prevailing type of intellectual culture. In speaking of clerical learning, we have directed attention more to the material, than to the formal side of the subject, because the intellectual tendency of the age is unduly to the form. Art is outrunning science. Rhetoric is destroying logic, as in some previous ages logic destroyed rhetoric. Style, instead of being the pure and austerely beautiful embodiment of an idea and a truth and a logic that is greater and grander than itself, exists too much by itself, and for itself. There is not enough of argument in the sermon. Men are not sufficiently *reasoned with* out of the Scriptures. Preaching is too often a play, and a display. It is not often enough a conflict of mind with mind, and a battle of the understanding of the preacher with that of the hearer. For the pulpit, like God, has a controversy with human nature. Hence the need and worth of scientific discipline. For this species of power springs from the rigor of a professional course; is drawn from the nether fountains of philosophical and theological science. He who expects that mighty reasoners and men of commanding power will be raised up without the discipline of institutions, and the learning of libraries, expects that the perturbations of the planets will be calculated without mathematics, and that the constellations of the skies will be mapped without observatories. Showy men, striking men, may be formed without the school or curriculum; but strong men cannot be.

The great majority of clergymen have received through the Church an amount and kind of aid that decided their profession for them, and their own position within it. Subtract this ecclesiastical agency and influence, and you subtract in an untold manner from the sum total of the clerical agencies and influences now at work in society. If this is true of the past, it will hold true with emphasis of the future. The time is coming, and now is, when the interests of the church and of Christianity will require a far broader foundation, and a much ampler apparatus for clerical education than now exists. As our own country fills up with population, wealth, and human knowledge, and as the globe wheels up more and more of its dark sides to the eye of the philanthropist and the Christian, there will be needed a permanence and an affluence in educational facilities, such as exists in the church establishments of the Old World. Suppose that all those foundations, and fellowships, and scholarships—all those edifices, and libraries, and museums, and faculties, and courses of instruction, which are radiating an influence from generation after generation of students—could instantaneously be transferred to the care and use of a church disconnected from the state, and supported upon the voluntary system, what a stream of fresh and energetic life would be poured through these veins and arteries, now clogged and in danger of ossification! How much more evenly and impartially would the revenues be distributed, and how much more advantageously would the power of this great educational system and apparatus be applied!

The Church, in this country, has now solved a problem, which, since the days of Constantine, had been deemed insoluble. It has convincingly proved, that Christian institutions not only do not need the support of the state, but thrive best, when left to the spontaneous and free support of that individual Christian heart and mind which wants them and loves them. The doctrine of a self-supporting church, now, has less of doubt and difficulty overhanging it, than the doctrine of a self-governing state. We think, and say, that the United States of America have convincingly proved, that a republic is not merely an ideal, but also a realizable form of government. We may be yet more confident, that the church of Christ in this country has irrefragably evinced the inherent and persistent power of vital Christianity to organize its own simple forms, and supply its own few outward wants. Visible churches die out of localities, far less often under the Voluntary System than under the Establishment. Go among the hills, where a sparse population wrings a bare livelihood from the thin and sterile soil, and you find a "feeble church," as it is called, but a church that never ceases to be among the hills, because it draws what life it has from free-will, and not from ancestral revenues. But how many a church, whose material, moneyed foundation dates back to the Plantagenets and the Tudors, has disappeared from the sum of national life and vital influences, and exists, now, only as an investment in the funds, or the national debt, because the invisible church, in the outset, was not laden with its proper responsibility, and as a penalty, in the end, ceased to exist altogether as a moral force in the nation.

It, therefore, now remains for the Church to complete what has been so well begun; to arm this voluntary system with the powers and resources of an establishment; to fill up its treasuries, that it may dispense with a liberal hand; to endow its institutions, that it may promote its own growth and prosperity. For, in this instance, it is not one party who gives, and another who receives and disburses. It is the church, self-governing, self-supporting, self-extending. It is a true evolution from centre to circumference, and back, by a reflex influence, from the periphery to the radiating point. There is no danger, therefore, that revenues will become too large, and the organization too complicated and massive; for the giver is also the treasurer and the almoner, and will know when to stop. There is no danger of maladministration; for they who administer, and they who endow, are both of one, and at one; of one body, and at one object.

www.ingramcontent.com/pod-product-compliance
Lightning Source LLC
Chambersburg PA
CBHW021829220426
43663CB00005B/176